Paths to Success

Paths to Success

Beating the Odds in American Society

CHARLES C. HARRINGTON

SUSAN K. BOARDMAN

Harvard University Press
Cambridge, Massachusetts
London, England
1997

Library of Congress Cataloging-in-Publication Data

Harrington, Charles C.
    Paths to success : beating the odds in American society / Charles
C. Harrington, Susan K. Boardman.
        p.   cm.
    Includes bibliographical references and index.
    ISBN 0-674-65794-2 (alk. paper)
    1. Success in business—United States.   2. Success—United States.
3. Social mobility—United States.   I. Boardman, Susan K.
II. Title.
HF5386.H267   1997
650.1—dc21   97-8380

For Jamie

Preface

This book is about people who are interesting because they have lived out an American myth. Born to poor and uneducated families, the subjects of this book achieved success. The myth has many names: "rags to riches," "Horatio Alger stories," or "born in a log cabin" are just a few examples. However rare, the stories of such people as Joycelyn Elders and Clarence Thomas reassure the democratic community that the myth can still become a reality.

Joycelyn Elders was born in Schaal, Arkansas. Her family survived by chopping cotton and trapping raccoons.[1] Her career goals were modest: being a laboratory technician was what a medical career meant to her. She was able to attend college because her church provided a scholarship and because her seven sisters and brothers picked cotton to finance her clothing and transportation. At college she met the first black woman ever to study at the University of Arkansas medical school, and "was totally impressed by her." The identification led to a goal to follow her into medicine. To make that happen, she entered the army on graduation, was trained as a physical therapist, and then went to medical school (also at Arkansas) under the GI bill. She became a physician, a pediatrician, a pediatric endocrinologist, and a professor at a major university medical school. Yet she also helped her siblings through school. She took a job as Health Director of the State of Arkansas where she waged a campaign for contraception because "I saw the massive suffering of so many bright young black women because of having unplanned and unwanted pregnancies. And I began to realize how much they had been exploited, not only by the religious right but also by their own kind with this talk of contraception being genocide." When nominated to become Surgeon General of the United States she reports that the American Medical Association didn't even think she

vii

was a physician. "They don't expect a black female to have accomplished what I have accomplished, and to have done the things that I have." During her confirmation process, a reporter in *US News and World Report*[2] described her as "intolerant, preachy, judgmental, and overbearing. She's bright, articulate, passionate, and kind." When asked to comment on this description, she told Claudia Dreifus that the description was "pretty good. I'm only overbearing to the people I need to be overbearing with. You've got to get people's attention before you can achieve change . . . You have to take a stand. People are either going to love you or hate you."

Joycelyn Elders is a "Pathmaker." She has overcome considerable odds associated with her race, her sex, her family's poverty, and her parents' low educational achievement, and found a way to succeed in spite of these obstacles. She shares these characteristics with the main subjects of this book. Her life also exemplifies some of the main themes we will discuss in regard to black female Pathmakers: the importance of family support, of taking advantage of serendipitous opportunity (the scholarship), of the role of modeling and mentoring in career choice and development, of the use of education to level the playing field with other more advantaged populations, and of the conscious need to pay back by helping siblings and others through altruistic public service. Even Elders's personality (as described in the press), a strong belief in her own ability, and a faith in herself independent of what others think of her are traits characteristic of black female Pathmakers.

But not all Pathmakers are the same. Clarence Thomas was born to sharecroppers in Pin Point, Georgia, the middle child of three. When he was two, his father left home. His mother worked as a crab-picker and housecleaner to keep her children together until he was seven, when their house burned down. She and Thomas's sister went to live with an aunt, while Thomas and his younger brother moved in with his mother's parents. This family was "strong, stable, and conservative . . . God was central. School, discipline, hard work, and knowing right from wrong were of highest priority. Crime, welfare, slothfulness, and alcohol were enemies."[3] His "barely literate" grandfather sent Thomas to a Roman Catholic school for blacks run by whites, which taught him to fend for himself in a hostile environment. "The nuns gave us hope and belief in ourselves when society didn't."[4]

The adult Thomas, most would agree, is a very different person from the adult Elders. In fact Elders herself describes key differences. In contrast to her own altruism she sees Thomas "want[ing]to move away from being black and associat[ing himself] with the white power structure . . . [He] put down black women . . . Thomas was a man who had used the system to get where he wanted to be, but then felt that everyone else should pull themselves up by their own bootstraps."[5] In her description of Thomas are themes that recur in our study for black males: strong family support of schooling, seeing racism as an obstacle to be overcome, a strong need for power for its own sake, and less need to pay back or to help others achieve the same level of success. Despite the similarity of their origins, Elders and Thomas created very different paths to success.

For more than fifteen years we have been exploring how people overcome negative predictions associated with childhood poverty and low educational attainment of parents. It is now our conclusion that the paths such people construct show certain consistencies with those taken by other successful people, as well as patterned differences, which this book seeks to describe. We also think that there is more than one way for Pathmakers to achieve success, and that differences and similarities between Pathmakers can be partially explained by race and gender. Indeed our findings will enable the reader to see that some of the differences between Elders and Thomas are not idiosyncratic to them as individuals, but rather represent general trends described in this book. Despite the attention of the popular press to individuals like Elders and Thomas, the literatures of the behavioral sciences have been relatively silent on the processes of such careers, and it is our central concern to fill this gap.

We compare Pathmakers with an equally successful control group from middle-class, educated families who are able to move into paths already constructed, and discuss the similarities and differences in their motivations and resources.

Our work has benefited from many influences. The idea for research on Pathmakers was originally conceived in the research planning group of the Institute for Urban and Minority Education at Teachers College, Columbia University. For their helpful participation in these meetings, we thank Edmund Gordon (chair), Curtis Banks, Peter Gumpert, and William Moody. The research project reported here was subsequently planned by Charles Harrington with Peter Gumpert, whose contributions as co-author of the original proposal to the Spencer Foundation, and as co-principal investigator in the first months of the actual research are acknowledged. Our research benefited from the collaboration of Sandra V. Horowitz, Lynn Mulkey, Robert Allen Orr, and Medria Williams; and the assistance of Robert Frenzl-Berra, Donnah Canavan-Gumpert (at the proposal stage), Mitchell Bakst, Joseph Dioso, Desmond Groarke, Christine Helm, Vernay Mitchell, Beatriz Morales, Judith Preissle, Gloria Silverman, Janet Skupien, and Dennis Young.

The manuscript has also benefited at various stages from readings by Sue Berryman, George Clement Bond, William Buse, Vivian Garrison, Olga Gonzalez, Judith King-Calnek, Robert Lafayette, Vernay Mitchell, Lynn Mulkey, and Judith Preissle, as well as anonymous reviewers.

The research reported here was supported in part by the Spencer Foundation as the grant, "Educational Antecedents of Success," made to the Institute for Urban and Minority Education of Teachers College, Columbia University in 1981. We gratefully acknowledge their generosity and patience. From 1985 to 1987, support for the work described herein also came from the National Center on Education and Employment funded by the United States Office of Educational Research and Improvement by contract with Teachers College, Columbia University. The hospitality of the Departments of Education and Anthropology of the University of Otago during the New Zealand spring semester of 1984 is gratefully acknowledged, with special thanks to Joseph Diorio, a thoughtful critic and gracious host.

Contents

Paths to Success

1

Introduction

Born and raised as the child of a sharecropper in the rural South, one subject of this book walked five miles of dirt road each day to a one-room schoolhouse to go to school. He became the owner and CEO of a business with net earnings of $50 million a year which pays him a seven-figure salary. Another subject of this book who grew up in city slums, with a mother too ill to work and a father nowhere to be found, lied about her age so that, at twelve or thirteen, she could get a job to bring home money for food and clothes for her mother, sisters, and brothers. She became a corporate officer and board member of a major multinational corporation. Another grew up not knowing what colleges are. When his high school teacher said, "You're going to college, aren't you?" he said, "What's a college?" He became the president of a major university.

This book is about such people's lives. It asks how people who originally came from such impoverished backgrounds can go on to achieve high levels of occupational success, and if their paths to success differ from people born more advantageously. We present data from an exploratory study designed to answer these questions for one hundred successful Americans.

During our research we called the subjects of our study "negative prediction defiers,"[1] since their success is in defiance of negative predictions based upon their social status. But we have never been fully satisfied with the term because of the multiple connotations of "defiance." Some subjects no doubt exhibited a defiant attitude toward their obstacles, others overcame them without it.[2]

Some researchers have opted for the term "resilient," but we find its meaning also not fully reflective of how our subjects described their lives. One of the few works to stress dictionary definitions of resilience is Rhodes and Brown (1991), who suggest that resilient children must go through a period of "dysfunctionality" before "turning their lives around." Vaillant (1993) also stresses that resilience is "recovery" (p. 284). Resilience has taken on a general meaning in the psychology literature of growing up "competent"[3] or "coping effectively,"[4] despite risks for pathological outcomes, which is quite a different matter from our research, though not unrelated.

Another, even stronger, metaphor frequently encountered is "invulnerability."[5] Literally, however, this would mean that the subject suffers not even short-term trauma. Indeed Rhodes and Brown (1991) distinguish invulnerability and resilience in exactly this way, and their invulnerable subjects experience no dysfunction whatsoever: invulnerability is the avoidance of dysfunction, resilience is recovery from dysfunction. But Vaillant (1993: 284) takes pains to assure us that resilient youth are not invulnerable in the sense of being unempathic. Hence "invulnerability," despite its frequent use to describe resilience, suggests isolation[6] and insensitivity, although this is not always implied by those using the term interchangeably with resilience. Werner and Smith's (1982) seminal research on resilience sees pathological antecedents as stressors creating "vulnerability," suggesting that resilients are in fact vulnerable, and refers to the subjects who survive as "invincible," suggesting indefatigability rather than insensitivity, but leaving open the question of the need to recover from negative effects. All of these terms refer to issues of resistance, but contain significant, and sometimes conflicting, assumptions about what resistance psychologically requires from, or does to, individuals.

Current and past studies of resilience, invulnerability, and invincibility also define the outcomes which are characterized as "normal" or "competent" behavior in the sense of "coping" and "making do." Competence is central to Garmezy's understanding of resilience (Garmezy, 1983). While competence can be linked to efficacy (through a competent involvement with one's environment) and self-esteem, and is thus both a behavioral and a psychological variable, the behavior marker of resilience in empirical research is often the absence of failure. Werner and Smith (1982) use as their marker "the capacity to cope effectively" (p. 4) with both internal (e.g., fear) and external (e.g., loss of parent) stress. While Rutter sees resilient individuals as those who "overcome adversity, who survive stress, and who rise above disadvantage" (1979: 3), the main thrust of his work is about surviving adversity without lasting damage.[7]

The literature on resilience all too often assumes that poverty and parental psychopathology are linked,[8] a position of class bias we do not share. However, there are social factors associated with being poor and having uneducated parents that place impediments on children's development: absence of financial resources, quality of schools, parental experience of education, and class prejudice, among others. Previous research on resiliency emphasizes resistance to the presumed pathology in family backgrounds,[9] rather than the transcendence of the social factors we are emphasizing.[10]

In this book we examine how people who rise above disadvantage not only "make do," but build highly successful careers. We study not just the absence of negative outcomes, but the generative behavior associated with a successful adulthood. In our last chapter we compare our findings on these people with previous findings on resiliency. We wondered at the absence from the behavioral science literature of a term which would focus specific attention on people who *succeeded* in the face of origin factors which *opposed* their success. We think no term exists because research is remarkably lacking. Apparently, Americans don't study the process of their own most cherished myth. Indeed the present study was explicitly designed to fill this gap in the literature, and, as such, is an "exploratory study," since there were few guides for our research.

Since our subjects had used more than one path to achieve success, we decided to call our book *Paths to Success*, and our subjects Pathmakers, a descriptive term that makes fewer assumptions about the nature of the self.[11] The making of paths focuses attention on a creative interaction of both social and psychological factors to define human agency, when individuals transcend their own situation. Pathmakers do so by constructing new outcomes in the face of the odds against them.

The Social Field: Opportunities and Impediments

The United States is a stratified society which presents a variety of obstacles to an equal distribution of its resources: gender, skin color, class, and language, for example, are characteristics people can use to give an advantage to some and a disadvantage to others. That such discrimination is effective is reflected in sociological literature showing that females, blacks, non-English speakers, and those growing up poor have lower rates of success. Yet despite these general societal tendencies, many women, blacks, people born to lower-class families, and non-English dominant persons do succeed, and in this sense can be thought of as "negative prediction defiers." In this book we examine people who faced negative predictions associated with both education and socioeconomic status (SES), specifically black and white men and women who grew up poor by local definition, with neither parent completing high school, but who achieved high levels of career success anyway. The purpose of our research was to determine how they found a way to succeed in spite of these obstacles, and whether they differ from more mainstream populations. We have concluded that to succeed, they often needed to create new paths to achieve in situations in which the route to success was difficult and uncharted.

For the past twenty years we have been engaged in research at Teachers College, Columbia University on a number of social and psychological processes that are useful in enabling Pathmakers to succeed.[12] Our impetus for conducting such research was two-fold. First, we sought to redress a balance in the literature which has examined failure for these categories of people more than it has the exceptions to that pattern (see Sewell and Hauser, 1980; Coleman et al., 1966; Jencks et al., 1972; Macleod, 1987). Second, we are convinced by work of Vaillant and Levinson (Vaillant, 1977; Felsman and Vaillant, 1987; Long and Vaillant, 1989; Levinson, Darrow, Klein, Levinson, and McKee, 1978) that examination of careers that are well underway is essential. We therefore focused on mid-life career status, taking a long-term retrospective view not measured by input-output studies of performance over brief periods of time.[13] The data necessary to assess these long-term processes and configurations have not been systematically available although a few longitudinal studies have been suggestive (Long and Vaillant, 1989; Werner and Smith, 1982; and Chess and Thomas, 1984). Indeed our study should be responsive to a call by Hallinan

(1985) for such data to allow better conceptualizations of processes which contribute to mobility.

Our study attempts to illuminate how societal opportunities, serendipities, and impediments intersect with personal resources, strategies, and choices of individuals to produce success. In considering this we do not make the assumption that quality will win out. Indeed, it is likely that most individual talent available is wasted because of the obstacles stratified societies place in the path of individuals. The purpose of our research is not to deny the enormous odds favoring "social reproduction," nor to argue, along with exceptional Horatio Alger stories, that anyone can make it. We do start from the premise that, however rare, some individuals succeed in spite of the obstacles, and that it is important to ask how they do it. They could be extraordinarily able, but able at what? They could also be lucky, or better connected to resources which turn out to be critical, but which resources? Our research examined the intersection of opportunity and resources (in which we discuss family, social networks, education, and serendipity), and character (involving an examination of personality, motivation, and strategy). Our research is fundamentally a study of human agency.

While the present study bears upon a more general concern for social mobility in the social science literature, it differs in that we are examining how individual persons create successful careers rather than how populations mobilize or the consequences of mobility for social stratification. In this sense we are studying individual achievement as much as social mobility.

Sociological Variables and Upward Mobility

Sociologically oriented analyses of social mobility (see Duncan, Featherman, and Duncan, 1972) have, however, identified correlates of upward mobility that are suggestive for the present study. Among the factors found to have a differential effect on occupational success are social origin, ethnic status, sex, region of birth, type of community, and other characteristics of the family of origin. Education is an important intervening variable: poverty, minority status, the size and stability of one's family of origin, as well as one's position in it, all have an effect on access to schooling, which is generally found to be the most important determinant of occupational achievement in America. We will discuss education in more detail below.

While for whites these variables were not seen as cumulative in their effect, Blau and Duncan (1967) found that for blacks they were. Even when differences in social origin, region of birth, and education were controlled, the chances of occupational achievement were poorer for blacks than for whites—making their comparative study all the more important. In addition, for all levels below college graduate, the more education blacks had, the farther they were behind whites of equal education in occupational attainment. While progress may have been made since their 1967 study in remediating these effects by public and private investments, the effects have not disappeared, suggesting that the career paths of whites who do defy these negative predictions will differ from those of blacks. Blau and Duncan suggest that the blacks in their sample who defy the negative predictions go on to obtain higher levels of achievement than those who did not originally face such difficulties. It seems likely that the distance traveled for minorities will be greater than for non-minorities when mobility does occur, but their study does not clarify whether this is due to greater motivation, as they seem to suggest, or simply because the previous generation was kept so low in comparison to ability.

Many would argue that Duncan's scale has different meaning when applied to female versus traditionally male occupations. Sewell and Hauser's (1980) findings show that women begin their careers in higher status occupations than men (about one third of a standard deviation higher than men on Duncan's scale). However, by age thirty-two men had gained and women had lost status so that the men were higher. This suggests to Treiman (1985) a pattern attributable to child rearing and problems of career re-entry in women. This point is reinforced by Rossi (1985), who argued that because of their additional role responsibilities, women tend to reach mid-career, and therefore their highest career achievements, later than men. This seems an important reason to examine a sample old enough to allow time for success for both genders.[14] While a number of such studies have examined entry points and career options for women, the study of these phenomena retrospectively for women with highly successful careers has been largely neglected (for exceptions see Nieva and Gutek, 1981). For these reasons it seems clear to us that women's careers must be studied separately, just as it seems clear from the foregoing that blacks' careers may be different as well. This highlights an important focus of our research: as we examine the paths of Pathmakers, we should also examine whether there may be different paths for blacks and whites, and males and females.

Family of Origin

Pathmakers become very different from their families of origin, yet little previous research addresses how this happens. With respect to the role of the family of origin on occupational achievement, Blau and Duncan (1967) found stability and size to be related to upward mobility, as well as birth order—with the oldest in small families and the youngest in large ones the most likely to achieve mobility. The father's aspiration for his sons has been correlated with upward mobility (Kahl, 1953). Ellis and Lane (1963) found the mother's influence to be greater than the father's for upwardly mobile sons. However, the problem with much of this research is that the populations studied were so young that upward mobility was not as extreme as that of the Pathmakers. Research into the career patterns of "upwardly mobile" women has found that the mother's occupation as well as the father's is a significant dimension of women's intergenerational occupational mobility (Rosenfeld, 1978), although the social distance traveled is again not great, and the differences in age between women studied and men studied may be having an effect.

Early research on the upwardly mobile focused on the emotional antecedents of upward mobility without much consistency. Training for independence and involvement with adults at early ages have been identified as antecedents of success (Goertzel and Goertzel, 1978), or resiliency (Werner and Smith, 1992; Werner, 1993). Ellis and Lane (1967), however, took the view (along with Adler, 1930; Horney, 1950; Sherif and Cantril, 1947) that upward mobility is an escape from or compensation for early childhood deprivation, especially emotional deprivation.[15] Lipset and Bendix (1959) have argued that it is only the extremely upwardly mobile that bear out the deprivation hypothesis, but other research has contradicted this (Ellis and Lane, 1967; Shaffer, 1968). We will discuss the relevant psychological variables as we understand them in Chapter 2.

In studies of blacks, there is a similar split between researchers who see families as access to networks of opportunities, and those who see families as obstacles to social movement. We believe both could be relevant to our findings. Billingsley's 1968 study of black families refers to what he calls "screens of opportunity." He observes four levels of opportunity corresponding to four levels of society: individual, family, community, and the wider society. He suggests that a strong family life played a major role in the background of black men and women of achievement, noting such factors as a family history of literacy, free status during slavery, lineal descendants from slave masters, special status of family ancestors during slavery, and "strong" parents. He notes further that members of the black community serve as family extensions in terms of role models, advocates, and supportive figures, and that black institutions—like churches and settlement houses—played significant roles in the lives of successful blacks. We examined these variables for all of our subjects. These notions as they relate to family network influences reinforce the need to examine the role of kin networks among Pathmakers. This will also provide an opportunity to fill a gap pointed to by Bott (1971), who argued that no detailed study of network change over the life cycle exists.

An alternative view stressing the negative effects of black families to mobility is provided by authors like Erikson (1965), who argued that black mothers kept their children, "especially the gifted and questioning ones, away from futile and dangerous competition, imposing on them a surrendered identity" (p. 200), and Rainwater (1965), who argued that black families fail to teach their children to "embark on any course of action that might make things better" (p. 310). Bell (1965) went so far as to write that since the reality of the urban ghetto is so negative, black families have little reason to encourage children, and the black mother "simply does not believe in success" (p. 449). Alternatively Kandel (1967) found for working-class blacks living in predominantly white neighborhoods that maternal aspirations were so high for their children as to be "clearly unrealistic . . . wishful thinking" (p. 999). Personal values and needs such as social life, community interaction, and children's school experiences are seen by these authors as impinging on opportunities for mobility. Loury has argued that family networks determine the resources available to human development, the social capital, and thereby create and perpetuate socioeconomic inequality (Loury, 1995: 103). Such researchers have argued that the low status of black families sets limits to the help they can provide even if they want to, which further restrains the degree of mobility possible unless the individual is willing to make a path escaping from these negative family influences. Instead of seeing black families as resources to be exploited, these authors see them as negatives to be overcome or settings to flee in order to succeed.[16] In terms of occupational mobility, black individuals' needs for security and a sense of belonging were therefore seen to be at odds with the need to take advantage of opportunities. It has even been argued that growing up black "does not encourage the belief that one can manipulate his [*sic*] environment or the conviction that one can improve his condition very much by planning and hard work" (Rosen, 1959: 55). Given these arguments, we chose to examine variables that should enable us to assess whether becoming a Pathmaker is helped or hurt by personal and kin ties.

Education

An important definer of paths to career success is education, including schooling. Our research was explicitly designed to enable us to address a perennial debate (see Bowles and Gintis, 1976; Collins, 1971) about education: Is it an equally effective path to success for both the disadvantaged and the relatively advantaged? To assess the role of education, we studied life histories. As Cremin (1976) has noted,

> individuals come to educational situations with their own temperaments, histories, and purposes, and different individuals will obviously interact with a given configuration of education in different ways and with different outcomes. Hence, in considering the interactions and the outcomes, it is as necessary to examine individual life histories as it is to examine the configurations themselves. An educational life history focuses on the experience of education from the perspective of the person having and undergoing the experience . . . (p. 38)

It is important to determine any relationship between educational achievement and career achievement. Measures of who will be successful in school have not been successfully applied to an understanding of who will succeed in the workplace, although Werner and Smith (1992) do link good school performance to resiliency. In fact, attempts to relate IQ measured in school to adult performance have not been fruitful. This result is not surprising since IQ was originally developed by Binet to predict school, not life, performance.[17] Success in school might be a powerful message that might carry over to other challenges, but studies that relate school performance to success later in life do not tell us why or how people succeed and tell us little about the processes through which success is attained.[18] School success might also lead to more schooling: essential for some careers, but less effective, or even counter-productive, for others. Race and ethnicity must also be taken into account: if a study showed that whites succeeded more often than better-educated blacks or Hispanics, it would not necessarily argue the ineffectiveness of education, but rather speak to the effectiveness of the social-stratification mechanisms of the larger society that keep people from fulfilling their potential. John Ogbu has also argued that if the society's inequalities are perceived, lower-status school students would lower their efforts, making school success for such populations even less likely.

Furthermore, studies which only assess schooling can never fully assess the role of education.[19] We take seriously the definition of education offered by Cremin (1970) as "the deliberate, systematic, and sustained effort to transmit, evoke, or acquire knowledge, values, attitudes, skills, or sensibilities . . ." (p. xiii). It would also include *any* learning that results from the effort: direct or indirect, intended or unintended. In an empirical study Cremin's definition needs modification because we must admit the impossibility of trying to recognize intent empirically, that is, to recognize which efforts are deliberate and which are not. It is important to determine what skills people say were needed to build their careers, and how they feel they acquired them. By relating the actual demands faced by people as they have built their careers to the resources these people had for meeting those demands, we aim to assess the role of the educative process in its broadest sense.

In addition, if Pathmakers have compensated in some way for their backgrounds, we know very little about their truly "compensatory" education, despite the billions of dollars spent each year on such programs (Title I, Head Start, Upward Bound, etc.). They are designed to be compensatory in their effects, and yet are conceived with no real idea about which real-life compensations are successful.[20] Our conceptual framework leads us to carefully examine the educational history of the subjects of our research, and determine the role of education in their career achievement. We review material on the educational attainment of their parents and siblings; the types and locations of the schools they attended and their ethnic composition; the subjects' performance in school, including relationships with teachers and peers; attitudes of family and peers toward school performance, including what encouragement they or others gave; and the role of extracurricular activities and social relationships.

In examining our data about schools as institutions, a number of issues will emerge that have to do with how individuals differentially experience the school environment (the size, SES and ethnic composition, rural or urban location, and the number of grades). These are aspects of the formal setting within which informal processes of education (for example, learning from peers and mentors) occur. These issues all emerge in literatures seeking an understanding of the education of blacks and other traditionally lower-status groups. We compare individual variations in coping with these aspects of institutionalized schooling, and specifically try to determine what impact can be discerned from subjects' reports of their experiences in segregated and integrated schools.

We also compare some aspects of formal with informal learning. The work of Scribner and Stevens (1989) highlights the potential differences between what schools teach and what people need to know in the world of work. Our study allows the examination of what many authors have distinguished as formal (curricular) and informal learning within schools and their relevance to later career success. It may be that informal opportunities to exercise leadership, manage conflict, and to learn from peers and significant figures other than teachers are important. Informal parts of the teacher's role (for example, taking the time after school to encourage children to attend college) may matter more to long-term outcomes than teachers' classroom organization or performance on formal tests measuring teacher competence.

The issue of mentoring has also been much discussed for the groups involved in our study, and programs designed to promote mentoring for minority and female scholars proliferate. However, there is little long-term confirmation of the actual benefit of mentoring, or how processes of spiralism may be critical to understanding mentoring programs (see Flaxman, Ascher, and Harrington, 1988 for a review). We examine not only who reports mentoring relationships as being important, but who mentors whom. Are there differences in who mentors Pathmakers, men and women, blacks and whites? Is race or gender an important variable in who becomes a mentor, and to whom?

Since career success was a prerequisite to be in our sample, a number of questions were also asked concerning other resources that people utilized in building their successful careers which might be useful in examining differences between Pathmakers and others, while at the same time assessing the effects of race and gender on these patterns. If Pathmakers have different paths to career success than more advantaged people, do these differences interact with race and gender differences to create even greater diversity of paths? While we might find job resource or career path differences between men and women, or blacks and whites per se, we might also find that interactions of these variables with Pathmaker status will be crucial. Therefore, our study should allow us to address whether differences in career success between men and women attributed in other studies to gender, or between blacks and whites attributed in other studies to race, may be misattributions resulting from not examining and controlling the class and education variables that for us define Pathmaker status. Regrettably, too much research on career success seems to assume that all blacks grew up poor (see Gary, 1981), and that the effects of being female can be studied without controlling for class differences (see Kanter, 1977). We disagree, and expect to find race and gender useful in better understanding differences attributable to being a Pathmaker; a point stressed by Scarr (1988), who argues that research investigating gender and race along with SES and educational background is needed and should be encouraged.

Redundancy and Spiralism

Our review of the literature on mobility strongly implies that the social supports and opportunities available to demographically advantaged individuals are highly redundant. If educated and middle SES parents fail to provide an appropriate, expected amount of encouragement and help which supports the person's advancement, other persons or institutions (e.g., other kin, families of peers, teachers, employers, or counseling services) are likely to fill in the gaps left by the person's own parents. In the case of the economically disadvantaged, in contrast, such support-and-opportunity-redundancy is far less common. The opportunities are probably more isolated, rarer, and hence thinner, while the obstacles to their achievement are plentiful. Furthermore, we speculate that obstacles associated with race and gender may require different solutions than those simply associated with class or education of parent. That is, as resources are spread over more obstacles, they become even thinner, and solutions to obstacles become necessarily more creative and different from the paths to success of those with redundant social resources and fewer obstacles to overcome.

The notion of spiralism is related to the concept of redundancy but is more concerned with how networks are utilized, and reminds us that small advantages can have big consequences over time. The term was first used in a political-economic context by Vincent (1971). She describes positive and negative spirals: a person gets a foothold on an ascending path that begins to acquire its own momentum. This reinforces our need to study the development of Pathmakers across their lives.[21] While spiralism is descriptive only of intra-generational mobility, it is interesting to note that Lenin deals with a related concept in *The Development of Capitalism in Russia*. Small advantages like a horse or an extra wagon were parlayed over time to larger advantages, more horses, more land, and the outcome was the differentiation of the peasantry into workers or entrepreneurs. Spiralism returns us to the relationship of individual achievement to social stratification.

It was our intention in carrying out this study to examine how the social variables just reviewed interact with the personal resources of individual actors to produce different patterns of career success. The examination of individuals within the social settings in which they become socialized is a longstanding concern of psychology and anthropology, but our developmental focus through adulthood for white and black, male and female Pathmakers in the United States is unique.[22] In the next chapter we turn to the psychological variables which define the personal resources that will help us understand Pathmakers and their success.

2

Personal Resources

Our study of the careers of people who, according to statistical predictors, should not have become successful, but who became successful nevertheless illuminates not only the obstacles, opportunities, and serendipities that have framed their world, but also the personal resources, strategies, and choices they brought to and made within that social field. Combinations of factors—cultural, social, familial, and educational— are no doubt important in determining the extraordinary social mobility and personal accomplishments of the persons we call Pathmakers. While we are fully persuaded that such accomplishments are unlikely without supports and opportunities made available by other people and institutions, we also believe that without developing certain personal resources, Pathmakers could not have utilized the opportunities to overcome obstacles. As Garmezy (1981: 249) stressed, "Life is not a matter of holding good cards, but of playing a poor hand well."[1]

We have argued in Chapter 1 that the social supports and opportunities that are available to demographically advantaged persons are, in effect, highly redundant. That is, if the parents of a demographically advantaged person fail to provide an appropriate, expected amount of encouragement and help to support the person's advancement, other persons or institutions (other kin, families of peers, teachers, employers, or counselors) will be more likely to fill in the gaps left by the person's own family. In the case of the economically disadvantaged, in contrast, such support- and opportunity-redundancy may be far less common. Therefore we expected that personal resources would be more crucial to Pathmakers' career success than to sociologically more advantaged people.

Certainly people born to different families acquire and practice different interpersonal skills. These interpersonal skills and opportunities should have consequences later in life.[2] But in addition to such interpersonal perspectives, the psychological literature suggests that we should be interested in two more classic, or endogenous, conceptions of personal resources that are relevant to people's ability to cope successfully with such adverse life circumstances: personal resources like motivation and personal orientation; and strategies for coping with, and defending against, stress and adversity.[3]

As Lois Murphy (1962) has pointed out, it is an unfortunate fact that psychologists of personality development have tended to neglect the study of unusually able, stress-resistant persons in favor of the study of psychopathology and failures of adaptation. The tendency still exists, but there have been some notable and important exceptions.

The concern of Abraham Maslow (1954, 1968) with "self-actualizing" persons—those whose degree of psychological development is extraordinary—sparked not only a popular concern with "personal growth," but also a rekindling of interest in the theories of adult development postulated by Jung (1963, 1964, 1969) and the ego identity theories of Eric Erikson (1950, 1959). Indeed, since Erikson's work, theory and research on ego and personality development have begun to attend to developmental successes as well as developmental problems.[4]

The work of David McClelland (1955, 1961), John W. Atkinson (1966), and Atkinson and Joel O. Raynor (1978) on motivational orientations toward issues of achievement, affiliation, and power, and on the consequences of identifying and pursuing long-term career paths represents an extensive program of systematic research on personal characteristics that presumably lead to positive outcomes.

Thibaut and Kelley (1959) and others have noted that an orientation to seeking out rewards in situations (as contrasted with an orientation to the avoidance of costs) may have profound consequences for learning, performance, and long-term outcomes.[5]

Rotter (1966) and others (Lefcourt, 1982; Phares, 1976) have examined the tendency of persons to see either themselves or forces external to themselves as the locus of control over what happens to them and to others. Those with an internal locus of control ought to be particularly resistant to the kinds of sociological expectations Pathmakers face, since they see their fates as determined by forces internal to themselves, not the social surround.

Riesman, Glazer, and Denney (1950), and Shostrom (1965, 1966) have pointed to a distinction between persons who are inclined to formulate and use their own standards for evaluating what they do and what happens to them, and persons who tend to adopt the standards of others in making such evaluations; "inner-directed" people may be presumed to be less encumbered by an orientation to pleasing others, and may therefore have an important advantage over people who are "other-directed."

Garmezy (1981, 1983) has emphasized that not all succumb to risks they encounter. But what can these variables tell us about those who not only fail to succumb, but succeed despite negative expectations? In the next section we briefly review theory and research on these personal orientations that may help people build new paths that defy negative social expectations in the world of work, and discuss their implications for our research.

Motivations and Personality Orientations Related to Mobility

Achievement, Affiliation, and Power Motivation

The work on achievement motivation begun by McClelland, Atkinson, and their colleagues in the early 1950s was intended to explain stable tendencies in certain persons to be oriented toward striving for "success in life." This group of psychologists devised measures of achievement motivation based on analyses of the content of stories told by persons in response to ambiguous stimuli such as pictures and brief "lead" sentences (McClelland, Atkinson, Clark, and Lowell, 1958). People whose stories reflect what these investigators called "competition with a standard of excellence" are seen as being more likely than others to have a consistent tendency to be motivated to achieve success. The research of these investigators (see Atkinson and Raynor, 1978 for a review) suggests that people who are relatively high in achievement motivation tend to attempt tasks that appear moderately difficult to them (rather than easy or extremely difficult); tend to be persistent in the face of difficulties they may encounter in their tasks; and tend, on the whole, to show evidence of good performance and achievement over a period of time.[6]

Winter (1973) has demonstrated that public speeches of national leaders can be examined for evidence of motives to achieve, affiliate, and seek power, and that the balance of these themes in such speeches is related to the international actions taken by these leaders. Likewise, we believe that the autobiographical utterances of our subjects can also be analyzed for achievement, affiliation, and power themes, and that the balance of these themes may well be related to the various ways in which these persons have managed social mobility and career advancement.

Extensions of achievement-motivation ideas by Atkinson and Raynor (1978) suggest that effective career striving on the part of achievement-oriented persons must involve a good deal of long-term planning. If a person's achievement motivation is to influence the quality of a particular performance, he or she must be aware of the relevance of that performance to long-term goals (Raynor, Atkinson, and Brown, 1974). This notion suggests that the lives of our subjects should also be examined for evidence of explicit career planning, including a tendency to be unusually aware both of future career paths and of the instrumentality of particular courses of action for movement along those paths.

Reward and Cost Orientation

John Thibaut and Harold Kelley (1959) suggested that it is sensible to distinguish between two personal orientations to outcomes that may be available. They speculated that some people are particularly oriented to the rewards they might obtain, and relatively insensitive to the costs they might incur in the course of striving for rewards. Such "reward-oriented" people were described by Thibaut and Kelley as tending to feel "confident, powerful, and oriented to success." In contrast, "cost-oriented" people, who are particularly sensitive to the costs they might suffer, were described as feeling generally "constricted, powerless, and oriented toward the avoidance of failure." Research on reward and cost orientations has indicated that relative to cost-oriented persons, those who are reward-oriented tend to overvalue outcomes they have not yet experienced (Gumpert, Thibaut, and Shuford, 1961). In addition, reward-oriented people have relatively optimistic perceptions of their past and future performances, are willing to undertake relatively difficult tasks, tend to learn more than cost-oriented people about those tasks, and therefore tend to perform somewhat better and reap greater rewards (Canavan-Gumpert, 1977; Sun, 1975).

It seems plausible to us that the unusual social mobility and career accomplishments of Pathmakers require, among other things, a particularly active stance toward the world—a willingness to see opportunities and to take action despite the possibility that costs may be incurred in the process. We could, therefore, hypothesize that Pathmakers are more likely to be reward-oriented than cost-oriented, yet it is also plausible to argue that because they grew up with less money they may be more cost-oriented than equally successful but economically better-off subjects. Due to childhood poverty, Pathmakers may be more concerned with holding on to what they have rather than taking risks to get more. In any event we consider it prudent to look for evidence of both reward and cost orientations.

Internal and External Locus of Control

The work of Julian Rotter (1966) and his students and colleagues (see Lefcourt, 1982 and Phares, 1976 for reviews) suggests that it is useful and important to distinguish between two major attitudes people entertain about the causes of things that happen to themselves and others. According to these researchers, some take the point of view that they are the cause of most of the things that happen to them—that the locus of causality for events tends to be internal. Others believe that forces external to themselves are more likely to exert the most important causal influence.

A great deal of research has demonstrated important differences between people whose "locus of control" is internal and those for whom it is external.[7] One of the more important findings of Coleman et al. (1966) was that the black school children studied appeared to feel less internal control than the white children. External locus of control may be realistic for blacks growing up in a stratified society, but Hillman, Wood, and Sawilowsky (1992) go further and argue that externality is self-protective for people in a "stigmatized" group. If so, the self-protection may also be self-defeating; Coleman also found that among black children, those with a higher degree of internal locus of control had higher school achievement scores. Webb, Waugh, and Herbert

(1993) found internal locus of control positively correlated with performance on medical boards of black medical students. Those who continue to believe that they are makers of their own fates appear to become more successful and creative individuals (see Lefcourt, 1976). Research on children at risk has also found an internal locus of control to be important to resilience.[8]

These ideas about locus of control are related conceptually to the notions about reward-cost orientations discussed above. We think it is highly plausible to hypothesize that many or most Pathmakers are likely to believe that their rewards are contingent on their behavior—to have a strong internal locus of control, in Rotter's terms. If they not did believe so, then it seems more likely that they would succumb to the negative predictor factors that surround them in their early lives. For example, if you are the son of a sharecropper in the rural south walking five miles to a one-room schoolhouse each day, it seems to us that only an individual with an internal locus of control, who believed his fate was in his own hands, could become a Pathmaker. Therefore it seems sensible to consider these orientations in our study.

In our study, we defined locus of control to be a personality variable that is fairly stable over time. Other authors have been more interested in demonstrating that such orientations are malleable and more situational. For example, Bandura (1990) has stressed that the likelihood that an individual will have control must be assessed for each new life situation. We assume that general expectancies arise from accumulations of such assessments, and these in turn play a role in future assessments. In this way there is a link between locus of control, competence beliefs, and self-efficacy.[9]

Inner- and Other-Directedness

In a well-known book about Americans after World War II, David Riesman and his collaborators (Riesman, Glazer, and Denney, 1950) suggested that a plausible and probably important distinction can be made among people based on the sources of their standards of behavior and performance.[10] The meaning of the terms inner- and other-directedness for psychologists (such as Shostrom, 1965, who has worked from the perspective of Abraham Maslow) is rather different from Riesman's original work: inner-directed people are seen as creating and using their own standards of performance and conduct in judging their own and others' actions and work, while other-directed people are seen as seeking out and adopting the standards of others in judging the adequacy of their own and others' performances and outcomes. Thus the inner-directed person, viewed from the perspective of personality psychologists, is autonomous, independent, and initiating. The other-directed person is more dependent on the standards of others, and presumably more strongly oriented to pleasing others and meeting their standards.

We believe that it is reasonable to expect that Pathmakers should be generally inner-directed—that they are not, by and large, over-encumbered by a need to discover and meet the standards of others, but rather more likely to adopt and maintain standards of evaluation of their own. This would seem to be an important attitudinal resource for achieving social mobility. We therefore considered evidence of inner- versus other-directedness in our investigation.

Styles of Coping with Stress and Conflict

The psychological literature on coping with stress, adversity, and conflict is large and particularly diverse. Most thinking relevant to our research has emerged from psychoanalytic literature, more particularly from the work of Anna Freud (1937) and Heinz Hartmann (1958). Anna Freud constructed a broad catalogue of mechanisms of defense used by people to protect themselves from unconscious conflicts—from unacceptable impulses, feelings, and thoughts. These "ego mechanisms of defense" were generally thought to be characteristic of neurotic functioning; even the more "productive" ones—such as sublimation and humor—were taken as somewhat distorted expressions of neurotically forbidden impulses and ideas. The emergence of the ego psychology of Hartmann (1958) drastically changed the views of many psychoanalytically oriented thinkers about ego defenses; Hartmann saw them as integral to the general problem of adaptation to life. Many psychoanalytic thinkers have adopted his point of view and seen defenses not solely as protecting against unacceptable endogenous wishes, but also as coping strategies in which the self deals with conflict in the external world.[11]

While ego defenses and coping strategies represent different theoretical perspectives, distinctions between internal ego-defenses and external coping styles are not always practically useful or easy to make, especially if ego defenses under investigation include the so-called mature "coping" ones (notably altruism, humor, suppression, anticipation, and sublimation). We believe that it is sensible to assume that the defense mechanisms that a person uses in dealing with intrapsychic conflicts are related to how one copes with the problems and obstacles encountered in the external world. Intrapsychic conflicts are, after all, often stimulated by real-world events, and the real-world consequences of defense mechanisms (such as projection in the case of authoritarian attitudes and behaviors) have often been documented. The distinctions that have been made, then, can seem indistinct and arbitrary.[12]

Most research on ego defenses has emphasized defensive styles that are maladaptive, rigid, or distorting: characteristics of pathological functioning.[13] It must be noted that the purpose of much of the work to which we refer has been diagnostic-clinical, and that these researchers have generally not been interested in the broader issues of surmounting realistic obstacles, coping with long-term adversity, or general adaptation to life. Cohler (1987) has argued that there has been little progress as well in developing instruments to measure coping, perhaps for the same reason.[14]

However, the results of a number of longitudinal studies have been concerned with these issues. For example, Haan (1963) and Kroeber (1963) have reported that defense mechanism preference among men and women is strongly associated with behavioral indicators of mental health and maturity. Haan (1964) has interpreted her longitudinal data on adolescents as indicating that defense mechanism preference in adulthood is associated with shifts in social class. Persons in her study whose styles of adaptation can be seen as productive or mature were more likely than others to move upward in social class. In a similar vein, Lengner and Michael (1963) have suggested that persons whose defensive styles are very immature are more likely than others to experience downward mobility. Some researchers have argued that maturity of ego functioning is a result as well as a partial determinant of social class (see Weinstock, 1967; Long and Vaillant, 1989).

The early work of George Vaillant (1971, 1975, 1976, 1977) on preferred defense mechanisms is relevant to our own interest in Pathmakers.[15] What seems to us most striking about the results of Vaillant's longitudinal study is that the preferred ego-defense mechanisms of the adult men in the sample, originally selected as promising Harvard undergraduates, discriminated between those whose life outcomes were particularly good and those whose career, interpersonal, and health outcomes were relatively poor.[16] In his descriptions of the lives of people who exemplify his points about maturity of ego defenses, Vaillant (1977) implies that many of those whose defenses were judged to be in the mature category started life in relatively modest circumstances, and a number of the men who were socioeconomically advantaged during childhood did not develop productive styles of adaptation.[17]

It seems highly plausible to us that Pathmakers would need to develop mature ego-defense mechanisms more than people in more privileged categories. On the other hand, since defense mechanisms are developed early, and since the childhood of Pathmakers may be much more deprived than the Harvard men studied by Vaillant, it is also plausible that Pathmakers might have higher rates of less mature defense mechanisms than people growing up in more economically and educationally advantaged homes.[18] However, if there are differences between Pathmakers and other subjects, they should be restricted in their scope. Psychotic or immature defenses are unlikely, according to Vaillant's work, to be associated with the levels of career success characteristic of our sample.

Vaillant (1993) has emphasized that maturity of defenses can come about as the subject ages and the ego itself matures, suggesting that ego defenses are not fixed but plastic. Vaillant's results can be interpreted as suggesting that certain immature or neurotic defenses are more likely to evolve into mature ones than others (Vaillant, 1977, 1993).[19] We should also stress that when one considers coping conceptualizations emphasizing skills in dealing with the outside world, the maturity metaphor emphasizing only intrapsychic energy management becomes less relevant, and even inappropriate. Some defenses can still be seen as more productive, not for their efficiency in managing internal forces but because they lead to better coping strategies interpersonally than do other defenses (see Moos and Billings, 1982; Cohler, 1987). Better coping can lead to higher levels of competence. Since competence is intrinsically satisfying, it can result in higher self-esteem, and more internal attributions (see, for example, Anthony and Cohler, 1987, Part II).

Costs of Success

One important topic which we considered was the cost of success to subjects we studied. While it may seem to some that success is its own reward, the literature does suggest that there are real costs to Path-makers which come about directly from the mobility they have exhibited. Typical of this literature is the argument that Pathmakers suffer from being marginal people who are in some respects out of tune with both their early family and their present environment.[20] This marginality is closely linked to the literature on family already reviewed in Chapter 1, but it does introduce some new dynamics which need examining: mobile people tend to be cool and distant from neighbors who are not usually regarded as friends (Stacey, 1967). The same study found that they have fewer friends, more brittle friendships, and "are characteristically isolated people who are never deeply involved with acquaintances, friends, or relatives" (Stacey, 1967: 7). On the other hand, Klein and Riviere (1964) argue that such people are capable of quickly making congenial social contacts. This trait is presumably linked to an earlier observation by Stacey, that mobile people have to improvise behavior which other people have learned.

If some studies find upward mobility linked with divorce, neurotic disorders, even psychosomatic disorders or suicide,[21] the literature is far from homogeneous. Upwardly mobile individuals have also been found to be healthier and more stable than the downwardly mobile individual (Hollingshead and Redlich, 1958; Myers and Roberts, 1959; Srole, Langner, Michael, Opler, and Rennie, 1962), but the differences may be due to the degree of mobility (extreme versus modest)—a variable on which there is little data. Also some of these studies are based upon comparisons of upward and downward mobility instead of inter-generationally stable subjects. This stacks the deck in favor of psychological health, since downward mobility is known to be associated with a higher incidence of neurotic disorders, schizophrenia, and suicide.

In general, there are few clues to the specific psychological and social costs that pertain to becoming a Pathmaker, but there is sufficient literature to justify our examining if costs are incurred by our subjects, and what these costs might be.

In Chapter 3 we turn to a description of the method of our study. It is clear from the literature we have reviewed in Chapters 1 and 2 that understanding how Pathmakers build their careers raises questions from several disciplines: anthropology, psychology, and sociology. These questions frequently intersect. Our study is therefore designed to examine some of these complexities.

3

The Study Design

In this chapter we first summarize how we designed our study of Pathmakers. Then we describe how we defined the cohorts to be studied, and how our findings are presented. A fuller description of the interview procedures and the analyses undertaken is to be found in Appendix A.

Defining Pathmakers

The problem of constructing criteria that define what origins are necessary to make someone a Pathmaker is not an easy one, particularly since the relevant disciplines of sociology, psychology, and anthropology all have different notions about which issues and variables are important. For most sociologists, the central issue has been inter-generational social mobility—movement from one social stratum to another. For psychologists, the central issue of interest has usually been "success," or "career success." Anthropologists have had both sorts of concerns, with American anthropologists placing a predictably greater emphasis, perhaps, on historical (sub-) cultural differences in routes to success (Ogbu, 1974; Alvarez, 1987) rather than class issues of rigidity to mobility favored by their English colleagues (Hargreaves, 1967; Lacey, 1970), or the social reproductionists (Bourdieu and Passeron, 1977). Our own inclination was to bypass the difficulties that would be involved in defining social class by concerning ourselves primarily with the question of occupational status of parents during childhood. We began, therefore, with the common-sense proposition that Pathmakers would have overcome the difficult obstacles to occupational success presented by growing up in a family who was poor by local standards.[1] Given the ages of our sample (forty to fifty-five at the time of the interview), Hollingshead and Redlich's (1958) index is an appropriate measure of national occupational status when our subjects were growing up. Our criterion of childhood poverty meant that the Pathmakers came from families from the bottom two strata of Hollingshead and Redlich's index of occupational prestige, and Pathmakers' parents must have remained in these low-status, low-income strata throughout the subject's childhood.

We also chose to limit the educational attainment of parents in order for subjects to be considered Pathmakers. An often used sociological variable—graduation from high school—must not have been achieved by either parent for the Pathmaker to qualify for our study. While the proportion of Americans achieving high school graduation has varied historically, we have restricted the ages of our subjects as described below. The parents of the subjects studied here were therefore most likely to have been in high school between World Wars I and II, and therefore we feel the variable has consistent meaning. This variable was important to us theoretically because it assured that neither parent would have had college experience, meaning that parental ties to colleges would be unlikely. Thus Pathmakers as defined in this study come from homes characterized by low income and occupational status, and have parents who were not high school graduates.[2]

To be a Pathmaker, of course, one must also succeed. The occupational status of Pathmakers at mid-career (at the time of the interview) would generally be seen as belonging to the upper-middle and professional classes, corresponding to the top two strata on the Hollingshead and Redlich (1958) index. Such a large jump in one generation is an appropriate criterion: our study was intended to examine extreme cases. Yet even within our sample there are many degrees of mobility and career success, as well as a considerable range in the number and severity of obstacles the person has had to overcome. As we explain below, in our judgment, such variation had to be permitted in the study.

For the purpose of this research, we further required that careers not just be in high-status fields, but sufficiently developed to be unambiguously recognized as successful by others in that occupation. For this study, panels of experts were used: academics who evaluated academic careers (i.e., university professors, basic and applied researchers, senior administrators); business people who evaluated business careers (i.e., managers and entrepreneurs in commerce and industry); and government people who evaluated careers in government (i.e., high-level local and national political figures). We believe that these occupations are representative of upper-middle-class and professional occupations in the U.S. (except for physicians, lawyers, and dentists in private practices, who were excluded due to difficulties in judging career success).[3] We chose this peer-defined, relatively broad criterion for career success rather than more narrow criteria because we were concerned that limiting our definition to include only people who are widely regarded as "superstars" in their chosen occupation might have overweighed our sample with people of truly extraordinary talent—people who might be seen as having been able to reach their positions on the basis of this talent alone, with little or no assistance from others and no unusual ability to adapt to adversity. In this context, one of the weaknesses of Maslow's interesting work on "self-actualizing" people is that he chose only people who had achieved "star" status in their professions (Maslow, 1954, 1968, 1971); for our purposes the subjects of his study (such as Beethoven and Einstein) could be viewed as simply too unusual.

Pathmakers, completely defined then, are those with successful careers in high-status occupations whose families of origin were poor by local standards, low in occupational status, and whose parents were not high school graduates.

Defining Controls

The primary purpose of our research is to identify factors that are particularly important in the unusual degree of social mobility of Pathmakers—factors that are, in a sense, unique to this degree of status mobility. For this reason, we had to be able to distinguish these factors from others that Pathmakers might *share* with persons who have the same degree of career success, but who are not inter-generationally mobile. To do so we compared Pathmakers with equally successful people who did not face negative predictions due to their backgrounds. Operationally such a comparison was achieved by studying subjects who were successful but who did not grow up in families of low status and income, and who had parents who graduated from high school.[4] These equally successful individuals from middle-class and educated families constitute our Controls.

It is important to point out that other control groups could have been selected for study. For example, persons with origins similar to Pathmakers but who did not achieve high career success or who failed in their careers could be studied. This would allow comparisons of Pathmakers with those from similar backgrounds who did not experience inter-generational mobility. We chose not to deal with the question of why some people facing negative predictions make it and some do not, however. Our control group was chosen with the main focus of our study in mind: what, if anything, differentiates how Pathmakers become successful from how other people who come from more traditionally middle-class backgrounds become successful?

Race and Gender Comparisons

As previously mentioned, we were also interested in assessing the additional negative obstacles associated with being black and being female in the United States. We assumed that members of subordinate (see Ogbu, 1974) categories who met our basic success criteria would have had to move through a greater number of obstacles to mobility and career success than others. Those commonly labeled blacks constitute at least two major groups. One is a recent migrant population and their descendants from various primarily West Indian countries, predominantly Trinidad, Jamaica, and Barbados. The other is comprised of the black descendants of slave populations who have been in the U.S. for much longer. We concentrated our research on the latter group by excluding migrants from other countries or their first-generation descendants from our sample. We felt that current or recent migrations pose different psychological challenges, and introduce self-selection variables that were best deferred for future research. This second group of blacks were chosen for our study because they are the largest group who have a long history of residence in the U.S., and therefore a rich history of dealing with subordinate status. We have chosen to continue to use the term "black" in this book since this was the usage at the time of the interviews. This allows us to preserve the integrity of the quotes, and to maintain consistency between the text and the quotes.

As discussed earlier, we also believe it is important to build a comparison between men and women because the traditional subordinate status of women in our society introduces obstacles—negative predictions—for levels of career success compared to men, obstacles which need to be overcome in ways analogous to obstacles associated with race for the black subjects. We also believe that women have not been studied enough in the general mobility literature. It is plausible and reasonable to assume that there are both commonalities and differences in the psychological characteristics of men and women regardless of how many and how severe the obstacles were that they have had to overcome.

We found it sensible for our comparison group to include both equal numbers of males and females, and black and white subjects in order to facilitate comparisons between Pathmakers and Controls within each racial and gender category.

Description of the Interview

The method employed in our study was a lengthy life-history interview asking adult Pathmakers and Controls to report retrospectively on their own lives. The interview (see Appendix B) was the sole data-collection device for our research, and therefore had to bear a great deal of weight. It had to allow us to discover the effects of the supporting persons and institutions that were involved over time in the mobility and career strivings of the respondent, directly or indirectly—family members, peers and families of peers, chance acquaintances, friends, co-workers, schools, church, the military, government institutions, employing organizations, and so on. We also needed to discover the events and the decisions that punctuated the respondent's progress—opportunities, obstacles, serendipity, choices made, successes, failures, etcetera. The instrument also had to reveal the role of the family of origin, the extended family, and other members of the community in providing the respondent with the material and psychological resources that may have helped. Finally, it had to enable us to assess the personal attributes of the respondent—ego defenses, adaptation styles, and other psychological characteristics described in Chapter 2—that may have helped or hindered the respondent's progress. The interview was constructed by the investigators through pretest interviews with older graduate students and mid-career professionals.

The resulting interview was divided into the following sections: biographical material (nine questions), employment history (twenty-eight questions), schooling history (twenty-seven questions), family and community of origin (nineteen questions), current family (thirteen questions), health (eighteen questions), and psychological/general (seventeen questions).

The first sections of the interview were designed to stimulate recollection of material not immediately retrievable as the interview began, and thereby functioned as a self-correcting procedure. We believe such embedded recollections can be highly useful, and could be reliably retrieved with a properly constructed instrument. To improve both the reliability and validity of our data a number of strategies were used. The employment, schooling, and family of origin sections were, for example, approached in sequence and chronologically; each section therefore started earlier in time and ran through the present, beginning respectively with first job, first school, and birth. The structure was designed to stimulate memories about important early decisions, people, events, feelings, and responses by going over the respondent's life three times from these different perspectives; the covered material also facilitated probing and triangulation in later sections with specific content from earlier answers. The order of jobs, schooling, and family was determined by what we assumed would be least threatening—jobs (since all were by definition successful), to more threatening—family (first of origin and later of procreation). We emphasize that a crucial key to assessing respondents' styles of adaptation during various times of his or her life is knowing what she or he did in response to important events, threats, obstacles, and so on. This format enabled a considerable amount of emphasis in the interview on asking the respondent to recall and describe not only events, opportunities, obstacles, sources of support, etcetera, but also the behaviors and feelings that these elicited. Each section of the interview, then, asked for a good deal of detail in the description of important incidents and people at several points in the life cycle, and the same time frame was often examined from different perspectives. By having our subjects go over their lives several times from different perspectives, we hoped to stimulate recollections of material not immediately accessible, and tried in this way to construct a self-correcting instrument.

Our long interview method, like any, is not without its limitations. Cohler has written about his concerns for the validity of such data:

"Little is known about the manner in which persons create a narrative that renders adversity coherent in terms of experienced life history, or of the manner in which presently constructed meanings of life changes may be altered in order to maintain a sense of personal integration" (Cohler, 1987). Although such self-reported data have their problems, we know of no other method suitable for our research purpose. To be sure, our method will be unable to address issues of the mutability of personality and defenses over time discussed in Chapter 2, as might a longitudinal study, but Pathmakers are by definition rare. A longitudinal design would require a prohibitively large number of subjects and extraordinary resources in order to contain enough Pathmakers to study.[5] Further, our primary purpose in this research is not to test issues of personality stability or change over the life course, but to determine whether Pathmakers report taking different paths to success than the Controls. Our data are limited to their retrospective accounts of these paths, but there is also a rich literature in psychological anthropology showing the value of this type of life history research.[6] The study of life histories is, in a sense, the study of individuals' myths about themselves. But we can learn much from this that will tell us what kinds of people they are, and that will locate them in their social context.

The Sampling Procedure

Since our study was exploratory in purpose, we believed that little was to be gained and much could be wasted by attempting to impose the criterion of national representativeness on the sample we interviewed. The convenience sample we used to initiate a subsequent snowball sampling procedure was, however, purposive in that it was framed by the three occupational categories previously described: academia, business, and government. The search for subjects for our research was initiated through the use of social networks of the senior researchers. These included contacts through board memberships in various educational and corporate institutions in the Northeast, present and past colleagues at a number of universities, and government officials encountered in such professional activities as grants application and lobbying. Points of entry were expanded through these people's networks via an informal snowball procedure in which, when subjects were nominated for study, the subjects in turn nominated other subjects from their networks.

Since it seemed desirable to maximize comparability between Pathmakers and Controls, Controls were selected from the same sources used to identify Pathmakers.[7] The Pathmakers and Controls actually studied, in fact, did not differ in their distribution among the three occupational domains, nor in their level of success. They are also comparable on rural/urban background, and parts of the country in which they grew up. They do not differ in age.

In order to have subjects with unquestioned career success we thought it best to sample subjects whose careers were well under way. Since we were interested in the careers of women as well as men, it was necessary to set the age requirements high enough to give women's later-developing careers (if Rossi [1985] is correct) time. We chose age limits ranging from forty to fifty-five (in 1982 when interviewing began). The period of growing up then varied from birth as early as 1927 and as late as 1942. This break had some other interesting characteristics. It meant that few of our subjects were in World War II, thus reducing the special effects of the GI bill on career redevelopment. At the younger end, it meant that our subjects were too old to be Vietnam veterans. Thus, military experience was largely limited to a few veterans of the United Nations' efforts in Korea. Hence special veterans' programs are not a major issue in our research.[8] Half of the total sample selected were white and the other half black so that comparisons could be facilitated on that variable. Similarly half were male and the other half female.

The in-depth nature of our study severely limited the number of people who could be examined. We felt that the number of Controls interviewed in each of the four categories could be somewhat smaller than the number of Pathmakers since they were the group of greater interest. Ultimately we studied sixty Pathmakers, and a control group of forty.[9] In all, we interviewed eight categories of respondents: fifteen each of black, white, male, and female Pathmakers, and ten each of black, white, male, and female Controls, for a total of one hundred subjects.

The names in Table 3.1 represent eight selected subjects we have used in this book to exemplify the findings we are reporting. How they were selected and a summary of their lives is given in the next section of this chapter. The names are constructed to the following code: last names beginning with P represent Pathmakers, and those with C in-

Table 3.1 The sample

	Pathmakers		Controls	
	Number of subjects	Example's name	Number of subjects	Example's name
Black males	15	Bob Price	10	Bernie Clark
Black females	15	Betty Powers	10	Bonnie Cart
White males	15	Wes Parker	10	Wendell Cu
White females	15	Wanda Perkins	10	Wendy Cass

dicate Controls. First names beginning with B indicate black subjects, and names beginning with W indicate white subjects. Gender is revealed by the first name. Thus Bob Price is a black male Pathmaker.

Presentation of Results

Our most basic finding is that the phenomenon we wished to study did exist. We were able to carry out our research as designed, meaning that we found sixty people who had achieved high levels of career success who grew up in homes characterized as poor by local definition and in which neither parent finished high school. Whatever one might make of the use of the Horatio Alger myth in our society, it has some basis in fact for both races and both sexes.[10]

However, the phenomenon we wished to study is not common. It took longer to find the subjects for our study than we had anticipated. Further, some categories of subjects were more difficult to find than others. Controls, of course, were the easiest to find. The Pathmakers were more difficult to locate, and of these the black female subjects were the most difficult. They alone had obstacles of both race and gender to overcome, and there are fewer blacks than whites in the overall population.

Our findings will first describe any differences our analyses show between Pathmakers and the Controls, and where they are similar. Then we will present the patterns that were found in comparing blacks and women to whites and males.

Since the purpose of this study is more exploratory than confirmatory, our findings are generally presented descriptively. But since we are primarily interested in knowing if Pathmakers are different from

Controls, how do we decide if there is a difference and when differences are statistically significant? We only report differences among categories in this book if the distribution would have achieved statistical significance in a confirmatory study using the same data (see Appendix A for a fuller description of the quantitative analyses). The text then footnotes the statistic (or table number) and p value for the finding.[11]

Our method leads us to search for and stress patterns shared among categories of subjects. We should remember that, whatever traits they share, the lives we study are unique. Therefore, in addition to presenting patterns based upon the quantitative data analysis, we felt that, for both methodological and theoretical reasons, it was important to present some subjects as they described themselves, even though their words were prompted by the interview schedule just described. So in addition to our descriptive analysis of the quantitative data organized by the major theoretical foci of the study, we include the actual words of eight subjects, each chosen from one cell of our design (see Table 3.1). Within each cell we made a list of those subjects who had given us permission to quote in published materials, then wrote to each person confirming this. Of those who responded to our letter, we excluded those careers so idiosyncratic that it would be impossible to disguise without enormous distortion. If there were more than one subject remaining in a cell, we selected the fullest interviews, giving preference to interviews we had conducted ourselves. If there were still more than one qualifying interview, we chose one randomly. These narratives are woven throughout the next five chapters and enable the reader to put our descriptive findings in the context of the actual words of the participants.

Individuals presented have been disguised to protect their anonymity.[12] Present tense in descriptions and quotations indicates an "ethnographic present": the time of the interview. All quotations are a transcription of the subjects' taped words with punctuation added by the authors.

Introduction to Eight Lives

Black Male Pathmaker

Bob Price, a CEO of a California investment banking house specializing in minority investment, was previously the president of a local bank in the Southwest. He started his business career in government service in a federally sponsored urban renewal project where he gained experience in housing and finance. Born and raised in the South, his father was a tenant farmer, later buying a small farm with his labor. His mother was "just a housewife, and that's it." He attended segregated rural public schools, a private, church-affiliated college (where he majored in business), and postgraduate education at a variety of institutions offering special courses in banking and finance. He supported his own college education with a variety of laboring jobs. One of fifteen children, with twelve still living, he is the only child to hold a college degree, let alone to have had postgraduate study. His parents were together throughout his childhood, and he has been married to the same woman for almost thirty years. He has two children.

His interview showed a life characterized by strong long-term planning, and a person with strong Achievement and Power needs, virtually no Affiliation needs, strong reward orientation (weak cost orientation), strong internal and weak external loci of control, and a moderately other-directed orientation. The interview revealed strong intellectualization themes, moderate use of humor and reaction formation, and a weak but present sense of altruism.

White Male Pathmaker

Wes Parker is about to retire from his second successful career, after four years as *pro bono* public servant, having built a successful business netting him, he says, over $50 million a year. Raised as one of two sons of a tenant farmer, he attended small rural all-white schools, and graduated from a small regional private college for which he paid out of earnings from jobs during and after high school. The skills acquired on these jobs became the foundation for the family company that he built as an adult (with his brother and father).

He married several years after college and has been married to the same woman for almost thirty years. He has two grown children, both beginning their careers. His individuality has been affected by the continuing ties to both his domineering father and his older brother, with whom he is still competitive. An indication of how central a theme this is in understanding his motivation is exemplified by his answer to the question: What in your life has given you the most satisfaction? He answered that it was the fact that we had chosen to interview him and not his brother! A workaholic ("if I didn't have nothing to do I'd go nuts"), he has a "terrible temper." His extreme independence, competitiveness, and hard work could be seen as defenses against an early absence of emotional support. Costs of this process are primarily relational.

His interview described a life of long-term planning, strong needs for Achievement and Power, weak to moderate Affiliation needs, strong reward orientation (and virtually no cost-orientation). Internal locus of control was strong, and external locus of control themes were absent. Inner direction was stronger than other direction. We thought the interview showed him defending against intimacy with strong altruism and sublimation themes, moderate displacement, anticipation, and dissociation defenses, and weak use of repression and humor.

Black Female Pathmaker

Betty Powers is a successful professor and college administrator who for ten years has also had a successful political career. Her alcoholic father left home when she was two. She has a younger sister who is a schoolteacher. Educated in Southern segregated public schools, she attended public colleges, and graduated from a publicly supported black college. She then earned a master's degree from a private university in the Northeast, and a doctoral degree from a newly integrated Southern state university. Except for the master's degree, which she earned in successive summers in time off from her teaching job, she worked whenever she was in school.

She was married for the first time while in college to a man who left college after two years. Threatened by her success, he became an alcoholic and they divorced, she reports. She has two children from that marriage: one college dropout already married and divorced, the other in school. After several years, and a depression over her loneliness, she married her present husband, who is a successful entrepreneur. She lives in the election district which she represents, and has thought seriously about holding national office, either as secretary of state or president.

Her interview suggested a person quite strong in long-term planning, with a strong need for Achievement, moderate Affiliation needs, moderate Power needs, moderate reward orientation (and virtually no cost orientation), strong in her belief that external forces were in control (with comparatively less internal locus of control themes), and moderate themes of both inner- and other-directedness. The interview suggested a life oriented around defenses against aggression, including strong intellectualization, altruism, and sublimation themes, as well as moderate anticipation. Concerning costs of success, both relational costs and the absence of play were noted.

White Female Pathmaker

Wanda Perkins is a professor of political science at a major university. Her father, a sometime factory worker with a sixth-grade education, left home when she was four (the oldest child, Wanda has a younger sister by him). Her stepfather, also with a sixth-grade education, was chronically unemployed, often taking odd jobs as a truck driver. Her mother was physically and psychologically abusive to Wanda from the time her father left (Wanda explains that she and her sister looked like him). The mother had three sons by Wanda's stepfather, but he left when Wanda was in college (following repeated infidelities by Wanda's mother) so that the family was financially dependent on Wanda and her sister until Wanda fled from home at the age of twenty-three. To make good her escape, made without her mother's knowledge, Wanda had to give up her teaching job to live with her biological father in another state. After living with her father for a year, she returned to teaching; then moved, following a mentor, to yet another teaching job in another state. All during this time and for many years to come she kept her whereabouts secret from her mother. Both male and female mentors encouraged Wanda on to her master's and then doctoral degrees. Some of the male mentors who were married were also her lovers, but long-term relationships with unmarried men have not developed, much to Wanda's regret. She reported suffering from eating disorders, including anorexia and bulimia, and was one of the fifteen subjects who exhibited overtly immature defenses. She reported a need for psychological counseling, however, except for brief interventions, had not sought it prior to the interview.

   Her interview showed her not to be a long-term planner, with strong needs for Achievement and Affiliation, with a strong internal locus of control focus (and a weaker external locus of control focus), moderate in her needs for Power and reward orientation (weak cost orientation), and moderately strong in both inner- and other-directedness. The interview suggested a person defending against intimacy utilizing strong intellectualization and sublimation strategies, moderate dissociation, humor, reaction formation, acting out, and displacement strategies, and having some passive-aggressive tendencies.

Black Male Control

Bernie Clark, senior vice-president of a multinational conglomerate, was born in the South. He was the grandson of the founder of a highly successful black business which was inherited and expanded by his father, who was himself a college graduate. He has one older and two younger sisters. His parents divorced when he was six years old, and he moved with his mother to the home of his mother's mother in another city. He returned to live with his father and father's mother at the age of twelve. Both grandmothers were important influences, his mother's mother for her strength and influence on his character formation, his father's mother for her contacts with the black elite of the country. He first worked following his parents' divorce, and continued to earn money thereafter. He attended a private prep school (boarding) and a public university, from which he dropped out and was then drafted into the military for the Korean war. He used his contacts from family and school to get a "soft and safe" job in the military. He finished his degree at a historically black college after working for three years after his discharge, living with his mother. After graduation he joined the family business, received a master's degree, and then left the family business to work in the same field but away from his family, who were active in the civil rights movement (and with whom he disagreed because he found their political strategy too mainstream). His career led him into visible national corporate work and he was called to Washington to work in the White House, a move which was more in keeping with his father's strategy than his own. He stayed in Washington through two administrations and then left to work with the company which now employs him, where he can utilize his international and national contacts to further corporate goals. He is married for the second time, having been divorced from a childhood sweetheart. He married his first wife when he was drafted, shortly after the birth of their now adult son. He has two teenage children from his second marriage. He tends to idealize his bosses and mentors and their influence, perhaps as a compensation for the six-year separation from his father following his parents' divorce. He credits his hard work ethic to his mother's mother with whom he lived after the divorce, when his dream was to do everything she expected of him without being asked.

His interview revealed a person with moderate amounts of long-term planning and Achievement needs (weak Affiliation needs), moderate to strong Power needs, and reward orientation (virtually lacking cost orientations), moderate beliefs in an internal locus of control (weak external locus of control themes), and with somewhat stronger inner- than other-directedness. Defending against dependency, and to a lesser extent aggression, the interview suggested the use of moderate to strong intellectualization, sublimation, and dissociation, with weaker altruism and humor motifs.

White Male Control

Wendell Curtis is treasurer and director of a large international investment concern. The son of a manager of a service company and a medical secretary, he was the younger of two children. His parents remained married until his father died when he was fifteen. After attending public schools, he attended a nationally ranked and highly prestigious undergraduate college outside his home state on a full scholarship. Upon graduation he entered the Air Force through its ROTC program. After service as a pilot he left the military and received his M.B.A. from an Ivy League school. He married the daughter of a successful self-made CEO of a financial subsidiary of a major international company, and had two children. He was employed by his present company as a result of an interview at the placement office of his M.B.A. school at the age of twenty-seven. By the age of thirty-nine he rose to the very high position he now holds at the same firm. His children graduated from prestigious private colleges, and he is still married to his first wife. Recovered from a nervous breakdown after her second child, his wife now runs her own business. Both are reported as deeply religious and involved in church activities.

His interview suggested moderate long-term planning, Achievement and Power needs (weak need for Affiliation), and reward orientation (weaker cost orientations). While there were moderate internal locus of control themes and inner-directedness, the external locus of control and other-directed themes were stronger. The interview suggested defending against aggression and dependency with strong to moderate

intellectualization and sublimation, and moderate suppression, dissociation, and altruism strategies.

White Female Control

Wendy Cassetta, a biologist, is a university president. The older daughter of the children of immigrants, she grew up with one sister and lots
of extended kin in the area. Her mother, a teacher, completed additional
graduate work when Wendy was in her teens. Wendy has been a faculty
member of both public and private institutions of note, and has also
served on numerous governmental commissions at both state and national levels. She received her Ph.D. in biology and her undergraduate
degree in anthropology. Never married with no children, she says she
never expected a career in academia: her preference was journalism.
Nevertheless her academic career has been meteoric, and she achieved
her present position before she was forty. While exclusively committed
to feminist goals in doing good works, she sees herself in her career as
non-threatening to men and able to be welcomed as an insider to the
various power centers in government and board rooms where she
chooses to play.

Her interview was coded weak in long-term planning, but showing
strong Achievement needs (weak Affiliation needs), strong Power needs
and reward orientations (weak cost orientations), moderate internal but
strong external locus of control beliefs, and both moderately inner- and
other-directedness. The interview suggested someone defending
against dependency with the following strong or moderate defenses:
altruism, sublimation, anticipation, intellectualization, suppression, and
reaction formation.

Black Female Control

Bonnie Carter heads a lobbying firm in Washington, D.C. active in
supporting hands-on projects to benefit urban and minority populations. She was previously an officer of a foundation which she entered
at a program officer level and worked her way up. Previous to the foundation, she was in various civil service research and program management positions. Her father was a college teacher with a master's degree,
her mother graduated from high school and now works as an admin-
istrative assistant. She grew up in college communities in the border

South and deep South and often attended private, college-connected schools. The schools were all black. She attended a black college, majored in sociology, and after graduation went to Washington to work in clerical civil service jobs. She earned an M.B.A. funded by a special fellowship program for minority students. Her way through the civil service was helped by an important mentor. She made her early choices in jobs in ways that added to her experience in different areas. She seemed to have had a vague, unspecified, long-range goal: knowing she needed various kinds of professional experience. She married once, for three years, but reports that they grew in different directions and divorced. She is single.

Bonnie's interview showed a moderate need for Achievement and use of long-term planning, strong Affiliation needs, and almost absent Power needs. Reward orientation was weak, but cost orientations were absent. Internal locus of control themes were strong, external themes weak to moderate, moderate inner-directed themes were detected but other-directed were absent. The interview suggested someone defending against aggression, in whom intellectualization and suppression were strong strategies, anticipation, sublimation, and altruism moderate ones, while reaction formation and repression were present, but weak.

4

Family Resources

The family forms the setting in which our subjects entered and learned about their world. Family members—their social networks, the resources they control—help to define the child, and help the child to define the world. The growing child will learn from his or her interactions with these people, and this interpersonal experience will have lasting effects. Indeed, it has been argued that the most significant role of the early family is in determining who will be available to the child.[1] The family, both directly in terms of its membership, and indirectly in terms of what networks of relatives, friends, peers to which the members link, constitutes the social field in which the child will develop. The theoretical importance of the family is fundamental to our study. The logic of anticipating potential differences between Pathmakers and our other subjects depends, in large part, on families having lasting consequences for the child. In Chapter 1 we reviewed literature suggesting that Pathmakers should have less redundant familial, social, and educational resources than our equally successful Controls. We need to determine whether families were resources or impediments to Pathmakers' success, and whether these patterns differed from the Controls'. While we are primarily alert to such differences in Pathmakers' descriptions of their families of origin, race and gender comparisons might also reveal powerful influences on the ways in which the self develops in the family setting.

Parents

In this conception of the family—important not just for the role models it provides, but also for the interpersonal opportunities it offers—if a child loses a parent through death or separation, it not only deprives the child of one half of his immediate adult resources for modeling and interaction, but also might break the social networks and resources linked to that parent. By happenstance of sample selection, a relatively high proportion (40 percent) of the subjects of our study lost a parent in childhood, but a trend suggested that this was more true of the Pathmakers (47 percent) than the Controls (30 percent). Further analysis revealed that this was probably a pattern more attributable to the women studied: only 25 percent of the Control females lost parents compared to 57 percent of the Pathmakers (see Table 4.1). Presumably the class and educational differences might account for the greater risk of parental loss for Pathmakers, although the lack of difference for males alone (38 percent versus 35 percent) is anomalous.

Exemplifying these patterns was Wanda Perkins:

> My mother and father separated pretty violently when I was about four years old. At that time I had a sister who was ten months and we proceeded to pick up a stepfather along the way. He was unemployed when he and my mother started seeing each other. Things went way downhill. We lived in a veterans' housing project, and we were on welfare and my mother received aid, and as long as I can remember we lived in public housing or worse through most of my adolescent years, all the way through the time I stayed at home. We also lived in one-room trailers or one-room apartments where we had to share bathrooms and [they] were pretty ratty in a literal sense with bugs and rats and crowded quarters and almost ghetto-style living.[2]

Table 4.1   Death of a parent in subjects' childhood for female Pathmakers and Controls

	Parent dies	No parent dies
Pathmakers (30)	17	13
Controls (20)	5	15
	(22)	(28)

X^2 (1, $N = 50$) = 4.88, $p < .025$

In contrast, consider the richness of the membership and the resources described by Wendy Cassetta for her stable extended family:

> I came from a big extended ethnic family and there were lots of [us].
> My father and mother had both brothers and sisters, and everybody
> lived in the same neighborhood. They were second generation; my
> grandparents came, both sides of my family came, from [the same
> community], so their families were friends, so that everybody was in
> and out of everybody else's house . . . I was some years older than my
> other cousins. My parents were the oldest in their generation. But I
> had all my cousins in and out so I grew up, I mean, the groupiness[3]
> probably came from, well, the groupiness of being in a big ethnic
> family. I probably liked group research because I grew up in a big
> ethnic family and I find the whole thing very loving and supportive.
> But I also like being alone. Someone visited me the other day at my
> [house] with their little kid, and the little kid said, "Mommy, why does
> Dr. Cassetta have three bathrooms and we only have one." The
> mother said "you answer that." I said it's because when I grew up,
> then we only had one bathroom, and I promised myself if I ever got
> rich enough I would have three. It's true, it's true. I love having bath-
> rooms!

At another point she reports that her parents' relationship to each other was quite distant:

> They stayed together for the children's sakes, but also because they
> were Catholic. But a lot of those marriages were not terrific marriages.
> No one beat anyone, but they weren't terrific marriages, but they did
> support each other . . . I remember more than anything else Christmas
> and Thanksgiving and the long tables and everybody eating together.
> The other thing I remember about growing up is that adults don't
> talk to children.

Unlike Wendy Cassetta's parents, Bernie Clark's parents did divorce (when he was six), but the family's other resources were deep. He lived with his mother's mother for the next six years, and ultimately his fa- ther's mother became a dominant force in his life, perhaps replacing his father's role, by linking him to the family's resources.

> The girls and I stayed with our grandmother on my mother's side.
> We had the influence of a very strong-willed great lady, my grand-

mother. She was just very religious, very hardworking. [When he was eleven] my father's mother used to travel a lot around the country, was a grand lady very involved with the National Conference, and she traveled with one of the great heroines of the black community, advising the kitchen cabinet of the President, and so they came through [our town] and visited . . . I guess it was decided at that visit that I should go to live with [my father's mother]. I think she said, "Hey, let's take him to [names city] and bring him up to my house and give him some more opportunities." My sisters later went to join my mother, but I [went to live] in a big family home . . . in one of the first middle-class black sections [in the South], and of course that was the result of Dad and those uncles and aunts who worked day and night in the [family] businesses.

So those who had lost a parent would be in different situations if they were Pathmakers (with less redundancy of resources available to fill the gap) than Controls like Bernie Clark or Wendell Curtis. Wendell's father died when he was fifteen; his parents' networks helped out in a hard time:

I had two big changes in my life. First was when my father died[4] . . . He had a stroke—a cerebral hemorrhage—at age fifty-two, when he had not been sick. But that was the age when you had high blood pressure but didn't know it . . . I grew up fast. Life was no longer fun and games but you had to do something to make sure you took on certain responsibilities and accepted others. Dad made decisions, so I began making decisions for myself and my mother at age fifteen . . . I was playing football at the time. Also immediately I went to work. And I really worked somewhere between twenty-five and forty hours a week as a soda jerk in a drug store [owned by a friend of his parents]. And I did that even on top of football practice. It only meant that I started at night instead of the afternoon. And I worked all the time I was in high school. My mother was forty-eight and she got a job and then worked until she was seventy-two . . . He didn't leave much insurance. He left the house so that it was clear of mortgage. But there wasn't really extra money beyond what my mother [received] . . . She got social security and widow's benefits for kids in school, which all went either to support us or support my sister through school.

We have said that black female Pathmakers are the category we studied with the most negative predictors. It is intriguing that they were also the subjects most likely to have lost a parent: 67 percent of the black female Pathmakers had lost a parent (compared to only 20 percent of the Control black females).[5] Betty Powers's families were typical of the black female Pathmakers:

> My parents were very poor, fairly well uneducated in that my mother went to the eighth grade, and my father to the seventh. She was a domestic at various times during her life, at other times a laundry worker, and later when we were older, seven or eight years old, my sister and myself, she went to cosmetology school and became a hair-dresser . . . She's worked all the time, never stopped working. I am the product of a broken home . . . I must have been two or three, very, very young . . . I don't remember much of [her father] until we became older; fourteen, fifteen, sixteen when we traveled to [another state] to visit him. He didn't move to [the other state] until we were seven or eight years old. He was there but would just stop by. We did not see him. He was an alcoholic so a lot of times nobody seemed to mind because it was always an unpleasant meeting and often times if he stayed around you never knew how your friends would come in the house and see him, you know, lying on the sofa. It was that kind of an early childhood. [How did you feel about that?] The thing I remember most about that was my friends coming by and I did not want them to see him.

How did black female Pathmakers overcome the loss of a parent if they were already in the toughest position? When we re-read their interviews we found that those who lost a parent were often among the 40 percent of the subjects who reported extended family in the home as they were growing up. Betty Powers, for example, says:

> I remember when I was four or five there was an uncle who just came from another part of [her state] to stay with us until he found a job, and when he found a job and married he moved out; that must have been after a year or two. And I remember that, since you asked [who she lived with as a child], because he was kind and gentle, and I think we just kind of—even though we called him Ben, that was unheard of for any of our other uncles and aunts: it was always Uncle Harvey or Aunt Mary, but we called him Ben. He was Mama's younger brother but we took him not as a brother even though we called him by his first name—we took him as a kind of father, he was that close to my

mother . . . He was very protective of us. He would do things with us, take us places.

Like 70 percent of the Control females, Bonnie Carter's parents were together and still were when we spoke with her. But she too had extended family at home. Following the death of Bonnie's grandfather, her father's mother lived with Bonnie's family. Yet, in her case, Bonnie Carter describes a drain on family resources rather than an addition:

Yes, she was a miserable person and you just coped with it . . . She will look for the worst in anything and she'd do things like let's say she was talking to [my sister] when she was about four about how she made cornbread, and [my sister] didn't like cornbread, and she [father's mother] said about how others in the family just loved it, and on and on and on about this cornbread until finally [my sister] said, "You know Grandma, you know what I think you should do with that cornbread? Why don't you just take it and [non-verbal gesture—gave her the finger]." My mother and my aunt were sitting at the table and we almost died. She could be very difficult, and you knew when she was coming that you had to try to continue the family existence as normally as possible.

Whether the subjects were Pathmakers or not, and whether their extended family were seen as additional resources or drains on resources, blacks overall—not just the black women—were more likely than white subjects to have extended family (adults other than parents) in the home (see Table 4.2). We observed no differences between Pathmakers and Controls, however, in this regard—with about 40 percent of both reporting extended families.

Another index of parental resources salient to the child is whether

Table 4.2 Extended family in the home during childhood by race of subject

	Extended family in home	
	Yes	No
Blacks (50)	26	24
Whites (50)	14	36
	(40)	(60)

$X^2 (1, N = 100) = 6.00, p < .025$

mothers, when present, worked. Seventy percent of our subjects reported mothers who worked during their childhood. We expected to find Pathmaker/Control differences because of the demands created by the Pathmaker families' poverty. But, surprisingly, there were no Pathmaker/Control differences in reports of working mothers for our subjects, who were all born between 1927 and 1942. We found that white male Pathmakers reported mothers working less often than did the females.[6] Indeed the white male Pathmakers reported mothers working less often than all other subjects, or other Pathmakers.[7] White subjects reported mothers working less often during their childhood than did black subjects (see Table 4.3). For example, Wendell Curtis's mother stopped working when she had his older sister, and only returned to work when her husband died, while Bernie Clark's mother worked throughout his childhood.[8] These findings suggest that whites, and especially white male Pathmakers, had more access to maternal time than did the black and female subjects, suggesting that this index of parental resources was more affected by gender and race. Working mothers might also be more able to provide role models for their daughters, and provide linkages through their jobs to other networks.

Beyond examining who was in the home when our subjects were growing up, we also examined what kind of parents were described by our subjects. We summarized our data by classifying responses relating to the strictness or "lovingness" of their parents. About the same proportion of our subjects reported being raised by loving parents (33 percent) or by strict parents (35 percent), and Pathmakers did not differ from Controls in this regard. Bob Price gives an illustration of what we, and our subjects, called strict parenting:

> As I grew up I was always a terribly obedient person to my parents and I never wanted to do anything that would displease them. I was

Table 4.3 Mothers working during childhood by race of subject

	Mothers worked during childhood	
	Yes	No
Blacks (49)	40	9
Whites (49)	31	18
	(71)	(27)

X^2 (1, $N = 98$) = 4.14, $p < .05$

a devil, you know, when they were not around, I was really a devil. But when they were around I really disciplined myself, the way that they felt and thought I should have been disciplined. I was a good kid in the family you know, I had the wool pulled over my Mom and my Dad. I really was a good kid. All the things I wanted to do, as soon as they left, I did it. And I guess every kid does that. My father was old, and he had very antiquated ways, and he used to say he was a strict disciplinarian . . . I guess I always sought my parents' approval. I always felt that it was important to try to do the things that they'd taught me, and so forth . . . My Daddy had a funny way of motivating people. He would say things like, "Son, you're going to regret this, but that's about the size of it." And he'd whip you if you did something bad. He'd tear you up. But my Daddy did the best he could, and I tease him about it now—we laugh and talk about it now . . . Daddy had a rule that everybody had to stay at home until they finished high school, but if they turned eighteen first, like my older brothers did, they left home at eighteen.

There was also a trend for white male Pathmakers to report less strict parenting than the other Pathmakers.

A related variable is how subjects described the atmosphere in their families when they were children as providing loving or tense settings: 62 percent described loving atmospheres and 37 percent described tense homes. We found no Pathmaker/Control differences. White males, however, were more likely to report coming from more tense, less loving homes than white female or black subjects, regardless of Pathmaker status.[9] This is, we believe, important to our understanding of resource redundancy. The finding should not be interpreted to say that white males more often have tense, unloving homes (a finding which is not supported by other research or by ethnic stereotyping since it is not true for white females); rather, the finding could be interpreted to suggest that blacks and white women who happen to have come from unloving, tense homes were less likely to become successful and appear in our sample[10] than white males who had a somewhat greater redundancy of social resources, and were not breaking as new a path. This presumably would also relate to the finding that blacks reported they came from more loving and less tense homes than whites (see Table 4.4). In any case, for family atmosphere we find ethnic and gender differences rather than Pathmaker/Control differences.

Bonnie Carter was an exception to these patterns in certain ways.

Table 4.4 Nature of homes of origin by race of subject

	Loving	Tense
Blacks (41)	32	9
Whites (42)	20	22
	(52)	(31)

$X^2 (1, N = 83) = 8.21, p < .005$

While she described a warm and supportive family with high expectations of her and her siblings, she also reported that

> a certain amount of tension in the household . . . revolved primarily around my father . . . because he is not the easiest person to live with. He could be a very irritable, abrupt, irrational person one moment, and then a very sweet loving person the next. You're never sure how much of it was due to [an injury from the military which left him with a steel plate in his head] and how much of it was just orneriness. It was very hurtful at times, and I guess it was the inconsistency that was most difficult to deal with. It was very hard for me because I adored him and it seemed at the time to be rejection, and it took a grip on me and during adolescence that period was probably more difficult than the norm.

Her relationship to her mother was no doubt an important balancing force: "She fills that void in the sense of being constant, consistent, open, communicative; you know, a very strong lady."

These findings concerning family membership give some hints that thinner resources may be even more characteristic of Pathmakers who are black or female. We feel that this shows that the variables making for resource redundancy—Pathmaker family background, race, and gender—may be cumulative.

Other Family Members

Another important issue for our study was whether subjects had siblings, and how many.[11] Overall, our subjects reported 2.8 siblings, but Pathmakers had more siblings than Controls, an average of 3.3 versus 2.1.[12] So not only were some Pathmakers, especially women and blacks, more likely to lose a parent, but Pathmakers generally had to share the thinner adult resources they had with more siblings. Wanda Perkins, for example, had a sister three years younger, and after her stepfather was on the scene, "son number one was born. And there were two other children, a son who was a hemophiliac, and another son two years later." Wendy Cassetta, in contrast, with all her extended family, only had one sibling, a sister. "My sister, who is far brighter than I am or ever was and is my soul mate . . . [is] a loner much more than I am, as is her husband. I mean they really like their privacy, love isolation." It also may be that, for some, siblings act not as a drain on resources, but can constitute a resource of their own that can compensate for the thinning of parental resources. Wendell Curtis, who lost his father at age fifteen, when asked about the significant people in his life, said:

> I guess first my sister. My mother and father were not particularly intellectual. But we had a warm household. But my sister is bright and I'm smart. She's smarter than I am. She's the only one who can intimidate me. She's done it all along. She doesn't understand that, but she does. So if there's ever anybody pricking me from behind, I suppose it was to a certain extent her, in a way that [had to do with] my doing as well as I might, but I don't mean [she was] pushy.

Perhaps when there are a lot of resources around, positive aspects of having siblings can emerge or dominate, but we don't have sufficient data to say more than that siblings are reported by individual subjects as having either negative or positive resource implications.

Only 15 percent of our subjects grew up in disintegrated homes, which we defined as involving abusive parent(s) or an extremely unstable (high turnover of people) family structure, but these were more likely to be Pathmakers' homes than Controls' (see Table 4.5). Wanda Perkins is an extreme example. Here she explains why she "ran away" from home when she was twenty-two:

Table 4.5 Pathmakers and Controls reporting disintegrated homes

	Yes	No
Pathmakers (58)	13	45
Controls (40)	2	38
	(15)	(83)

$X^2 (1, N = 98) = 5.53, p < .025$

I had been beaten pretty severely from the time I was four until the time I was twenty-two. And the beatings were getting worse. [By whom?] By my mother. My mother was the major person in all this. The beatings were getting worse, the psychological beatings were getting worse, and there was one point where my mother had a series of boyfriends who were in and out of the house over all those years. From far back as I can remember, there were men in the house, at night when my stepfather was working the night shift and so on . . . The turning point for me in terms of deciding to leave home was when she accused me of seeing one of her fat sloppy boyfriends and this must have been March of the first year I was teaching. And not only was I supporting this family [her stepfather left home the year before] and trying to be responsible at that, but she was making more demands on how we were making use of the little bit of money I was making. So the house was being filled with things and my name was on all those contracts as the responsible party, and the beatings would get worse. When she accused me of this that was the turning point for me.

Colleagues at work encouraged Wanda to leave, supported her emotionally, and on the last day of classes she fled the state to her biological father.

The family resources of the Pathmakers were not only thinner, but as this finding shows, were less stable as well as more fragile in their ability to provide emotional and physical nurturing. It is interesting that the white male Pathmakers were more likely to describe disintegrated homes than the other Pathmakers,[13] but they are the Pathmakers least likely to have lost a parent. Perhaps being white and male helped, in later life, to offset the effects of what should have been an especially debilitating childhood, or parental social resources helped overcome parental quality.

Family Resources and First Jobs

A key argument for the importance of family is whether or not family resources, if they existed, could be exploited by our subjects in pursuing their careers. We will review here only findings concerning the effects of family on early job patterns (other findings concerning family influence on jobs after college graduation are discussed in Chapter 6).

A variable we thought of special interest to our understanding of how

Pathmakers might differ is how our subjects reported getting their first jobs. We expected that Pathmakers would less often obtain early jobs through family connections because of the place of their parents in the community. We thought this would be true for jobs both before and after college, although graduation from college might make family influences less important than the graduate's own networks.

In fact, 43 percent of the subjects reported family connections. However, male Controls obtained jobs through their family connections more than male Pathmakers.[14] Bernie Clark went to work at age eleven for the family business after school, and during prep school in the summers. Family connections could also help get a job. Wendell Curtis, for example, described how he got his first soda jerk job: "I think a friend of the family knew the druggist and said that if he ever had need of somebody industrious and hard working . . . [Did you ask him to?] No, he was my mother's and father's close family friend and it kind of just evolved. He knew the situation." He stayed in this job until leaving for college. His next job also came through family connections: a summer neighbor of his grandparents took him on for a summer of commercial fishing.

Despite finding our expected differences between male Pathmakers and Controls, we found no such differences for the females. There were apparently family resources all women could exploit even if they were Pathmakers that were not available or used by male Pathmakers. Perhaps male Pathmakers couldn't or wouldn't take advantage of them because the opportunities were for work associated with females. As we have argued, since all our female subjects had careers it is interesting that they were more likely to report mothers working. Working mothers could have been role models, and links to new resources as well. As Betty Powers reported, even her mother's part-time cleaning experience could be used: "My very first job? Babysitter. Babysitter, and I guess I was eleven or twelve years old and babysitting for a white lady that my mother worked for; oh that goes way back, maybe ten or eleven." But she got her next kind of job through a teacher:

> And then around fifteen years old I was a secretary, believe it or not. This was [for] a black lawyer, well, more or less a typist job, but I would answer the phone and do all that. I remember being very excited about that kind of thing because I've never been in that environment before. I don't even know that I had even met a lawyer per-

sonally before then. And his wife was one of my teachers, Mrs. S., and she was a very dear woman and she said, "Well, how would you like to work for Mr. S during the summer?" I said, well, I did; you know I was just beside myself with excitement and I remember doing things, mostly typing and answering the phone, but that was a special time.

This job was a critical entree to jobs she used to support her college expenses, not only because it solidified her secretarial skills, but also because she later had the temerity to seek a job as secretary to her college's president.

In another potent early experience, one female Pathmaker reported being taken to the home in which her mother worked as a cleaning person to help her and realizing, for the first time, how differently these people lived. She attributed some of her motive for success to this experience, as well as talking about how the family helped her find other employment when she needed it.

In another example, Wendy Cassetta said of her first salaried job at fifteen:

My mother knew the director of Parks and Recreation, and I also hung out at those tennis courts and they were looking for someone. The alternative was whether I was going to hustle at tennis or not. I once got caught by my mother hustling tennis for a dollar a game with the men players because I looked like a little squirt but I was really a very good tennis player . . . But my mother got me out of that one. So I got this paid job and it was a tough job only in the sense that I had to work out and negotiate agreement with the gangs that controlled the park.[15]

Finally, Bonnie Carter described why she got her first job picking fruit at the age of four or five: ". . . Because my grandfather told me to do it."

In sum, though we had anticipated that Pathmakers would not have family resources to use to get early jobs, this was true only for male Pathmakers, and no general differences were noted for gender or race on the role of family in obtaining early jobs. Female Pathmakers were almost as able as the male and female Controls to report family resources. This is perhaps linked to the fact that among white Pathmakers, females were more likely to have working mothers than the males, showing perhaps different effects of working mothers on male and female subjects.

Once subjects were working, regardless of how they got their jobs, what did they do with the money they earned? Here again we see the effects of Pathmakers' less redundant family resources: there was a trend for Pathmakers to share the money they made on these early jobs with their families. Wanda Perkins said:

> I was a responsible little kid; I lived in a neighborhood where there were many children and so when you became fourteen you started babysitting, just like the normal thing to do. A lot. It was important to bring money into the household. I don't remember specifically but I'm sure I must have gone around looking for jobs because my sister worked in a number of factories, sewing, working on machines. It was just a terrible thing for her, I mean she hated it. I worked at the local KMart as a salesperson and then a cashier, and I thought my jobs were kind of fun—not heavy labor as was my sister's, and I remember not feeling good about that for her . . . During college I was bringing in money. I had some scholarships, but I also took an NDEA loan which I took for the maximum, but that didn't pay for my college, it went straight into the household, which satisfied my mother that there was still [a similar amount of] money coming into the house, and that allowed [meaning mother allowed] me to go to school. I still worked at the store and I still did babysitting too.

On the other hand, Bonnie Carter said that all the money she earned, even as young as four years old (the pattern continued through high school jobs), was hers to keep: "As kids growing up we were always hustling something, whether it was Christmas cards or paper flowers, but all kinds of little things to make money. Beyond that, I guess in junior high school I worked during weekends and during the summer at a variety store." Black Pathmakers were even more likely to share their early job earnings with their families than white Pathmakers.[16]

Following both white and Control patterns, Wendell Curtis did not share his earnings even though his father had just died: "I had the responsibility for the house in terms of upkeep, but not the monetary. My mother had enough money." The keeping of earnings relates to the more redundant resources available to the families of the Controls, but our findings also show different patterns among white and black Pathmakers.[17]

Family resources also affected why subjects left jobs before college.

Our findings suggested that Pathmakers' careers before college were more affected by family factors. We found a trend for Pathmakers to report having to leave jobs before college for family reasons (for example, family need for a better-paying job, need to move, etc.) more than the Controls.

Families and Schooling

Other examples of different paths may be found in some findings linking family and schooling. A characteristic of parents we thought to be crucial was educational attainment. Our data on the number of years of schooling completed by each parent revealed a trend for black subjects, Pathmaker or not, to report higher educational attainment for mothers than did white subjects.[18] This anticipates another finding: black subjects in our study reported more education than their equally successful white counterparts (see Chapter 5 for a description of this finding and other education findings).

Turning next to how supportive families were of our subjects' schooling, 67 percent of our subjects said that their parents were supportive by having high expectations, encouraging, and actively helping the subject with schoolwork. There were no differences between Pathmakers and Controls on family support for schooling, but white female Controls reported less family support for schooling than did all other Controls.[19] In contrast, the families of black males were the most supportive of schooling; in fact only one described his family as unsupportive.[20] Bob Price's father kept his kids living at home until they finished school, and tried to "motivate" them. His father had less education than his mother. Of his mother he says:

> She would get in with you and listen to you read and read to you and try to help you with your lesson and do all those kinds of things, whereas my Dad, he was always tired, he was always bushed and somehow he never really found the time. [Did he value school?] Yes, he valued it. My father was not academically oriented. He would . . . if you did something constructive, he probably wouldn't bother you. But he could never stand to see a child idle. An idle mind was the tool of the devil's workshop or something.

Bernie Clark's grandmother transported him to her house to improve his opportunities and then enrolled him in prep school.

A lot of love emanated from this. I knew I was loved. I left to go to prep school . . . , one of two major black minority prep schools at that time. My grandmother was friendly with the lady doctor who was the founder of that prep school. She traveled east to raise money for the school, she was a driving force. She'd come back and raise thousands. The school catered to the middle-class blacks. The kids came from all over the world: we had kids who later assumed leadership in their respective countries.

Of course, one could argue that a black male whose family didn't support schooling might be highly unlikely to appear in our study—it may approach being a sine qua non for the black male group. White female Controls, on the other hand, had other resources to call on, as well as some societal stereotyping (for example, that women are expected to do well in school) that would encourage their schooling. Bonnie Carter reported strong family support for education. Her father was a college professor, and she grew up on college campuses:

[To my mother] the only thing was that you've got to get an education, and everything you do you will need that. I think my mother's greatest objective in life was that her daughters get a college degree, because then you can take care of yourself, and it was something she had wanted very much, but came up in a household where her father really didn't see why she needed to go even to high school. [What did your parents expect from you at school?] To do your best. [Whatever that may be?] No, they had a very definite notion of what your best was. And I got A's more than B's, and when the B's came they wanted to know why and what the problem was, and they had no qualms about getting in touch with the teacher, and you knew that.

We will return to issues of schooling in Chapter 5.

Religion

Much has been written about the potential importance of religion and religious training in social mobility, and in developing resilience in children, especially among blacks. Sixty-four percent of our subjects reported coming from very religious homes. We found a trend for Pathmakers to describe themselves as having come from more religious homes than did Controls. Wanda Perkins said:

Religion is very important. My real father is Catholic, my mother was brought up Methodist. My mother insisted that I not be named Madeleine and my sister not be named Cynthia, that we be named non-traditional non-Catholic names. We did not go to a Catholic church even though I was baptized in a Catholic church, but she wanted us to go to a Methodist church, but if a Baptist church was close by, that was OK. I went to a Baptist church for many years, I went to a Seventh Day Adventist church, I went to a Methodist church. Church was very important, but my sister and I were the only ones who went, and we went religiously. We were very active: I was there two times on Sunday and Wednesday, active in the youth organization. People in church were very significant. Up until the time we really needed them. Always the minister, the head of the youth group, they kind of knew this was a family in trouble. They never got involved in any way . . . I was on the point of suicide or killing somebody [her mother], and went to the minister and said I need some help, and they just didn't want to touch this matter at all. That's when I thought, what is the church for anyway? I had a hard time dealing with that. Even now there's an uprising of emotional response when I'm in churches that look like those churches.

Blacks reported coming from more religious families than did whites.[21] Bob Price said:

Religion plays a very significant role in my life, and yet I can't even explain it because I have never believed that God was this blond guy with a halo around him. I've always felt that there was a supreme being holding this whole thing together, and so throughout my life I've been very, very involved in church-oriented kinds of activities. My mother, my father were very religiously involved, old Southern Baptist stuff, and so I worked in church at an early age: joined church, Sunday School teaching, singing in the choir. You name it and I did it, Sunday school conventions and wherever I did it. I went to a religious-supported [college], Methodist persuasion, and I meditate even today. It's a very important part of me. I get strength from it, and it helps you when you have to stand alone. And yet if I had to describe Christ for you I'd be lost for words in the process.

No differences on family religiosity were found between males and females, but black females reported coming from the most religious homes in the study,[22] and white females came from the least religious homes in the study.[23] As Bonnie Carter said:

> We went to church, the Episcopal church. I got a good spirit because my father's mother was Baptist, and my mother's mother was Baptist, and my mother's father was Methodist, so when we were visiting them we went to those churches, but my immediate family churched with the Episcopal church. We sang in the choir, headed the youth group, said grace before meals . . . Well, as kids you knew every Sunday you were going to church, and you certainly did not go out on Saturday night and not go to church on Sunday.

In contrast Wendy Cassetta says: "My mother and father sort of [were religious], but they were the least religious [members] of their families."

These patterns of family religiosity suggest ways in which different paths to success were taken. Black females not only came from the most religious homes, but they were also more likely to say that religion had a very great role in their lives at the time of the interview.[24] Conversely, white women were more likely to say that religion had no current role in their lives,[25] as well as reporting to have come from less religious homes. For example, Wendy Cassetta said of her current contact with the Catholic faith of her parents:

> I'm very anti-contact. The Cardinal in town and I play this little chicken game in which he tells people he'd be happy to see me if I'd call and I tell people when he calls me I'd be happy to see him. I'm not involved with organized religious organizations. The Cardinal would like very much [for] a prominent Catholic head of an institution like this to be more vocal on a certain set of issues, but the set of issues he wants me to be vocal on I absolutely disagree with the church on, so I am not about to be helpful to the Cardinal.

Yet each of these very different kinds of paths, in terms of orientation to religion, led to the same place: success. Perhaps these differences in religiosity once again reflect differences in redundancy of resources and social supports. For example, as we described, blacks and to some extent Pathmakers were more likely to come from religious homes than whites or Controls. Black females, relatively less advantaged on race and gender comparisons, were the most religious of the sample. Therefore it could be argued that religiosity was a characteristic of the relatively less advantaged groups. Whether this represents simply correlations with larger social trends of religiosity in the larger society, or whether these less advantaged groups found in religion, and the church, resources they could utilize in making their paths (or whether religion fostered feelings of self-confidence and control) is impossible for our research to determine.

Siblings and Subjects Compared

Now we examine how our subjects reported they compared with their siblings. We were especially interested in what patterns of success were established within the sibling group. Was everyone ultimately equally successful, a kind of corporate success, or did our subjects stand out, a kind of singular success? We first examine how our subjects' education compared to the levels of education achieved by their siblings. If resources were scarce, did Pathmaker families differentially invest in their children, or did they spread resources equally? Remember that, on average, Pathmakers had one additional sibling compared to Controls. Did Controls get more individual attention? We found no differences between Pathmakers and Controls with respect to differences in their educational attainment and that of their siblings. This suggests that neither were characterized by more singular successes than the other, and that neither more often represented a corporate-familial kind of accomplishment, insofar as educational attainment was concerned.

The thinness of family resources seems not to result in educational inequities within families for other comparisons either. While whites, men, and Controls may have had more family resources than other subjects, the fewer resources that the blacks, women, and Pathmakers had seemed to be fairly shared. We did find a trend that women more often than men reported siblings with higher educational achievement than themselves, but that is the only suggestion of difference. We discount this difference as attributable to sexism rather than our resource argument since no differences were found predicted by status or race, and the female subjects reported lower educational attainment than their often male siblings. In accounting for educational differences between himself and his siblings, Bob Price used his personality and motivation to explain why he went to college and his siblings didn't:

> That's a tough question. I don't know, maybe since a kid I've had a big mouth. I always talked about being somebody. I used to tease my Daddy by telling him that I was not a cotton picker. I just detested

that kind of life; there had to be another way, and so I finally talked myself into going to school. I saw that education would enable me to drive a pretty car. I saw that education would enable me to get a little pretty wife and all of that. I saw that education was the key out. There were a few teachers in those days who dressed nice, drove cars, and I'd look around at all those other people and they were driving beat up buggies, trucks and things, and somewhere along it occurred to me that you had to have education if you really want to drive this new shining car, and that kind of thing. Really I was pretty old, before college, before I became really obsessed with it.

We will address issues of motivation again in Chapter 8.

Another index of whether resources were equally shared is the current occupational status and prestige achieved by our subjects' siblings. While there were again no Pathmaker/Control differences on occupational prestige of subjects and siblings, female Pathmakers and male Controls reported having more siblings with the same occupational prestige as they had attained than did male Pathmakers and Control females.[26] This suggests that female Pathmakers and male Controls reported other siblings who "made it" more often than female Controls and male Pathmakers, whose success therefore was more idiosyncratic to themselves. For example, Wanda Perkins's sister became a registered nurse, but Wendy Cassetta's sister never had a career separate from her husband's business, and none of Bob Price's fourteen siblings finished college or had careers that compared with his.[27] Bonnie Carter's siblings all got college degrees but none were as successful as she.

We suggest that what we are seeing in these occupational success of sibling data are the two different kinds of success described earlier: one a singular pattern of an individual subject, and the other a more corporate pattern in which the whole sibship is characterized by success. But the difference is complicated and shows a powerful interaction with gender: female Pathmakers and male Controls are part of a corporate family pattern of achievement while male Pathmakers and female Controls appear more often to be singular cases of achievement.[28] As an example, albeit an extreme one, we offer one male Pathmaker who is a natural scientist holding a Ph.D. degree and prestigious international prizes. He had six other siblings, none of whom graduated from high school, all with numerous children, and none of whom went to college (neither did this Pathmaker's children). At a family reunion, with more than a hundred relatives in attendance, he was the only one with a college degree. In contrast, a female Pathmaker, also the holder of a Ph.D. in the natural sciences, was the youngest of seventeen children, and described them all as successful.

We had anticipated that resource redundancy would have predisposed Controls to be part of a familial pattern, while Pathmakers might be more isolated within their families, but our findings indicate that this was not so simple. But why should female Pathmakers and male Controls be more often parts of corporate family success, and male Pathmakers and female Controls represent more singular achievement? Male Controls are quintessential path-followers, as were their (presumably male) siblings, but female Pathmakers shared their (presumably newly made) path to success with their siblings, suggesting that these siblings were resources from whom they gathered support—after all, it was more unusual for women to pursue careers than for men.

More male Pathmakers were able to stand alone, as were, paradoxically, female Controls. This paradox perhaps is linked to the fact that the female Controls were taking routes not taken as often by women in their families, and thus were to some degree Pathmakers themselves. We feel the patterns are another important example of the different paths our subjects have made or followed. These findings on group or isolated success are also informed by certain findings presented in Chapter 8 for these four groups, and they offer another explanation of these patterns than the sociological ones just given.[29]

Feelings about Home and Leaving Home

Our final variables concerning the influence of family and family resources concern the way our subjects reported feeling about the homes and neighborhoods in which they grew up, and the salience of their families of origin in their current lives. With regard to questions concerning the current place of their family of origin in their lives 28 percent reported regular (i.e., at least weekly) contact with their families of origin. Controls reported this more than Pathmakers (see Table 4.6), and this makes sense given how far Pathmakers have come from the lifestyles of their families.[30] As Bob Price said:

I'm very humbled when I go back home because I see not only relatives but also others who have not moved beyond the station which we left off back in 1957 when I left that part of the country. That's

Table 4.6   Daily or weekly contact with family of origin for Pathmakers and
Controls

	Daily or weekly contact	
	Yes	No
Pathmakers (54)	13	41
Controls (33)	15	18
	(28)	(59)

X^2 (1, N = 87) = 4.29, p < .05

sometimes depressing, when you see people that didn't take care of themselves health-wise and it's really an experience that gives me even greater ambition to come back and try. It sort of rejuvenates, but I have mixed feelings when I go back home, very mixed feelings.

In contrast Bonnie Carter said: "I see my mother and father two, three, four times a year. My sisters and brother about the same. I see my youngest sister much more now because she's moved [to the same city]."

Like Bonnie Carter, black Controls reported more current contact with their family of origin than did black Pathmakers.[31] This finding returns us to the question of whether the families of blacks in our study were a help or a hindrance. Our findings show that both patterns (and subsequent attachment or separation) are in fact to be found. Black Pathmakers do seem more often to become isolated from families of origin, while black Controls more often keep in contact. We take these contacts as signs of generally positive influence by the family upon the subject. For example, his father's family's network of relationships among the black aristocracy got Bernie Clark placed in prep school. He met most of the black leadership of the country in his uncle's office. He selected a college his uncle had graduated from. The family got him jobs before and after college; indeed he worked in the family business. Even after leaving the family business, his family's connections continued to matter even in Washington:

Some of the other people who knew my family recommended me [for the White House job] and they knew my family was Republican. We went Republican under Eisenhower. And part of that preaching during the nights at the office [was that] we needed a two-party system, and we [blacks] were locked into the Democratic party and you couldn't vote; you could vote for the national, but it was a lily white primary on the local or state level. Our position was to free ourselves from the one-party structure . . . I guess I probably agreed with the philosophy that was espoused over the years by our family—the need for a two-party system so that one party wouldn't take you for granted.

Later, when being interviewed by his present company, he was introduced by the white male President of the company to a female black member of the Board of Directors. Bernie knew her husband from meetings he had had with his family when he worked in the family business, and said to us: "That was the advantage of being a middle-class black. You know, it's a small community in America." Played against Billingsley's (1968) arguments about the role of the black family, it may be that different roles should be examined for black families' effects on the careers of Pathmakers and Controls.

As an index of their feelings, we asked the subjects how they felt about returning to the place where they grew up. We found Pathmakers more likely to express severely negative feelings.[32] For example, Wes Parker said when asked what feelings returning home evoked:

None. Hatred. Because so much work my mother made me do . . . was unnecessary. [Q. Have you been back recently?] Yes. Kind of a weird feeling. I went to my aunt's funeral a couple, three or four months ago, and of course my mother's sister grew up right in my old neighborhood. All these people I grew up with and my cousins and all were there. And they looked so much older, and so much more— well I want to be kind. I didn't realize that I had progressed so much greater than they had. I didn't realize how bad it is to go to the church that I once went to, and it brought back memories of "God, I thought this was good!" And boy, this was the worst thing I ever heard in my life. The people—and the basic things that you and I do every day, keep up your teeth, and have a suit of clothes, and that sort of thing, and there were people I went to high school and grammar school with, and they didn't own a suit of clothes. And the poor manners they have . . . And of course everybody knew me because I'm on television every day. And they all, you know, talk about me. I bet you a hundred people came up to me and said, "I'll bet you don't remember me, do you?" What do you say? No, I don't remember you or yes, I do. And if you say yes, then it's "Who am I?" I couldn't quite comprehend it. It's probably the first time I've been back there in that light, although my father's buried down there. And how little they know about what's going on in the world, and their attitudes and so forth was just absolutely amazing. They want to expound on what the economy is doing, and all that, but they don't know what is going on.

Contrast this with the low-key response of Wendell Curtis to the same question, after he tells us that his mother still lives in his old home:

My mother's been retired eight years now and still lives in the same house and the same town. She's lived in only two houses all her life: the one she was born in and the one she moved to when she got married . . . [Home]'s no different than what you remember it to be. I went back for my twenty-fifth high school reunion which was great fun. Most of the people still live within a thirty-mile radius of [town]. It was the next generation that moved.

On the other hand Bonnie Carter felt disengaged: "I feel kind of strange—I get lost because they've put in an expressway and so all my landmarks are gone, and when I'm there I spend most of my time with my family and visit a few friends who are still there. It's usually not for a very long time, so I'm really not that much concerned."

Wendy Cassetta talked about some frustrations in visiting the people in her large extended family. "Their view of me is still as a sixteen-year-old. My family still thinks of me as that age because I never returned home for more than a summer again after that. Darn it, I'm a completely different human being, absolutely shaped by other kinds of things." Yet she returns home frequently:

They'll drive me nuts. I'll have a headache when I get back because there's just too much noise. I'm overwhelmed. What happens when I go home is interesting in that my cousins, who are ten years younger, see me as a role model. They'll gather round, mostly I'll tell them funny stories. Increasingly as I've gone home, and I've said this to my sister and she has begun to notice it, they treat me like I'm a famous person. My sister finds it very amusing because I don't act any different than I've always done. But even my mother is a little taken aback and a little more careful and I find it very amusing, but the truth is that they believe my press notices!

Blacks, on the whole, also expressed more pleasure on returning home as an adult than did white subjects, whether they were Pathmakers or not (see Table 4.7). Bob Price said:

Table 4.7 Reports of pleasure on returning home by race

		Pleasure on returning home	
		Yes	No
Blacks	(33)	20	13
Whites	(25)	8	17
		(28)	(30)

$X^2 (1, N = 58) = 4.67, p < .05$

As a matter of fact I went out home this past summer—I took some pictures. I had to go back to the old home place, I just had to go back. And I went down and took some pictures of the old chimney that is fallen now, and the well still stands, so I took pictures of that just to let my fourteen-year-old daughter know that there's another place in the world besides New Canaan. [He points to a picture hanging in his office of a girl in a cotton field.] That's symbolic of the kind of experience I came from. When I saw the picture I just couldn't resist it . . . It doesn't fit in with anything else in this room, but I couldn't resist the picture so I just bought it and put it on the wall.

Bernie Clark, who when visiting the town where his family business had been started, was brought to the business's original building:

This lady came up to me after my remarks on behalf of the Republican party there and said, "Mr. Clark, I'd like to come by and pick you up tomorrow morning and drive you around. I was in the same college as your aunt." So I said I'd be delighted and she took me by the black business district and we stopped off at some businesses and she said, "This is young Clark; you remember his father," so it was a good feeling from that respect because my Mom and Dad divorced early on and it took me awhile to reconcile that, which I did. But it gave me a warm feeling because my Dad stood for something, his parents stood for something, I was catching up on some of his past. And finally we came to this dilapidated two-story brick building. She said, "Come on, get out of the car," so we walked across the street and I looked up and she said, "Look up at that cement," and there was "B.A. Clark II, 1886" which I found remarkable because I had heard people talking about grandpop's business . . . , this building that he had actually put up, which was a little radical for that time in history for blacks, so it was a good feeling. I took photographs of it and everything and sent it to my kids.

Wanda Perkins hasn't spoken to her mother in many years, let alone visited her, and she talks wonderingly of a recent visit to two high school friends:

> Here are these two women, they knew me and all the family history, and one woman in particular was always brilliant and beautiful. And the other had real capacity too, and we all three were dating these [three] guys and we all probably would have married these men and lived happily ever after . . . and they did marry their high school sweethearts, they each have four children, took out many years to raise kids, and now they're going back to work, and they're being "rif'd" ["reduction in force"] right and left. I'm the only person with a doctoral degree that these two women know! That reunion was bizarre, like on the one hand we're the same as we were before, on the other hand we're light years away from one another. If I had stayed I might have married [her high school date] and become a fifth-grade teacher for the rest of my life. But now Wanda's different.

We will return to issues of friendship in Chapter 7.

We now turn to other findings concerning the reasons subjects gave for leaving home. Like Wanda Perkins, 10 percent of our subjects say they left home to get away from a bad environment: they were all Pathmakers (see Table 4.8). No gender or race differences were noted. These findings parallel and extend our findings for abusive or unstable homes, and suggest that Pathmakers were not only more likely to come from such backgrounds, but also the only ones to report leaving home because of it.

Not surprisingly given the age of our subjects and the nature of our

Table 4.8 Pathmakers and Controls reporting leaving home to get away from bad environment

	Yes	No
Pathmakers (60)	10	50
Controls (39)	0	39
	(10)	(89)

$X^2 (1, N = 89) = 7.23, p < .01$

society, only males reported leaving home to go into the armed services. Given the literature suggesting the use of the armed services as entry occupational points for otherwise blocked minorities and women (see Berryman, 1988), it is interesting to note that in our sample it is a route only reported by men. There were no differences in the use of the armed services by Pathmakers and Controls, or blacks and whites. There were, however, individual differences in the ways in which military careers were experienced. Bob Price was drafted after college:

> I didn't like being made to feel less than a human being, and that's what the army does to you to a large extent. Now you don't have to do a whole lot of other things but by really locking your heels, calling you, doing whatever they want to on you as often as they want to do it to you just because they outrank you is a very dehumanizing kind of experience for me and one that I wouldn't give a dollar for if I had to do it again. That was really the dehumanization associated with the discipline you have in the army, and yet I understand the necessity for it. They threw me right into the infantry. I was commonly referred to as a ground hound, after which I went to California. They gave me an option. They said I could go to OC [Officer Candidate] School if I was prepared to enlist for an additional fifteen months. And I said no thanks, I'll take my chance. So I went to California and took advanced training in the weapons platoon, and that kind of stuff. I went to Germany and stayed eighteen months as a company clerk and liaison officer for newly shipped housewives of soldiers.

Clearly an army career poses some problems for someone like Bob Price. Contrast his reaction to the army with Wendell Curtis's:

> I went to Texas—everybody in the Air Force goes to Texas. Bought my first car. First time I ever owned a car. Brand new convertible, aged twenty-two. I had flight training and all that jazz. [Q. Served three years?] Yes. One year in Texas, one year in Mississippi, became an electronic spy, and then a year and a half in Europe flying Gary Powers–type missions. Met my wife in Texas, got married. I got my wings on the first of May, my birthday was on the third of May, and we got married on the fifth of May. I went off to my next assignment . . . We enjoyed the service, other than my job which gave my wife an ulcer because of what I was doing. [The main reason he left the service for graduate school.] I had no problem with the military as a career at the time because it was an important job.

Bernie Clark quit ROTC at the end of his sophomore year because a "lot of the second lieutenants were getting killed at the outbreak of the Korean war." He was drafted, as he had been warned he would be, and served as a private. He avoided receiving his draft notice for six months because he wanted to spend Christmas with his girlfriend. When he got to Korea, he found the worst of the fighting over, and that his commanding officer had been a former roommate of his varsity teammate in college.

> That's why I put great stock in contacts . . . When he realized that I knew Bill, I was his guy. All I had to do was keep that darned haircut short and play chess with him. Everybody has played chess in my family over the years. At the end of the day he wanted me to play chess with him, so he really took care of me. I worked in supply. I drove the company commander around. So if you ask me what my job was, it was taking care of him. I was playing politics, he liked me. And I kind of had it made in Korea . . .

Finally, Pathmakers—certainly tautologically—reported coming from lower SES neighborhoods than did the Controls.[33] If you're poor by local definition it affects where you live. But blacks overall did not report coming from lower SES neighborhoods than whites in our study, and there were no gender differences either, reassuring us that there were no hidden SES differences among these other cells of our sample. Bob Price makes a point about his original SES:

> We were poor, but we thought everybody lived like this so we were rich. I grew up on a farm, and we all, back in the back country, benefited from hand-me-downs. I used to tell this joke about it, how I don't know my shoes from my feet until I was about twelve, because I went through my brothers' shoes and that kind of thing. We were all very poor. We grew up in a four-room house with one room being the cooking kitchen, so you know the fifteen kids plus Mom and Dad slept in that four-room-type house . . . We had our own social club within the family and we were a backward-type family in the sense that a lot of the people didn't want to associate with us. We weren't too polished. As a matter of fact we were sort of rough-edged. We were not the kind of people that you get in the front line to be with and so forth. But we had plenty to eat—we raised for the most part all our food. So that's why I meant we were rich. We had plenty of food, we never went to bed hungry or anything like that. And we

didn't have television so we didn't know how the other world lived and we didn't have radio until Joe Lewis got ready to fight and we had a battery radio for that . . . so we didn't have much exposure to the outside world. And so we thought everybody lived like us. We got some education from books and from reading the Sears Roebuck and Montgomery Ward catalogues. That's where we saw how people were living and we began to realize we weren't doing it right or something. They weren't in quite the same world.

In summary we have learned a great deal about the role of families in the beginning of our subjects' lives. Pathmakers were somewhat more likely to have lost a parent in childhood, to report coming from disintegrated homes, to report strong negative feelings on returning home, to say they more often left home to get away from bad environments, and to maintain less contact with their families of origin. Pathmakers had more siblings, were somewhat more religious, were somewhat more likely to share money earned with their families, and came from poorer neighborhoods than Controls. Male Pathmakers were less likely to obtain their first jobs through family influence, but the same was not true for females.

A number of differences were also found between black and white subjects: blacks were more likely than whites to have had mothers working, to have had extended family in their homes, to report more loving and less tense homes, to report warmer feelings on return to homes of origin and stronger religion in the home of origin, and were somewhat more likely to report having more highly educated mothers. Black Pathmakers were more likely to share early earnings with their families than white Pathmakers.

In contrast, very few findings differentiated men and women overall on these family of origin variables: women tended to have more siblings with more education than themselves, and to have maintained more contact with their families of origin than men. Pathmaker women were more likely to be able to get early jobs through family connections than were Pathmaker men. In addition we have distinguished two patterns of success within families: singular and corporate, and discovered that the first pattern typified female Controls and male Pathmakers, the second female Pathmakers and male Controls.

These findings allow us to suggest that the less redundant resources of Pathmakers and blacks are having some effects on the early careers of our subjects. In addition we have been able to show situations in which families either contribute to, or limit, the success of Pathmaker and Control subjects, both black and white. Since all of our subjects are equally successful, it is apparent that we must continue to consider that different paths may characterize the way to success for the various categories of people studied. We turn next to a more detailed examination of the educational histories of our subjects.

5

Education and Schooling

After the family, the next set of formal opportunities and resources encountered are those linked to schools. In our study we were fundamentally interested in the role of schooling, and the more inclusive variable education, in the careers of Pathmakers. In reviewing the literature on education relevant to Pathmakers, we encountered a by now familiar question. Do schools open opportunities for Pathmakers, or do they block their advancement?

In presenting what our subjects told us about their education we will first describe the ways in which Pathmakers are different from or similar to our other successful people. Then we will discuss whatever differences have been observed between blacks and whites, and between men and women.

Educational Attainment

The two defining characteristics of Pathmakers—that they come from backgrounds of poverty and that their parents lack high school degrees—correlate with restricted access to superior educational resources. The findings concerning other family differences for Pathmakers, reported in Chapter 4, seemed likely to accentuate their restricted access to quality education. Certainly such variables do not augur well for the quality of schools that will be available to Pathmakers, or for the family's ability to support and knowledgeably advise about education.[1] According to previous research on these variables, one should expect powerful differences on educational attainment between Pathmakers and Controls. Yet Pathmakers defied these predictions.

We found no differences between Pathmakers and Controls in how, or to what degree, they reported their families' positive influence upon their education, or (as presented in Chapter 4) in whether families supported schooling. Of the subjects studied, 89 percent reported one or both parents as a positive influence on their schooling. The similarity between Pathmakers and Controls may suggest that many Pathmakers came from families that were themselves resisting sociological expectations. Despite differences in background, both Pathmakers' and Controls' families much more often positively influenced their children's schooling than not.[2] This apparently was effective: 95 percent entered college.

But they did not attend the same colleges. When we examined published data for the selectivity of the colleges our subjects attended, we found that Pathmakers both started in and graduated from less selective schools than Controls.[3] This is confirmation that the social obstacles Pathmakers faced, including their families' lesser financial resources and lesser familiarity with issues relating to school choice, were having an influence on their ability to know about or enter top-ranked schools. There were no differences by race or gender on the selectivity of colleges attended, suggesting to us that the Pathmakers' special characteristics (low SES and low parental education) were germane.[4]

Whatever difference in quality of school attended, the Pathmakers made the most of what they got: they attained the same levels of education as the Controls. They did not differ in years of educational attainment or degrees earned, despite the odds that could be expected in favor of such differences. Of the people in our study, 87 percent finished college, while 74 percent went beyond college. There were no differences in either indicator between Pathmakers and Controls. Any doubts about the importance of schooling may be settled by considering these data, which suggest that higher education might have ameliorated the large differences in social background for Pathmakers, helping to level the playing field in later life. Indeed, education seems to be the first arena in which many of the Pathmakers beat the sociological odds, in this case against their own school achievement, and began to make their own way. Wes Parker put it strongly:

If I attribute anything to my success, it is my college [rated quite low in selectivity]. I've served as president of the foundation, I've given them a considerable amount of money, I still am very active in their alumni affairs, and I still do a lot of guest lecturing up there, although all the people I knew at the time are gone. [Q. Why credit your college?] Well, it told me that I didn't have to be a truck driver the rest of my life. I used to dream of marrying the girl next door at the farmhouse, and going to their house on Sunday, sitting on the porch and killing flies. And driving a truck. And it made me get some ambition and then to move forward—that I was better than that.[5]

Pathmakers and Controls also shared the kinds of feelings they reported about college (55 percent gave positive and 33 percent only negative reports) and about college teachers (of those reporting a feeling, 42 percent reported liking them, while 19 percent disliked their professors). It would appear that while Pathmakers attended less selective colleges than Controls, their experiences of college teaching and their levels of attainment were similar.

Teachers and Schooling

We turn next to a discussion of variables having more directly to do with schooling prior to college, and how our subjects got to college. If there were no differences on the numbers of Pathmakers and Controls graduating from colleges and universities, and no differences in their levels of final educational attainment, we did find powerful differences between Pathmakers and Controls in how they made their way in school and how they got to college. The most theoretically and practically important finding showing differences between Pathmakers and Controls is that while most subjects said teachers were influential in their school success by their own accounts, Pathmakers more often reported teachers as positive influences on their schooling than Controls (see Table 5.1). This is in line with our resource redundancy argument: teachers should be more important to students with thinner resources. The black male Pathmaker referred to in Chapter 1 who went on to become a university president reported that in his last year of segregated high school in the rural South he had not heard of college, let alone applied to one. When his teacher asked him about his college plans and he said this, she took him to her (all black) college, two

Table 5.1 Pathmakers and Controls reporting teachers as influential on school
            success

	Yes	No
Pathmakers (55)	41	14
Controls (40)	21	19
	(62)	(33)

$X^2 (1, N = 95) = 4.96, p < .05$

hundred miles away, the next weekend. She obtained an interview for
him, helped him apply, and he was offered a scholarship. The following
September, with her encouragement, off he went, and the next year he
was offered a position in an exchange program at an elite Northern
school from which he ultimately graduated.

Controls not only mentioned teachers less often as positive influences, they even gave negative evaluations. For example, Bonnie Carter
could not remember teachers by name in the early part of the interview,
then unhappily recalled her first exposure to public schools in sixth
grade:

> I had very negative attitudes toward the school administration and the
> teacher. The teacher, the principal Mrs. [gives name]—I remember
> her name—had this bell which she clanged. She was a very big,
> abrupt, abrasive kind of a woman and not too long after we were there,
> they were dedicating a new cafeteria. And she kept thanking this su-
> perintendent of schools [remembers name] for giving us the cafeteria,
> and I couldn't understand what she was talking about—what does she
> mean he gave us the cafeteria? You know you pay for this in taxes,
> and she said "shhhhh, be quiet," and they beat the kids with the straps
> . . . I [missed my previous school] and I didn't know why we had to
> be there in the first place—where my father was working that year
> they didn't have dormitories and didn't have a campus and we were
> living in the city. I didn't like it at all, not at all.

We infer from this Pathmaker/Control difference on the role of
teachers that the Pathmakers needed, or noted, the support of their
teachers more than the Controls like Bonnie Carter, who probably had
other resources, like her academic parents. Wanda Perkins's relationship to protective elementary school teachers is an example:

In the first grade I couldn't learn how to read. First grade was a transition. My father left home and there was a lot of tumult. There was no job, we traveled, lived in trailers with no water. And that's when the beating had started too. So I started and couldn't read and I remember crying about that an awful lot. And I remember teachers coming to the house for interviews, talking with my mother. I must have become like a teacher's pet through those years. I remember the teachers' names. I remember positive kinds of things after I learned how to read. I started to spell really well and I was in those local spelling bees and so I became a local contest winner . . . The teachers had to know, knew I was being beaten. It was so obvious. There were visits to the home, especially at the elementary school. And I think there must have been teachers who must have [said] "should we do something here?" But there was no actual intrusion in terms of actually doing anything, ever.

In describing her high school teachers she said:

I remember teachers all along the line. I could almost name every one of them who had major influences on my life and career choices. Mr. T . . . was the adviser of the school newspaper, and I thought that was where I was going to be going. He would counsel me in that direction as well as teaching. There were a number of teachers, especially the English teachers, some of the social studies teachers. There were fairly overt messages that I was getting. I think most of the girls were being directed in the same direction. I was not aware of boys being directed at all.

The data concerning teachers are especially important since there was no probe or question specifically about teachers: the open-ended question asked who had been an important influence on their schooling. Of the overall sample, 65 percent voluntarily mentioned elementary and secondary school teachers, usually by name, as positive influences some thirty years or more after they were in school. This seems to us to speak to issues of teacher quality and effectiveness more eloquently than shorter-term evaluations of teachers, and the findings would make us wary of evaluations based solely on short-term data.[6]

Wendell Curtis fit the control pattern by never mentioning any teacher by name. His sole response to our question was "Teachers were good." Nor did he mention college teachers or graduate-school teachers as important influences in his life or career.

Turning to other variables, Pathmakers and Controls had similar feelings about schools, whether grade school or high school (study-wide 61 percent reported positive feelings while 5 percent reported only negative feelings). Nor were there differences between Pathmakers and Controls on how they responded to education obstacles when they occurred, or the ethnicity or gender of educational mentors. Furthermore, there were also no differences between Pathmakers and Controls on the described levels of extracurricular activities or leisure activities after school. We will discuss some of these variables in more detail below. There were also no differences as to whether or not black Pathmakers and Controls attended segregated schools.

Concerning how our subjects did in school, Pathmaker women reported they were better students than Pathmaker men,[7] but, surprisingly, the same was not true of Control women versus Control men. Wanda Perkins, for example, said of her elementary years:

> I had always done well in school. I liked going to school. Maybe it was an escape for me. I think it was in many ways. I was a different person at school, and I was getting the emotional satisfaction and feedback that made me feel like a capable human being because I wasn't a capable human being at home. I don't know whether I was consciously aware that was pushing me, but I had good feelings in school all the way through. Lots of those emotional responses kept me liking school . . .

School for Wanda Perkins, perhaps with the active collusion of her teachers, became an alternative universe separate from the problems of home. It is interesting to note that she was not able to leave home until she had herself become a teacher.

Wendy Cassetta described herself as fitting what would appear to be a more typical Control pattern. "I just liked school. I wasn't a terrific student. I wasn't very good in math. I was also a mediocre college student, but then I was in the middle of the civil rights movement and running the place [a small liberal arts college]. I bet I graduated with just about a B average from college. I had A's when I had a great teacher, otherwise B's and C's. I wasn't a great college student." We feel the gender differences in school performance among the Pathmakers but not among the Controls suggest the existence of multiple paths to success: Pathmaker women are less likely to appear in our sample if they hadn't been good students. Success in school is a prime route to a successful career, perhaps because it facilitates bonding with teachers who are so important to Pathmakers. Male Pathmakers report teachers as equally important, but they seem to form other links with the teacher than the good student role. Controls might either have faced fewer obstacles or created other paths to success than through teachers.

Private versus Public Schools

Not surprisingly given their parents' relative poverty and lesser experience of education, Pathmakers attended private elementary and secondary schools less often than Controls (see Table 5.2). In fact 38 percent of the Controls (among them Bernie Clark) attended private elementary or secondary institutions, compared with only 15 percent of Pathmakers.[8] Bonnie Carter attended private schools before and after her public school experience. Given the cost of private schools, these differences are not surprising, but it should be noted that private schooling as defined here would include Catholic and religious schools, which could cost less, presumably explaining why even 15 percent of Pathmakers could attend private schools. In addition to strictly economic arguments then, the Pathmaker/Control difference here might also suggest that Pathmaker parents might have been less able to find alternatives to public schooling for their children. Some readers might find both rates of private school attendance high compared to the general population, suggesting that private schooling may be over-represented among these successful subjects. No race or gender differences for private schooling were found, suggesting that black families were as likely to make use of private schools as white families, and that for these subjects males were not selected more than females.

Table 5.2 Pathmakers and Controls attending private elementary or secondary school

	Yes	No
Pathmakers (59)	9	50
Controls (39)	15	24
	(24)	(74)

X^2 (1, N = 98) = 6.84, $p < .025$

If Pathmakers more often had to rely upon public schools than did Controls, their teachers apparently responded. Wanda Perkins said:

> Somehow I was in this college track with no concrete notion that I was ever going to go to college, . . . but I sort of liked these courses and I was doing well in school and that fit. But who knew what the next step was going to be? . . . I was getting this counseling in school [from teachers] that I was going to be a teacher. You know, then, thinking then that there were a number of state colleges, and I knew that there were state scholarships that paid all that whatever the low tuition was. And a number of folks [at my high school] were going on to [what became her college] and so I just sort of fell in with applying for school and so on. It was a teacher preparation, a normal school. And so it was sort of the obvious thing to do. You were going to be a teacher, as were the masses, I mean all my friends were going to be teachers. And so a big clump of us went on from that high school to get state scholarships in teacher education, not really having much comprehension of what I was getting into.

Betty Powers also credited her public school teachers for encouraging her to attend college (as well as her boss, a lawyer's wife), but their support didn't change the economics:

> I was so disappointed because I thought I was number two or three in my [high school] graduation class, and I had a lot of plans about going to college and I was just so shocked to learn that my mother didn't have money to send me to college and I had a couple of scholarships. I remember one was to [a particular] college, and [one] of them [was somewhere else, both predominantly black schools], but neither was enough [for all expenses], and she [her mother] didn't have enough money to match either [offer]. For instance, most people who gave black scholarships gave it for small amounts so they could help as many as possible: you know, so many young people needed help who decided to go to school. But she just couldn't match any of them so I was so disappointed, I didn't know what to do. So I went to New York. I went to a friend in New York, on my own, a friend from seventh, eighth, and ninth grades. She had left and gone to New York, and she was married, had a husband, and had her husband's child and an apartment.

Turning to public/private distinctions in higher education, 77 percent of the Controls went to private colleges or universities while only

44 percent of Pathmakers did (see Table 5.3). After Betty Powers lived and worked in New York for a year after high school, she attended a city college, then reentered her own state university and finished there, supporting herself all the while. The percentages for private colleges, however, were still larger than one would expect, especially for the Pathmakers. The highest proportion of private school attendees was in the black control group, where 85 percent attended such schools, but this finding is difficult to interpret: remember that many all-black schools attended by our subjects were privately funded as alternatives to limited public options in higher education. Some of our subjects preferred black schools. Bonnie Carter's father wanted her to attend prestigious predominantly white liberal arts colleges like Oberlin, Bryn Mawr, or Smith, but she said, "I just wanted to go to a black school, and [where she went] was supposed to be the best, and after all . . . [her father] had started there so it was the great compromise. I just didn't find anything terribly attractive about those [other] schools."

When Bernie Clark returned to college three years after leaving the military, he also chose to go to a predominantly black private college rather than returning to the integrated Midwest state university (which he had selected based upon his uncle's attendance) where he had encountered obstacles about his race.

Among the white Controls there was a clear majority again, with 68 percent attending private colleges. In spite of his father's death when he was fifteen, Wendell Curtis never even applied to any publicly supported college, although living in a state renowned for such schools:

What money was left that was extra for education finished my sister's college [she was a sophomore when he was applying to schools]. So it in effect finished up her education. And there was no question. I went where I got the largest scholarship. I got accepted at [all five of] the schools. [One] gave me a year's scholarship, possibly renewable.

Table 5.3 Pathmakers and Controls attending private college

	Yes	No
Pathmakers (59)	26	33
Controls (39)	30	9
	(56)	(42)

X^2 (1, N = 98) = 10.35, p < .01

Dartmouth accepted me, but with no scholarship. [Where I went] gave me a full four-year scholarship—a memorial scholarship, which is the one they gave to a select few who meet academic and extracurricular requirements. I had never even seen the school . . . I graduated sixth out of seven hundred in high school . . .

After serving in the armed forces Wendell Curtis went on for his prestigious M.B.A.:

The first year I used the balance of my savings, and my mother lent me a thousand dollars. And I borrowed a little from my sister, and I allowed my father-in-law to pay the rent [$105 a month]. It used to blow his mind, because he wanted to send me money and I wouldn't take it. I bugged him on one side and made him pleased on the other, so he had a mixed reaction . . . The second year after my funds were exhausted they give you a stipend which is equal to what they say a married person with one child with a wife not working [needs], because they don't think the wife should work. I think it was about $4600, so I graduated in two years.

Wendy Cassetta had the following to say of her small private women's college, and her public school teacher's role in selecting it:

It turned out to be perfect for me. I went to school [college] with a lot of rich kids. Went to school with kids that went to girls' prep schools and I got enough polish in college to help me climb out of [my home city]. That's what it really did for me. I went there because a high school teacher said, "You know, you might get a little polish and a little class there and that may make a difference for someone like you." It turned out they were right . . . It gave me a different world—the first time I ever met Jews. I had a couple of black friends in high school. The first time I ever really met people from foreign countries. It turned out to be very useful, very useful.[9]

For the Pathmakers, the least likely to attend private colleges were the white females (33 percent) like Wanda Perkins. If one assumes this to be the result of a decision about allocating scarce family resources, there is the hint of a gender bias, since Pathmaker females reported doing better in their elementary and secondary schools than did Pathmaker males. For example, within her family, Wanda Perkins reports a definite gender bias: her mother never hit her brothers, and she and they "were treated in two distinctly different ways." The remaining Pathmaker groups were evenly distributed, with around 50 percent attending private colleges.

How should these findings be interpreted? Given the racial divisions of society, private colleges could be assumed to be more important for blacks than traditionally advantaged whites, and the black Controls were most able to know about alternatives or be able to afford them. The white Controls exercised traditional privilege but its exercise was perhaps somewhat less essential to the outcome of the child. That many Pathmaker children were tracked by some process into private college (remember they say they were good students) results in about half of them attending such colleges. The notable exception is the white female Pathmakers whose good performance in school might have been more stereotypical and therefore less likely to result in such unusual interventions, or perhaps whose parents were less willing to further sacrifice for them. Then too, Wanda Perkins's mother didn't want her to go to college because she was afraid it would interrupt the income she received from Wanda's work. Under any circumstances, clearly seen from these data, by the time these Pathmakers reached college age, they had begun to show promise recognized by those around them.[10]

School Obstacles

A number of schooling variables produced Pathmaker/Control differences, which return us to the redundancy of resources argument. We saw our subjects facing many obstacles to school success. How did they perceive them? How many did they report? We found a trend for Pathmakers—with their less redundant resources—to be more likely to report obstacles to school success than Controls. Bob Price said of the segregated black schools he attended:

> If you can imagine a four-room school from grade one to twelve, you can actually graduate from this school, it was an accredited "C" school, but you couldn't get into college if you finished from that school . . . Somewhere along it occurred to me that you had to have education if you really want to drive this shining new car and that sort of thing. In [his area] blacks could do two or three different things. You could drive a car, chauffeur, you could drive a truck, work on a defense plant, and those were the better jobs. Education was the only way and I had

always said that I could never be a farmer. That's a hard job, cotton picking . . . [When he was fourteen his parents moved to the city and he attended a larger high school.] So I was going to a "C" school all those years and all of a sudden I was going to a double "A" school. There was a vice-principal [black] who came from a family almost as large as mine and was the first to go to school . . . I asked him if he thought . . . I was college material. He said of course, but it will be difficult . . . because I didn't have the kind of background that many of the kids in the double "A" school had, having gone to a good school all their life, but I demonstrated that I could match wits with most of the kids, and so if I was prepared to put in a little more time then, perhaps, I'd be all right.

If Pathmakers faced obstacles associated with class and the low educational attainment of parents, Wendy Cassetta reported no obstacles to school success, even though she had parents with a strong ethnic identity: "The ethnicity in school, as I was going through elementary and secondary school, was not a problem because everybody was ethnic and we went through periods when we wanted to hide our ethnicity but mostly we liked the food so we visited each other's houses."

Obstacles of Race and Gender

Female and black Pathmakers would have to spread their resources over even more obstacles—sexism and racism—than white male Pathmakers. Bob Price said: "Not being able to go to school on a regular basis [except for rain he had to take two months off for harvest and two months off in the spring to break ground] was a big disadvantage. I think the teachers felt sorry for me . . . It was a difficult process to keep up . . . I was able to get A's and B's but some I knew I didn't deserve."

Not surprisingly, it is the white male Controls who reported the least obstacles to school success than any other cohort.[11] In fact, all the blacks in our sample, Pathmaker or Control, acknowledged more obstacles to school success than the white subjects (see Table 5.4). Of all blacks, 48 percent voluntarily reported racism of whites to be one such obstacle. Bernie Clark said that being black was "absolutely" an obstacle at his first college, a large midwestern state university, except at the house where he lived, which was integrated by university policy. He left this university after two years, and selected an all-black institution when he returned to school five years later.

Table 5.4 Obstacles reported to school success by race of subjects[a]

	Yes	No
Blacks (61)	50	11
Whites (51)	28	23
	(78)	(34)

X^2 (1, N = 112) = 9.63, p < .005
a. More than one obstacle could be reported by each subject.

But blacks faced other obstacles as well. Bonnie Carter said of her public school (which was further south than where she had grown up), "Inasmuch as I had all black teachers, not racial prejudice, but again part of it was my skin, but it had more to do with custom. For example, I did not say 'Ma'am, Yes Ma'am, No Ma'am,' 'Respectful Yes and Respectful No,' and 'Yes Sir' to an elderly gentleman, and that was not allowed, so I did have the experience of being taken to the office because I wouldn't say 'Ma'am' to the teacher." She also reported being penalized for her accent. As Bonnie Carter learned, obstacles can also be linked to regional patterns of manners and speech. Racism can involve judgments of lightness or darkness of skin or class among blacks, and not always white prejudice, as Betty Powers reported for her segregated all-black grade school:

It was a public school, of course, it was a good school. It was about a mile from home. I walked there and back and it was very cold in the winter although that's not a long period of cold. But teachers—I don't really want to see this in print, but since I feel so strongly about the truth I'll say it . . . There was a lot of discrimination among the blacks themselves on the basis of color. I remember I was always in Group 2 [of three ability groups in school] but I was the best reader in the class. [She has moderately dark skin.] You know the teacher—not always in every grade but in enough grades for it to be still in my mind today, forty years later—I remember the teachers always came to me and said, "Read this," "How would you pronounce this word?" but they always had to come to me in Group 2 to do that [even though she was the best in the class], and the children were placed [in groups] supposedly on the basis of their reading abilities! One, two, and three—we always had three groups; that happened to me and that hurt me . . . You could walk into the class and see that [the grouping] was on the basis of color . . . I was conscious then, because the children would talk about it. And then there was certain talk in the home about it, because it was practiced a lot in other parts of our society, not just in school . . . Overall I always liked teachers, even the ones that treated me like that because, well, they didn't treat me like that, they treated me nice. They just had a special kind of different niceness for some of the others in terms of their going to the blackboard and writing, in terms of sending them on little errands, in terms of going to the cabinet and getting the books out and passing out this and passing out that. It was always that, but there was never a time when any of my teachers were not nice to me. But in elementary school I ended up in Group 2, and you could see; you could see all the real, real dark children in the third group. I remember being very quiet, not talking much, reading and writing.

Overcoming Obstacles

An important set of findings has to do with how individuals responded to these obstacles to school success. We classified the reported responses into the following categories: assertive or aggressive responses (e.g., fighting back when teased), purely emotional responses (e.g., cry), goal adaptation responses (changing one's goals in the light of the opposition), "walk around" responses (keeping the goal in sight, but finding an alternative way to get there), and finally compensatory responses (working harder to overcome the obstacle). As previously mentioned there were no differences between Pathmakers and Controls in the nature of the response made to obstacles even though Pathmakers were more likely to encounter obstacles, suggesting a uniformity of strategies across these categories.

However, responses to obstacles were predicted by race and sex. Specifically, blacks were more likely to report aggressive or assertive responses to school obstacles than whites (see Table 5.5). As we saw ear-

Table 5.5 Aggressive responses to obstacles to school success by race of subjects

	Yes	No
Blacks (33)	13	20
Whites (22)	1	21
	(14)	(41)

X^2 (1, N = 55) = 8.45, p < .005

lier, Bonnie Carter attended private, college-related schools until her father changed jobs when she was in the sixth grade, and she began public school:

> That was the first time that doing well was not necessarily rewarding among your peers. I think that was one of the biggest problems . . . [Q. How did you deal with it?] I don't know, I think I did a lot of crying and kind of worked it through . . . They were always threatening to beat me up, and at home our parents took this reasonable psychological approach because they were trying to make us independent thinkers so there was not an awful lot of violence, you know, at home and hitting somebody was not the way to solve problems, and these kids used to scare me to death. So finally I got up enough nerve to decide that I'm tired of this . . . every day something would happen, every day. So finally I had enough from Bobby Jean, and so what I did was to follow her home from school and threaten to beat her up, and she wouldn't come out, and that was a turning point when they left me alone. I'm sure a lot of it had to do with the kind of support that I got at home, from my mother, but I can't give you an ABC of what I did . . . The [social] class situation was different because there was a broader spectrum of kids. It was the first time that I had been made aware of my complexion, and I had never known what "high yellow"[12] was before, so I got introduced to that, and it was probably very healthy in the long run—my mother decided we should not go back [to her previous school] because we were about to become little snobs and that the public schools would be the best thing. So it is not a good memory.

Conversely, white females made no assertive or aggressive responses to obstacles, and the typical white female Pathmaker response to obstacles to school success (more than any other cohort) was to work harder.[13] Wendy Cassetta reported working to head off responses to her ethnicity in college: "In college everybody was really into ethnicity for one reason or another: we had a lot of foreign students around and my [rich] college friends loved coming to my house for [ethnic] foods and at Christmas there was a kind of tradition that I started that I invited everybody from the town that was going to college to my house to meet my friends and my mother would cook."

Compensatory response patterns were reported by Wendell Curtis when he had his first problem in school—in graduate school for his M.B.A.:

I got one of those pink slips which said if you don't improve by the end of the first year you're out. And for somebody who was laying out the kind of money that I was laying out that meant something to me. I thought this was great stuff . . . I thought I was doing great until I got this piece of paper. Well, that was a shock! [Q. How did you respond?] I guess like everybody. I think I worked harder and I was more diligent, but I don't think I really did anything. But I tell you it really wakes you up. It makes believers out of you, especially when you're buying . . . At the end of my first year though, I was probably in the lower half, and I graduated in the top third.

Extracurricular Activities and Peers

One of our themes has been that resources for Pathmakers, blacks, and women were less redundant than resources for Controls. We thought that an important way to construct access to additional resources in school might be through extracurricular activities, and that they might constitute an important resource for the Pathmakers by offering networks of friendships and relationships outside of one's immediate circle, as well as opportunities to test oneself, and to learn social and leadership skills. But, as we mentioned earlier, we were surprised to learn that Pathmakers did not report extracurricular activities more often than Controls.

However, there was a trend for white males overall to report less extracurricular activities, suggesting that extracurricular activities were used more by blacks and women. Wendy Cassetta, for example, became editor of her high school newspaper, and used that experience to get summer employment as a "copy girl" on the city paper. She also edited the college paper, and her referral to the summer job she obtained at her college came from the newspaper adviser, both good examples of the utilization of constructed resources. Bonnie Carter also reported that she was in "the Math Club, the Yearbook, whatever the girls' organization was, the band, really whatever they had." She links this to the fact that her teachers "really liked me, and that was in some ways a disadvantage in that you were singled out for being good, and that wouldn't really help you out an awful lot with your peers, and I didn't like being [her father the professor's daughter]. I was very anxious to establish my own identity." One explanation for the Pathmakers' similarity to Controls is that Pathmakers might have needed extracurricular activities, but may have been blocked from participating by their families' backgrounds. White males had the easiest access, but less need, perhaps explaining the greater use of extracurricular activities by blacks and women.

In some cases, however, we found that extracurricular activities could help in more personal ways, like testing oneself. When we asked Wendell Curtis about extracurricular activities he said he only had one, but that it was psychologically important:

> My name is Wendell and I played football because my name is Wendell. I'm not a fighting person but there was this connotation of sorts. And I only say this now. I never knew why I did it then. But that was probably why. I had to prove that Wendell could play football. And I made first string in my junior year in high school and I weighed only 160 pounds. But that pushed me in that area. [Q. Other sports?] I sailed. I skied, but only football at school. [Q. Did you play football at college?] Two days. I got my scholarship because of my combination of athletics and academics, but I didn't have to play it. [Q. Why didn't you continue football?] Because they played for blood and not for fun. My roommate in college was an All-American guard, and the difference between him and me . . . [was that] he was there to play football and I was there for education and fun. It only took me one day to find that out. I make decisions quickly.

Dating

Moving to activities and peer relations outside of school, we asked the subjects to describe their dating behavior while in school and college. Pathmakers were more likely to say that they seldom dated until they met their spouse (see Table 5.6). Wanda Perkins never married, but fit the pattern of delayed dating since she reported that she did not date during high school. Her first date was well into college, and her first

Table 5.6 Pathmakers and Controls reporting dating before meeting first spouse

	Yes	No
Pathmakers (58)	43	15
Controls (37)	35	2
	(78)	(17)

X^2 (1, N = 95) = 6.43, p < .025

"relationship" was when she was a college senior. Controls dated more widely. For example, Wendell Curtis said that he'd "always dated girls since I was eight or nine. I've always played the field." And Wendy Cassetta said, "Yes, I dated a lot [in high school]. And in college. Well, we did a lot of group dating in high school. I went with someone in college, but we really moved around in college and it was always on a different level. In the Peace Corps I fell madly in love with someone and that's the person I traveled with for a year after I left the Corps. And I lived with someone in graduate school, but I didn't marry him." Bonnie Carter described a pattern of dating she thought peculiar to the South where she spent her high school years:

> With Southern mothers, initially your parents take you and they pick you up, and on special occasions . . . We're very sheltered until your senior year, and then you get a little more flexibility. But to the extent that we could go, I did, and another thing that was different from my peers is that we could always bring people home. We've always, since junior high school, been able to bring different boys home, but you didn't go anywhere with them. And high school, the big thing was having company . . . You waited for the guy to come over to your house—he could come over and stay forever, but you couldn't go nowhere.

At college, she led an active social life after learning how to beat a 7 p.m. curfew imposed because the college "was entrusted with so many of these Southern darlings."

Pathmaker children may not have felt in a strong position to make dating claims on others. Their stricter parents may not have allowed it. They may also not have been able to afford to date. Pathmakers also reported more siblings than Controls. Perhaps this makes early dating less possible because of sibling care responsibilities or less necessary to develop peer interpersonal skills.

It is also possible that the dating findings, and the absence of the greater expected use of extracurricular activities by Pathmakers, may signal an avoidance of failure in arenas outside the home and not under the protection of teachers. In support of this interpretation is a finding that Pathmakers were more likely to describe themselves as loners in grade school and high school than Controls (see Table 5.7). They may not have felt extracurricular activities would welcome them. Wanda Perkins said:

Table 5.7   Pathmakers and Controls describing self as loner in high school

	Yes	No
Pathmakers (56)	11	45
Controls (30)	0	30
	(11)	(75)

X^2 (1, $N = 86$) = 6.76, $p < .01$

I was fat and ugly [in high school], I had terrible dental problems, and my mother used to cut my hair and it was terrible and, Oh God, I was ugly. And I felt fat and ugly and the way that I made friends was I used to give them my Latin homework or my algebra homework— that's the way you win friends and influence people. Because they were all out having a good time and didn't do their homework, so I'd slip them my homework. I remember that very well . . . I was reclusive and shy in high school, and while I starred academically, was in National Honor Society, the junior play, Latin club, I didn't go to football games, and I didn't have a boyfriend, and I didn't belong to a social club . . .

It is interesting to note that Wes Parker chose a college that had a uniform: "It was important to go to a place where I wasn't socially outclassed. But there I didn't have to worry about how I dressed, because I had to wear their uniform all the time . . . So my dress code was taken care of." In contrast, Bonnie Carter learned from her mother very early how to dress and felt comfortable that she was dressed appropriately.

[Going to college] was a very big thing of [her mother's]; it was instilled in us that you had to go to school, you had to get an education. Beyond that they really gave us a pretty free rope, and yet when you're consciously aware of doing things to get ahead and it goes back to some of those basic values that they instilled, like being on time, being dressed appropriately for wherever you go . . . But they didn't drill us in terms of "you've got to do this, you've got to do that," but it was a part of living whatever you were going to do.

Indeed, 100 percent of the white female Controls said they were liked by their peers; on the opposite extreme, only 33 percent of the black female Pathmakers so said.[14] Since female Pathmakers more often reported being good students, this could have come at the expense of peer relationships, apparently especially for the black female Pathmakers.

Educational Attainment: Race and Gender

Returning to the issue of overall educational attainment, we did find race and gender differences for blacks and women. As we reported in Chapter 4, we found different paths for family support of education by race and gender: white female Controls reported less family support for education—here we defined support as having high expectations, encouraging, and actively helping the subject—than did all other Controls. In contrast black Controls received strong support: Bernie Clark's grandmother virtually intervened to send him to prep school, he had enormous family support for his education, and even chose to attend the same college as his uncle because he had talked about it so much. Black males, whether Controls like Bernie Clark or Pathmakers, were the category most likely to describe their families as supporting their schooling. These findings argue that for these variables different paths to success were taken by black males and, in some instances, white females.

In this context we note here an important finding concerning race and educational attainment: black males reported more formal education than all other subjects.[15] While we reported earlier in this chapter that there are no Pathmaker/Control differences on educational attainment, this is evidence, as predicted by Blau and Duncan (1967), that black males, in the face of societal prejudice and with parental support, must achieve higher levels of educational attainment to achieve equal success. This finding contradicts popular criticism of affirmative action programs as synonymous with a drop in standards. It is also evidence that education has been used by black families and black males themselves as an important mechanism to achieve success in the face of racial obstacles.

The finding concerning the higher educational attainment of black males is intriguing since, like Bernie Clark, they were not as likely to mention teachers as important, nor did they describe themselves as better students. We feel it is another indication of multiple paths: black males did not see themselves as doing well in school as often, nor did they credit teachers as often, but despite this they reported higher levels of educational achievement than the others in the sample, Pathmaker or not. The fact that teachers were less important for the black male

Pathmakers than for the other Pathmakers is perhaps related to the fact that the black male Pathmakers, like all black males, had strong parental support for education, making teachers less critical.[16]

We also obtained findings relating to the racial segregation of the larger society and the segregation of schooling in that society, which could have multiple effects on motivation and performance. Virtually no whites (one out of fifty) attended schools which were predominantly black, and only three whites reported any black teachers. One was Wendell Curtis, who reported black teachers in his integrated junior and senior high schools, another attended a predominantly black high school, and another reported black teachers in graduate school. On the other hand forty-four out of the fifty blacks in our study attended predominantly black schools at some time in their lives. The segregated nature of the education system of this country when these forty- to fifty-five-year-old people were growing up is much in evidence in our data.

Mentoring in Education

There has been a lot written about mentoring as a technique to facilitate people who start out as our Pathmakers did to achieve success. Here and in the remaining chapters we follow Flaxman, Ascher, and Harrington's (1989) definition of mentor, which distinguishes it from parenting by stating that a mentor cannot be a family member. However, a few subjects like Bernie Clark use the term specifically to encompass family members. We follow their usage in presenting quotes, but use ours in statistical analyses.

Aside from their already reported greater reliance on teachers, Pathmakers did not report more people influencing their education than Controls. Nor, as we wrote earlier in discussing people influential to their schooling, did we observe differences between Pathmakers and Controls in the race and gender of the person they reported influencing them. There was, however, a high correlation between the race and gender of the subject and the race and gender of the person exerting the influence. Specifically, blacks reported being influenced by blacks, whites by whites, and women more often reported being influenced or mentored by women and men by men (see Table 5.8a and Table 5.8b). Given the literature on social modeling and identification (see Bandura, 1977) this "match" between race and gender is not surprising.

Teachers mentoring Wendy Cassetta were white females until she

Table 5.8a   Race of influential figures on education by race of subject

	Race of mentor[a]	
	Black	White
Blacks (55)	50	5
Whites (46)	0	46
	(50)	(51)

X^2 (1, N = 101) = 82.81, p < .001
a. More than one mentor could be mentioned by each subject.

Table 5.8b   Gender of influential figures on education by gender of subject

	Gender of mentor[a]	
	Male	Female
Males (40)	28	12
Females (39)	13	26
	(41)	(38)

X^2 (1, N = 79) = 10.63, p < .001
a. More than one mentor could be mentioned by each subject.

got to graduate school, where she was mentored by a white male. Since not all of our subjects grew up in segregated communities and since all communities contain men and women, these two findings speak to certain basic loyalties as well as the race and gender stratification of the larger society. Betty Powers talked about her English teacher:

I always thought I was unattractive, dull, in the way. I never had a very high regard for myself until I guess seventh grade when I started writing, yes, when I started writing. And I guess it was after that that Mrs. S used to encourage me. You know, she had no children, but I used to go to her house and do little things around her house, not for pay . . . I always had strong feelings about things and I never could [express them] . . . I remember feeling different but those essay papers, I used to say a lot of strong things in there and maybe it was coming out that way but I felt I really started feeling alright about myself then.

Her home economics teacher is linked to her successful career:

Mrs. L, who is a dear friend now, got me involved with New Home-makers. We started in tenth grade—the sewing projects—and we had to travel once a year to a convention, but then I went out of state for the first time with Mrs. L and the girls to Louisiana. My first trip out of the state. I was in eleventh grade. And I was made president of the New Homemakers, of our little school chapter there. But you had to conduct meetings . . . the New Homemakers was the one that I re-member, as far back as I can remember, saying now you have to have order, and you have to have a parliamentarian, and the president does this and this one does that, and that probably shaped my understand-ing . . .

Such descriptions of teachers as mentors also speak to the arguments currently heard for increasing the numbers of minority teachers. The argument is usually framed in the context of providing role models for students. However, our findings would suggest that such teachers would also be more likely to influence and mentor their minority students and that they could produce lasting effects. Mentors are seen by us as an-other replacement for thin family resources, just as we have argued that teachers are more important to Pathmakers than to Controls.

In his discussion of what he called "mentors," Bernie Clark men-tioned only family members. "I think that mentors are needed. I am one of those that believes that. I think that I've had mentors up and down the line. I had my grandmother. I always knew my mother and father were there even though they were apart—they were mentors. My grandmother was a central focus of my life. Several of my uncles I loved and admired . . ."

In contrast, Wanda Perkins's early mentors were a white female pro-fessor and a white female school superintendent who made her a dem-onstration teacher so that she "worked with teachers and kids simul-taneously and thrived on it." She then says that her relationships with male mentors have been complicated:

There are men in here all the way along, either men or significant people along the line. [So I've had] some mother figures and some, you know, lover figures. One relationship was with a professor [when she was getting her master's degree]. I had him on this pedestal, and I thought he was really brilliant, and he continued to give me en-couragement that I should go on to a doctoral degree, and that I had never thought about. And for two years he kept talking about a doctoral degree and more and more it seemed reasonable to me. And he kept telling me I could do this. [She subsequently did go to graduate school, but elsewhere. We asked why.] Well, even at that stage of my relationship with him I knew that he was married and that made me think that I shouldn't go back there, but I ought to be close enough [to see each other] if we wanted to, and the program [where she went] was really superlative. And their offer was really marvelous.

For Wanda, being mentored, like being parented, came with a price.

Summary

To review, we have found that Pathmakers share the same levels of educational attainment as Controls, and that education is appropriately thought of as an effective equalizer between the two groups. We found, perhaps because of their thinner home resources, that Pathmakers reported that teachers were more important to them than Controls. Given the state of urban schools that are heavily populated by today's Pathmakers, this finding should generate enormous concern. If good teaching matters more for Pathmakers than the Controls, are they likely to get it? We know that Pathmakers have less access to resources of private schooling, both in elementary and secondary schools and in college, and that they face greater obstacles to school success than Controls. Yet, in the face of all these obstacles, they still achieved. We also found that Pathmakers were more likely to say they dated little before meeting their spouse.

We found that black males in our sample reported higher levels of educational attainment than the other subjects, despite the fact that blacks reported greater obstacles to school success to which they were more likely to make aggressive responses. White males seem to use extracurricular activities less than the traditionally under-represented groups across the board, and white male Controls not unexpectedly reported fewer obstacles to school success than all other subjects. Female Pathmakers were better students than male Pathmakers. White female Controls had better relations with peers compared to the black female Pathmakers.

Given these varied findings, we believe research that allows for comparisons between and among subjects of different genders, races, SES, and educational background should be encouraged and strengthened.

Important differences in the nature of the paths followed to achieve success may be masked by studies that aggregate across these characteristics. As we shall see in the next chapter there appear to be differences between men and women in their orientation to and expectations of work, what they can get out of work, their fellow workers, and their own success. Further, we shall see that Pathmakers account for their success in fundamentally different ways than Controls. We turn now to such concerns.

6

Work and Careers

In this chapter we explore the paths made to build careers despite the social constraints Pathmakers faced: what opportunities and resources they utilized or created. We also examine how central their careers and work were to their lives, how they dealt with bosses and employees, the role of mentors and their relationships with them, what obstacles they faced in building their careers, how they dealt with these obstacles, and how they coped with any failures.

Getting and Leaving Jobs

An interest in spiralism focuses our attention first on how our subjects began working. We have reported in earlier chapters how family and education influenced the shape of early careers. Fifty-six percent of our subjects used family resources to get jobs before college. But we reported in Chapter 4 that male Controls reported family connections to be important in obtaining these early jobs more than male Pathmakers. For example, we showed how Wendell Curtis utilized his parents' friends to get work after his father's death. Like many Controls, he was also able to widen this base by using as resources neighbors and friends he had made in his neighborhood and school:

> When I was in high school after my father died [and while he was working in the drugstore job obtained through his family] one of my

friends' father was [in the theater], and his son and I worked for him, fixing up costumes, running errands all around. By convenience I chose to go away to school even though my mother was home alone, therefore I also chose [summer] jobs at home instead of going away. So that [for] the three months in the summer I also painted houses in the neighborhood for neighbors as second jobs to save more. I worked seven to four in the warehouse and would come home and paint the houses. They were getting a steal . . .

Despite finding support among males for our expectation that Path-makers would find family and family resources less useful than Con-trols, we did not find such a difference among women: as we reported in Chapter 4, female Pathmakers were about as able as female Controls to report resources of their families as important, but females were linked to different kinds of jobs.

Another variable related to the use of whatever resources were avail-able to Pathmakers and Controls is what goals motivated them to enter these early jobs, and here we find, not surprisingly, that Pathmakers were motivated to get a job to make money to help support their fam-ilies, or for their own use. Bob Price, for example, from the time he could walk was helping his father bring in crops. He got his first job when he was ten. "The thing I'm talking about is having a hand-me-down shoe or something else. I began to look at those Sears Roebuck and Montgomery Ward catalogues and see all the different things peo-ple had and the only way I could get those things was work myself. So I did the same kind of farm work for others that I was doing for my father . . ." Talking about a later job, he said: "The purpose of taking that construction job was to . . . save enough money to go to school. My parents were not able to send me to school or least didn't place that much value in going to school to cough up four, five hundred dollars or whatever the tuition was at the time. Therefore I had to go myself."

In contrast Bernie Clark's motivation for working before leaving for prep school had a great deal to do with family moral tradition and role models:

Work . . . it wasn't something you really think about. Not working: it wasn't something in your mind set. I might sneak out to a movie and come back. I'd make sure Mama Clark wasn't there, or one of my more severe uncles wasn't around. I'd pick my shots. It was just an expectation. You want to do the right thing. You work hard. But to put it in perspective, I grew up watching [prominent black political figures]—they'd all come to the family office . . . They had to have some impact on me growing up as a youngster. So I had positive images out there, going back to images and symbols.[1]

Bonnie Carter was told by her grandfather to get a job picking fruit when she was five! The first job she chose was when she was thirteen:

[Q. How did you get that job?] I asked the owner if I could get a job. It [a variety store] was in our neighborhood, and I was in and out of there from time to time and asked if I could get a job. [Was he black or white?] Black, he's a black minister. [Why that job?] Well, they had this marvelous ice cream contraption there and I had always thought it would be great to work behind a soda fountain. That was the only one I knew of nearby and particularly in [that city] where you had a chance of getting a job. It was still very segregated at that time. [Were your parents supportive of you doing this?] Oh yes, very.

Wendell Curtis, on the other hand, did not think of getting a job until his father died when he was fifteen, and then worked to have spending money. While Wendy Cassetta was clearly motivated early by getting money, when asked if she liked her tennis court job at fifteen she shows the difference between her getting money and Pathmakers' needing money:

Yes, I guess I did, it was a lot of fun. I liked the money, I think. It was an enormous amount of money when you're fifteen years old [$160 a month for three months]. And I think it was the first time I ever got a chance to buy clothes by myself or else I absolutely ruined myself on hamburgers or things like that because my parents, my father was very smart . . . he/they said I could spend the money any way I wanted to. I didn't have to save it for school. I didn't have to do anything else, and I said, could I eat anything I wanted and they said absolutely. So I think for the first two months I ate nothing but horrible junk food, and really got tired of it.

We said in Chapter 4 that Pathmakers more often shared the money they made with their families than Controls. Sharing of money was also more true for black Pathmakers than white Pathmakers. Such Pathmakers came to feel that their work was part of a family corporate necessity. Female Pathmakers could get a job through their family more often, while the male Pathmakers were more on their own. Controls could use family contacts to get jobs, but felt less family need for their income, and were more individuated in their motivation to seek work.[2]

We also found an additional variation in paths among Control subjects: black and female Controls were more likely to leave jobs before college graduation for school reasons than white male Controls.[3] Resources were plentiful enough for the Control subjects to allow other variables to be decisive. Wendy Cassetta explains why she left a job she loved as a copy girl at a major newspaper in her home city:

My junior year I stayed [at college in the summer] because I wanted to take part of my senior year off and go to Washington [on an exchange program with a college there] and to do that I kind of had to get my requirements out if I was only going to come back for my last semester of my senior year. I stayed down there and worked in the president's [remember she became one] office, and gave people tours of the college and stuff like that while I went to summer school.

Bernie Clark said:

I was buying a car, and giving Mom some money to help her on the bills at home. Mom had her own apartment building which she had bought. I'd bump into some of my old buddies from [my father's family's town] doing [their] master's [degrees], doing this exchange student in Europe thing, and I said, "Geez, I've got to get myself together here," so I quietly started putting applications together to go back to college. I didn't say anything to Mom. I decided to go to the only school in my field for blacks at that time. I thought, let me try this experience. So one morning I started to pack and she came into the room: "What are you doing son?" I said, "Mom, I'm getting ready to head out to college." And she came in and embraced me. "I'm so glad you got it together son."

An important variable perhaps more related to the current career of the subject is the question of whether families were important to how jobs were obtained *after* college graduation. We thought, as we had for jobs before college, that family should again matter less for Pathmakers than Controls, and matter even less than for early jobs. However, there was also the possibility that family resources might matter less after finishing college for both groups. This would follow from the fact that there were no differences in years of educational attainment between

Pathmakers and Controls (Chapter 5), suggesting that education was an equalizer for Pathmakers by opening opportunities beyond family connections. In fact, the latter was true. While 56 percent of the subjects reported any family sources for jobs before college, only 13 percent said families were sources of jobs after college. The difference between Pathmaker and non-Pathmaker males in the use of family before college disappeared in the after college data.

When asked about their most important route to jobs after college, twice as many Pathmakers as Controls reported being offered jobs that they hadn't applied for, and were also more likely to create their own jobs than Controls (see Table 6.1). The other ways to get jobs— through non-family connections (45 percent), by applying (45 percent), or through school networks (29 percent)—did not differ between the two groups. Being offered jobs more often than Controls suggests that, once the Pathmaker's talent was noted, they might have been sought out, pointing toward the beginnings of a spiralism pattern.[4] Wanda Perkins's first teaching job was offered to her:

> I had done my student teaching there, and as you know it is a substantial middle-class community. The communities I had lived in were pretty ethnic, blue collar communities, and this was really a notch different from there. But I had done my student teaching there and it was a really positive experience, probably the first positive experience I had with schools. [Earlier practica in public schools] were depressing experiences. They were in communities I had lived in, were depressing situations, and I thought, Lord is this what I'm going to be doing? So the woman with whom I did my student teaching was a dynamo . . . I had a person who inspired me and encouraged me and took an interest in me. I got assigned there by accident, but they asked me to stay.

Table 6.1   Most significant way of obtaining jobs after college for Pathmakers and Controls

	Created or was offered jobs	All other ways
Pathmakers (58)	27	31
Controls (40)	10	30
	(37)	(61)

X^2 (1, N = 98) = 4.68, $p < .05$

Bob Price describes his first post-college graduation jobs as initiating a spiral:

All the jobs that I had in [names city] with urban renewal sort of fell on my shoulders. In the sense that when I first got the job through an employment service, not a professional personnel type thing, but just go stand in line and filling out a form that I want a job. But after that, after six months my supervisor decided that he wanted to do something else, so there were three other people working in the same space as I, and I was the youngest, but somehow they failed . . . I had demonstrated some qualities which [his bosses] felt would have been good, so they promoted me as opposed to these other people on the job. A hard-working person who had demonstrated the ability of not being afraid of work, coming early, staying late, doing whatever was required, always having ideas pretty close to what was finally decided upon, exercising reasonably good judgment; working for the federal government didn't require anything but common sense. If you have common sense you can be President of the United States! If you're white. I just had to put that there. In any event I got to know more about that job than anyone else, and I was promoted, and then I knew more about that than anyone else because I've never liked anybody to tell me what to do.[5] I always like to tell other people what to do. So therefore I had to always prepare myself so no one could tell me anything.

Turning to the Controls, Wendell Curtis entered the Air Force after college, and on discharge completed his M.B.A. His first job on grad-uating was obtained through an interview in his business school's place-ment service, but the job was in a line of business in which his father-in-law had made his fortune:

My father-in-law is more of a role model I guess than anything. I saw what he had achieved and I saw that it could be done by somebody from his background [his father-in-law was a Pathmaker as defined in this book]. And the respect that he had in the community. It was the character of the person. [Q. Did he help you get the job?] No. I did not ask him in any way for the position or anything like that. I didn't want that kind of thing. My brother-in-law (his wife's brother), their father bought him the business that he runs. Now (I know) he couldn't have run it for twenty years unless he was good . . . But *he* still asks the question: could he have done it without [his father]? Which is sad, because the answer is yes, but he asked that question. And I never had that problem.

We have already seen that Bernie Clark is one person whose family has been a resource throughout his career. On graduation from college he returned to the family business, where he had increasingly responsible jobs and quick promotions until he split politically with his family. "And besides, not being paid what I thought I deserved" he left the family business for a job with national visibility:

> So I talked it over with my young lady [his wife] and she said, "Bernie let's do it." She knew I was unhappy in this situation and I didn't see it changing, and I didn't see any opportunity either. I guess in the back of my mind, to move up and take over and change policy, and head up the company one day, but this uncle, he was in his fifties, and I thought of all those things.[6] And then the driving desire, maybe a fascination, was to move a step up as the first black in [the new company] . . . But I wasn't frightened by the non-presence. I dug in.

After this Bernie Clark gives many instances of campaigning to get jobs, a pattern quite uncommon among the Pathmakers:

> What happened was that my predecessor [in Washington] announced he was going to step down. He had been with the President during the first four years . . . I wanted his job. And a lot of other people wanted to be it, around the country. So I started lobbying. I got all my contacts writing, several key contacts whom I had gotten to know and I felt respected my abilities . . . So letters are coming in from all over the country. Everybody wants to be on a winning team. I wrote a conceptual paper on what I thought the job should be. A couple of close colleagues worked with me on this paper, and I got this paper in the right hands, and sure enough, when the deal went down I was the guy.

His contacts included key White House personnel, figures from Capitol Hill, and key contacts from his home states, many through family networks.

Wendell Curtis still works for the same company he started with after earning his M.B.A. He said:

At that time most significant things in the Middle East were happening and I wanted to get into the middle of that. I decided that I wanted to do international finance. And I really decided, this had nothing to do with my father-in-law [who was already in this business]. He was retired—at that point he was chairman of the board of a company. But he really had an influence on me in that sense, and I just interviewed for international banks . . . I got two offers—I always graduated in recessions, so I only got two offers—one from here. [He interviewed at one where his father-in-law had been but did not get an offer.] Much to the consternation of my father-in-law, but I didn't really want to work for them. I suppose we all wanted to be loved by everybody, but I suppose it probably showed up, that I didn't want to run up his coat-tail. [Q. So it came down to two offers?] Yes, I chose here because we didn't have the depth of people that the other had. [Q. Depth of people?] Every time they had an opening they probably have five or six people to choose from who could adequately do the job. They staff themselves that way . . . Here, that's not true with us, and so every time we have an opening it's a learning experience for whoever's hanging on with his fingernails, and we do not have more than one or two people for every job. If we move one we have trouble replacing, we just have fewer people. A much leaner staff. [Q. So that means you move up faster?] Yes.

Despite this long-term planning, a Control pattern as we shall see in Chapter 8, he attributes all his subsequent promotions to "being in the right place at the right time," which is also illustrative of the external locus of control typical of Controls we will discuss in Chapter 8.

Turning to the issue of leaving jobs after college, we found that Pathmakers—more likely to be motivated by money to get a job before college—were more likely to leave jobs after college for reasons concerning money (presumably due to their thinner resources) as well; Controls were more likely to leave such jobs because they were bored.[7] Bob Price exemplifies the Pathmakers' reasons for leaving, and their more often being offered jobs they hadn't applied for, in explaining why he left government for banking:

I was working on a night, cold like tonight, in a basement of a church explaining real cases and benefits of the whole urban renewal program that the people would need to move from one spot to another, or in order to rehabilitate their homes . . . One night [his future boss] walked up to me and gave me his card and introduced himself as the founder and president of [names bank] and said, "I like the way you handle yourself; I'd like to sit down and chat with you some time. I'm always looking at new people coming into the city and I'm impressed with you." Well, for this guy to tell me something like that—this was a legend talking to me, like John Wayne or somebody. Well, I filed his card away and forgot about it, but six months later I was at a convention and got this call saying that this president wanted to talk to me. Well, he wanted me to start off as a teller, and I said, "Gee, no, my hands are too big and I'm not dexterous enough to use one of those machines"; I could never do that. And so I turned the job down and so he called me back and said he wanted me to meet the chairman. To make a long story shorter, after two meetings and after two rejections of his offer, he came back to me with an offer that was very difficult for me to turn down. He offered me more money than I ever thought possible. It was really double what I was already making—Jesus Christ—and I said to myself, are you crazy? I joked with him and told him, "I'm having a hard time keeping my checkbook balanced, and you want me to come down and work at your bank . . . ," and that's how I got into it. It was one of those situations where he saw me in action, if you'll pardon the expression, and he liked what he saw and went after me, and so that's how I got to the bank.

Of course this account is another instance of spiralism. This man became a mentor, and Bob became president of the bank when his mentor retired a few years later. When Bob Price left that presidency for his current one, he was also recruited on the basis of performance, but his reason for accepting was different, and much more a function of his personality:[8]

I simply wanted a bigger challenge. I have never been, I guess I have never really played it safe. When you grow up with nothing, from my perspective it's not hard for me to become satisfied or complacent with that; you continue to look for bigger challenges, you continue to look forward. I was president of this bank before I was forty, and so you know a lot of people really can be satisfied with that, and yet I don't work for money now, although money helped to keep your wife in the style she would like and grease your wheels. It's just the drive, the ambition, that you have and that is reinforced when you look at the job that still remains to be done, and I will continue to work ten, fourteen, fifteen hours a day on Saturdays and Sundays—whatever is required as long as work remains.

If, rather than for money, Controls were more likely to say they left jobs after college because of "boredom," the fact that Wendell Curtis still works for the same company after twenty-five years may be linked to his involvement in the job for its intellectual excitement. He had the following to say when he was asked what has been the most satisfying thing about work:

> Every day's different. It is involved in the world and a lot of things that are happening in the world. It has given me the opportunity to travel widely, participate in a whole wide variety of activities and circumstances that have been very exciting by anybody's standards. We get into these mergers and acquisitions and battle and whatever that is done by a relatively small handful of people . . . So very small groups of people in a highly concentrated period . . . But it's nonetheless fascinating.

Bernie Clark said of his career:

> I think one of the most enjoyable aspects has been the opportunity to do things that I wanted to do. I can truthfully say that I never had a job that I didn't like and that includes being a dining car waiter at that point in my life, which was exciting and provided me an opportunity to meet people and get to know people: blacks, browns, blues, and greens, all people . . . The opportunity when I was in Washington to see the world, to get a front porch seat in history, to see those heads of state . . . to actually meet some of them, to interface with some of the best thinkers in government and in the country . . . working with the family.

Bonnie Carter said, "My pattern seems to be to find something that's challenging and interesting and do it, and then look around and see what I want to do next . . . I do like being in a position where you can help things happen, now that's the best part of it all." Wendy Cassetta, when asked about what satisfied her about her current job, said: "I think I guess seeing the institution, finally—it's a very fine institution with really first-class faculty—seeing them finally excited about the place, turning them on, feeling the place actually changing as an institution . . . and it's kind of fun, it's kind of fun. Well, the students are cute." But she also said the thing that bothered her most about her current job was that she didn't have first-class minds working with her. She also volunteered that she has no loyalty to institutions. The typical Control solution to boredom in a job then—to take another—we might interpret as a sign of their more external locus of control; that is, the cure for boredom is to change one's setting and external stimulation (as opposed to reorganizing the job, or developing new interests from within).

However, there were also strong sex differences here: men were more likely than women to say their first reason for leaving jobs was for better opportunities (see Table 6.2). This may be linked to other findings presented in Chapter 8: males were stronger in reward orientation, need for power, and long-term planning than our female subjects. Women subjects overall also seemed to have some different career patterns than the men: specifically, rather menial entry-level jobs were used to gain access to larger opportunities. For example, Bonnie Carter said:

> The [government unit where she was working] was a complete bust. I learned after a while that it was never intended to do anything and there was this office down the hall and at least they looked busy. So I talked to a friend there and I asked her what they did, and she told me, and it sounded good and they had this opening for an administrative assistant, and so I went down to ask them about that. I told them that I could type, which I couldn't. And it worked out this deal was so good, she'd do the typing for me and I'd do some things for her, and once I got there, then I was able to demonstrate some ability and I was promoted eventually, and I became a program analyst, and it was a great place to work . . . I now worked for a [white male] sociologist, and he took me under his wing, and I went everywhere that he did . . . a fantastic experience in terms of learning about government.

He became a mentor and was instrumental in her getting her next three jobs (see below for other material on mentoring).

Table 6.2 Reasons for leaving jobs after college by gender of subject

	Better opportunity	Other reasons
Males (49)	34	15
Females (49)	22	27
	(56)	(42)

X^2 (1, N = 98) = 6.00, $p < .025$

Relations with People at Work

If families became less important as careers developed, and patterns of spiralism could be discerned in the careers of Pathmakers, other patterns developed involving personal contact with people at work. From our data on relational costs of success reported in Chapter 4, we found Pathmakers to have paid some relational price for intergenerational mobility in their careers, leaving behind family and early friends. Given this mobility, how do Pathmakers operate without such easy continuity with their past? For some, relationships with people at work took on personal importance. Pathmaker females were more likely than Control females to say that contact with people at work was a motivating factor in job decisions.[9] Wanda Perkins, for example, selected her third teaching job totally for personal contact reasons.

> It got to the point where [her second job] was not a good place for me anymore and professionally it was time to leave, because [the principal's] crowd was leaving and I was one of [his] crowd. We had all been involved in making major innovations: toward teachers making decisions, major organizational changes. It was very successful. But there was this core of fairly young, mostly single people who were in search of a dream. And we wound up with a carload of us driving to [another state] to apply for jobs. [Q. Why there?] Because that's where [he] went. We didn't know anything about the state . . .

In contrast Wendy Cassetta said of her current job:

> They also know they've got to keep me happy if they want me to do some other things I might set my heart on. I don't lose my heart to institutions or necessarily to people because you have to keep your— you can't get . . . as deep emotionally, as you did when you were younger. Like what you did about the civil rights movement, or the peace movement, or the women's movement. It's too complex for that and you have to live with ambiguity.

It is significant that women Pathmakers used work and career as a place to make friends, which Wendy Cassetta says she does not do. This finding is the first clue for us that female Pathmakers may define the work place differently than Control females, or the males in our study. Due to relational costs of success, for female Pathmakers work fills

some of the functions of family and friendships. As their careers develop, these Pathmakers are increasingly different from their origins
and networks, and work becomes a place to build new networks.[10] As
Stacey (1967) discussed, upward mobility can bring a stressful disruption of early friendships, home, and community. Many Pathmaker
women in our study reported feeling unable to relate to people associated with their early lives. This perceived disruption of identity with
early support systems may lead Pathmaker women to rely more on work
as a source of interpersonal support as well as a means of furthering
their mobility. This may explain why female Pathmakers were more
likely to report contact with people as a motivating force in their decisions about careers. We have also reported (in Boardman, Harrington,
and Horowitz, 1987) that these female Pathmakers cited friends from
work as being an important part of their social network more often
than did women from more affluent backgrounds. Wanda Perkins exemplifies this pattern:

> For a long time I operated on the basis that I only needed work: I
> needed teaching to acknowledge who I was as a person. I don't think
> I realized until the middle of my doctoral work that I was getting all
> my kicks from teaching school. It provided me with all of the reward
> systems for me to acknowledge that I was a capable human being. I'm
> a pretty good teacher and I like to teach and I would get great feed-
> back. There were opportunities for people-to-people relationships
> and I liked that and it was stimulating to me personally. I was satisfying
> my needs for emotional bonding, I was satisfying whatever recogni-
> tion needs I had—even publishing and seeing my name in print was
> rewarding. So I think that a lot of my own personal sustenance needs
> were satisfied for an awfully long time in a work setting. And even
> today, I must admit, it feels good. I like what I'm doing, I sometimes
> think it is funny that they pay me to do what I love to do! . . . I'd like
> to live a balanced life, where my personal life was in balance with my
> professional life, but I get out of balance real easily because all I do is
> school. I jog, I play, drink beer, go to movies, all with friends from
> work. When I travel, it's to conferences.

She met her closest friends in her doctoral program:

> There was a large group of females, probably the biggest group of
> females that were ever there in a doctoral program, and we started

using our birthdays for getting together socially. Because our birthdays were spaced out nicely it was perfect. And now we see each other as often as possible, we talk to one another; it's really a strong network where we support one another and like one another and we're behind one another. They are really important to me.

The use of career to fill functions normally filled by family and networks of origin has some interesting consequences (for current family patterns, see Chapter 7). Current friendship networks came from work, and this means that even their play was work-related. This constellation of variables—reliance on work for formation of personal friends and support networks, and an overall blurring of distinctions between personal and business relationships—would appear to have profound implications for what expectations these women had of work and what work may have reasonably demanded of them. It seems especially likely that they would have wound up devoting more time to their work than did Controls, which may not be incidental to their overall success. One of the costs of success—the disruption of early friendships and continuity with the past—became an asset as it directed more and more energy toward work and the people with whom one works. Note too that there were no differences between Pathmakers and Controls on the number reporting close friends as important: the differences are in the networks from which friends are made.

Wendy Cassetta again exemplified the Control patterns in her choice of friends from her early days and not from work: "I have some college friends, a couple of college friends that are still friends, and I have a couple of friends who are at my level [at other institutions], and I guess I'd say I got about six [friends] . . ." Contrasting this with her large extended family of origin, she says: "I have not repeated that, certainly not in the work place. I think it's a little bit of reaction in the sense that I require more privacy personally."

Obstacles Encountered and Overcome

We turn to an analysis of the obstacles our various categories of subjects encountered at work. While most subjects reported obstacles at work, we found trends for Pathmakers to more often report obstacles (92 percent versus 77 percent), and to report more work obstacles per person than Controls.[11] Of course, blacks reported racism as an obstacle more than all whites, but black males reported racism as an obstacle more than black women.[12] Black women in fact reported sexism to be an obstacle more often than racism. Therefore, these data suggest not only that sexism is a major career obstacle for women, but also hint that for many black women sexism is a more salient obstacle than racism.

White male Controls, the most privileged group in our study, less often reported encountering any obstacles when compared with all other subjects.[13] Wendell Curtis, for example, mentioned none. Yet white females do report obstacles; in fact *all* white female Controls reported encountering obstacles. Wendy Cassetta did not find gender to be an obstacle, but she understood its potential in part of her answer to the question, "How do you account for where you are now?" "I'm very much a part of the establishment in this country, and the city . . . And the women's movement really gave us a set of breaks, whether or not you like [its leaders] personally . . . They made an enormous difference in our lives and really gave us a set of breaks." She also mentioned ethnicity and religion as variables limiting her advancement in a city highly charged with ethnic politics among groups, none of which she was a member. But when she talked of obstacles at work, Wendy Cassetta talked about none of these variables, but rather the nature of her institution: "It really is a bureaucracy. The nice thing about the federal executive branch was that when the secretary asks us to do something our attitude was 'let's figure out how we can do it.' Here when you ask someone to do something, they tell you all the reasons you can't do it. My deans say, 'ah, you can't do that.'"

Not only were different obstacles encountered by different categories of respondents, but how our subjects responded to obstacles also showed differences. While we did not find that Pathmakers confronted job obstacles differently than Controls, there was a trend for white females to be less likely to confront obstacles directly when compared with white males. This pattern suggests the possibility of different styles for dealing with confrontation between men and women. Wendy Cassetta offered this response to conflicts at work: "The same way everyone else does, I try to run away from them, then I realize I have to deal with them . . . I usually personally get angry and figure out that I'm going to fire someone, and never do it. Usually end up trying to figure out a way to try never to get closure when people are really angry. So I try to just either give it enough time or talk it through and figure out how we can handle it."

Mentoring and Work

As with education, a variable often cited in literature about career development is the importance of mentoring.[14] Pathmakers and Controls (75 percent of Controls and 77 percent of Pathmakers) both reported mentors as we defined them to have been most influential to their careers, suggesting that processes of mentoring are equally important to both categories. Bob Price, for example, named one mentor in particular: "The gentleman that I spoke of who was president at the bank that recruited me—that would be the individual who really took me under his wing and really made something of me. If I had to pick just one, that would be the individual. There are many people." Nor were there differences between blacks and whites on numbers reporting with careers being influenced by mentors (75 percent and 76 percent respectively).[15] However, race again exerted a powerful effect on who the career mentor was. Of those influential figures for career decisions we were able to classify according to their race, whites reported having only white mentors, while blacks reported mostly black mentors (see Table 6.3a).

Women did not report mentoring more often than men with any degree of significance (78 percent and 72 percent respectively). But of those mentors who could be classified according to their gender, men more often reported male mentors. Women reported a higher percentage of female mentors than men did, but still reported more male mentors than female ones (see Table 6.3b).[16] Like many women, Wanda Perkins reported both female ("mother surrogates," she called them) and male mentors: "There have always been significant people in my life—significant people who have encouraged me ever since I can remember, who have been terribly important for me. There have been

Table 6.3a   Race of mentor by race of subject

	Mentor[a]	
	Black	White
Blacks (29)	22	7
Whites (39)	0	39
	(22)	(46)

X^2 (1, N = 68) = 43.74, p < .001

a. Mentor is defined as a non-kin adult mentioned as influential to the subject's career.

Table 6.3b   Gender of mentor by gender of subject

	Mentor[a]	
	Male	Female
Males (35)	30	5
Females (28)	18	10
	(48)	(15)

$X^2 (1, N = 63) = 3.94, p < .05$
a. Mentor is defined as a non-kin adult mentioned as influential to the subject's career.

surrogate mothers and fathers all the way along the line. Who have said 'you're OK, you're OK,' and those messages have had a cumulative effect."

Wendy Cassetta gave a description of one of her mentors, a boss as well as an academic adviser:

I eventually became a personal assistant to [a dean at her graduate school] who is my mentor. And that was a very important relationship because [he] for some reason or another—he certainly didn't have a liberated marriage—was a liberated man and loved having women research assistants and really thought that the future was going to be very bright for women scholars. So he always had a whole group of women around him. We also worked harder, and we were better than everybody else. I actually shared an office with him because there was a scarcity of offices . . . My early publishing is all with him.

He also introduced her to the foundation people who awarded her first grant. She said of her next mentor, her boss at her second job after her doctorate:

He was very helpful, in part because I got a better sense of him, from him, of what excellence was all about, not because he knew much about my field but it was a little bit of style and just kind of standards that he set and he believed in younger faculty. He had a really profound influence on my own attitudes and my value system about the academic world, I guess. I guess that was it.

We have already reported a male mentor for Bonnie Carter. The use of male mentors by women may reflect any one or a combination of the following: societal sexism, in that more males may have been in a position to help these women than were females; respondent sexism, in that women still looked to men for help more than women; or differences in helping behavior between men and women. Perhaps it was male seniors who more often acted in altruistic, helpful ways than did females: we report in Chapter 8 that men in this study were stronger in the use of altruism than women.

Wendy Cassetta and Bonnie Carter were not the only subjects to report bosses as mentors. However, compared to all other subjects, black males did so less often.[17] This was true for both black male Pathmakers and Controls, suggesting again that race (in this case interacting with gender) is having potent effects on mentoring and the development of influential relationships. Black males appear to have a very different, perhaps more competitive, relationship with their bosses than all the other subjects, whether or not they are Pathmakers.[18]

In contrast, Wendell Curtis talked frequently about the influence of various bosses on his career, always in positive terms:

> The guy who hired me . . . I learned a lot from him in terms of business finance, international finance. I've been pushing it always to work for people who have progressed and done well and [have] evidently given them confidence in the work that I did. Which helps in an organization like this where you don't have ten people you're choosing from each time something happens. He carried a big stick but I could get along with him. Our present [names collateral position] has been my boss twice; he is about to retire. Probably he taught me a lot about business and finance.

Pathmakers then did not differ in their feeling that being mentored was important to their careers, but the networks from which mentors come likely differ across categories of subjects. This is reminiscent of the finding reported earlier for close friends being important to most subjects, but that the networks from which friends are chosen differ for Pathmakers and women.

Conflicts and Their Resolution

We turn to the related issue of how conflicts are handled at work. There is a large literature on conflict and conflict resolution strategy (see Boardman and Horowitz, 1994), suggesting that, while conflicts are endemic to social life, how conflicts are resolved (either productively or destructively) has lasting consequences for individuals and relationships. It is likely then to matter very much how our subjects resolve conflicts with their bosses. Bonnie Carter gives an example of a strategy we coded as "direct reasoning": "If there is a point of disagreement with superiors I try and leave the door open a bit and to come back in another way if I can with a stronger or better case."[19]

Bob Price explains his direct reasoning approach:

> Whenever you have a conflict with your superiors you have to be very careful . . . You have to really spend a lot of time with your superiors to get your point across . . . If I know that my board is headed in a direction that is not in the best interests of the bank then I have to be very persuasive, be very diplomatic in the process. I have to use all kinds of techniques in order to guide and direct them in that way. And there is no set way to do it . . . So I guess to some extent you have to be like a piano player that plays without music or plays by ear. You have to be somewhat of a psychologist, a sociologist, a politician, an economist, all rolled into one. And that is really a great part of a CEO's job. I have fifteen directors and I have to be able to get along with all of them. And they call me up with all sorts of funny stuff. Some of it legal, some of it illegal. I have to be able to deal with that and I have to be able to say no, when it's not in the best interests of the bank, and I have to say no in such a way that won't be offensive, that they will not feel threatened, and will not anger them because if it does I've got a problem on my hands.

It is interesting to note that when we asked Bob Price how he came by his diplomatic skills, he answered: "When you grow up in a family of fourteen or fifteen and they're all bigger than you are . . ."

He is typical of black male Pathmakers, but not the black male Controls: we obtained a trend for black male Controls to less often report using direct reasoning approaches in conflict with bosses than black male Pathmakers. Half the black male Controls used aggression, denial, or suppression in dealing with conflicts with their bosses instead of direct reasoning. It is perhaps part of why black males overall were less likely to mention their bosses as influential resources. But in this case it would mean a very different working style than that used by black male Pathmakers. Thus even though Pathmaker and Control black males behave differently, bosses may anticipate one style from all black men.

These differences in relating to bosses between black male Controls and Pathmakers is of considerable theoretical and practical import to managers who assume that a certain kind of relationship will develop between bosses and their subordinates, given that apparently black males do not reciprocate bosses' expectations that they will influence their subordinates' career development—or else bosses don't mentor them the way they do other employees. The former could result from a distrust of often white managers, but it could also lead to either a reputation for being self-starting or a reputation for being difficult to influence. The latter could be interpreted as racism, except that black women have a different pattern. Perhaps bosses perceive black males as more of a threat. They may be: we will report in Chapter 8 that black males share a concern for competition, power, and winning more than the other subjects. For example, when asked what he liked most about his job, Bob Price replied "bossing people." It is likely that this strong need for power is at least partially responsible for black males failing to cite bosses as mentors, and black male Controls using aggression, denial, and suppression to handle conflict with bosses.

Turning to other relationships at work, only 25 percent of our subjects considered an autocratic approach to subordinates to be effective, and 75 percent of our subjects did not. However, the 25 percent who did were more likely to be Control females and Pathmaker males, the same groups which were loners in their adolescence (see Chapter 4). Control females were also more likely to prefer autocratic styles with subordinates than Control males.[20] Bonnie Carter said: "My resolution to conflict usually is to try and reason through, and then to assert authority if that is not possible." Pathmaker males were more likely to prefer autocratic styles than Pathmaker females.[21] When Bob Price was asked about his relationships with subordinates he said: "I don't care, if everyone knows that they should do what they're required to do. It's probably safe to say that since I've been here we have more than 100 percent turnover in the officer rank at this institution mainly because people didn't work out. And I'm not the sort that yields: I just say, 'Listen, pack and move on, we can't use you.'"

Bonnie Carter's and Bob Price's styles are certainly a contrast with Wendell Curtis's, who said:

> If work can't be fun, then I'm willing to help that guy find something that he wants to do. I've seen too many people who can't stand coming to work on Monday morning and just can't wait till they go home on

Friday night. If that's how their job feels, then we've got to find something else for him to do. There are lots of things more important [than work]. I think business is a game. There are too many businessmen who think that it's all-consuming and the beginning and the end. People take life too seriously. The one thing I learned from my father-in-law at a very early stage . . . is that we are all the same. My religious background also brings that out too. I am not overawed or hold in awe any businessman, regardless of title . . . I keep getting shocks from people who think my position is one of such power and presence that they shake. I know if I speak in a loud voice that they shake and that bothers me because I don't think in those terms. I'm not different than they are.

Wanda Perkins, as a white female Pathmaker, is like Wendell Curtis in her descriptions of her relations with subordinates.

Working Hard and Setting Limits

If Wendy Cassetta didn't accept hard work by itself as an explanation for success, one of the things that struck us as we were doing the interviews was how hard-working many of our subjects said they were. While we have avoided the word workaholic in writing about our study, it was clear to us that a tolerance for hard work was important, but that subjects did vary. We coded our interviews for the presence or absence of this tolerance. The only people judged by our coders not to exhibit this trait were Control males. Admittedly, they were few, but their presence is suggestive that a tolerance of hard work is not always required to get ahead for some categories of subjects.

Further, male Controls seemed to set limits even if they had a tolerance for hard work. Wendell Curtis set the boundaries he sees for work:

I have a set of priorities and the first is Jesus Christ and salvation. The second is my wife and my family, and the third is my job, the fourth is my ministry, whatever that is. I don't know what that is yet. That is my set of priorities. I get up about five-thirty in the morning. I'm a commuter [from a town fifty miles from his office]. I love commuting because that gives me two and a half hours a day that's mine, that's not anybody else's . . . I'm five minutes from the train on each end. And all the time I'm on the train is mine. And I leave the house at six-thirty in the morning and I start working, and I work until I get home, somewhere between seven-thirty and eight. And I close my briefcase, I get off the train, and at that time from then until next morning, is my family's or my church's or whatever I'm doing. And weekends, unless I'm in the middle of a marathon or whatever which I've got involved in and all, on weekends I don't even crack my briefcase from Friday night to Monday morning. So I haven't ever given up my family for my job, even though you might say I do for twelve hours.

Wendy Cassetta may be reforming in Wendell's direction. While in Washington she had worked sixteen or more hours a day for seven days a week. Now she says she will no longer do that, and she makes a point about the development of careers that appears quite different from Pathmaker patterns:

There's always other jobs that don't have anything to do with working weekends. Now I could not have, I don't think that being more protective of my life earlier on would have been helpful particularly. I think I really did have to put those years in of working very hard. It's just that most of the people that I know can't stop. And since I can, I intend to . . . People offer me five thousand dollars to go out and make major speeches and I will turn them down out of hand. I just want more control of my life, and the other thing I want to be able to [do is] read some things . . . And I don't have the kind of anxiousness that some of my friends do, my prominent friends do, where they just accept everything . . . I mean it's just at some point that you just decide that you just don't want to be that tired; and it, in terms of your career, it doesn't make that much difference—a little bit more of visibility, it doesn't matter. I'm well enough known, and visibility causes you security problems and personal problems and I just don't want to worry or put up with that.

Controls, it would seem, find it easier to stop or set limits on their careers than Pathmakers.

Failures and Their Meaning

Another intriguing variable concerned career failure. Had this group of successful people encountered failure in their careers? Not surprisingly a number admitted that they indeed had, and there were no differences on this variable between Pathmakers and Controls or blacks and whites with the exception of black male Controls who all admitted failures. We then asked our subjects about their responses to the failure. We classified the responses as to whether they reported positive or negative outcomes to the failure episode. Pathmakers were more likely to make positive outcomes of failures than Controls (see Table 6.4). This suggests that the Pathmakers' earlier adjustments and frustrations with the social obstacles associated with their status might have been good training—as adults they were better prepared for failure and could make something positive out of it. Wanda Perkins was quite explicit about this:

> I wouldn't wish the traumas I've had on anybody, but I think some of that does equal something else. Like I think there are many positive things that I've come out with. Like, I think I'm much more sensitive to people, to the human dilemma, to people with traumas in their lives. Much more sensitive to kids being beaten. So I think there are a lot of strong affective kinds of things that I've come out with. I know it's different but I may know something.

In contrast, Bonnie Carter, when asked if there had been failures in her work, replied, "No, not really. Which is not to suggest that everything has always gone through for me—up, up, up. But there are no major catastrophes yet." One is almost tempted to pity the fast-track Control achievers who encounter their first frustration or failure well into their career.

Wendy Cassetta saw her only failure in her current situation:

> I'm now at the top of the heap, but that in a sense is very frustrating. It's one of the reasons I won't work seventy hours a week anymore because I would drive these people all crazy, it would be too much for

Table 6.4 Positive outcomes for failures in career for Pathmakers and Controls

	Yes	No
Pathmakers (27)	16	11
Controls (24)	6	18
	(22)	(29)

$X^2 (1, N = 51) = 6.07, p < .025$

them to absorb. In fact, if there's any failure, any disappointments, I suppose it's that I miss, I miss the substance and I miss coming up against first-rate minds. But you get that in only a handful of places.

Futures and Future Careers

Did our subjects ever report worrying about their careers? "Big worries," when they occurred, unexpectedly had much less to do with work for Pathmakers than did the worries of Controls (see Table 6.5a), suggesting that Pathmakers were more troubled by issues other than work (100 percent of the white female Controls who cited worries worried about work). What do the Pathmakers worry about? Pathmakers said they worried about the future, where Controls didn't as often (see Table 6.5b). Wanda Perkins worries, for example, about her personal future, and her absence of a secure relationship with a man (see Chapter 7).

Male Pathmakers showed an even stronger finding versus male Controls[22] concerning worries about the future. Since there was no difference in their job or career satisfaction, the difference in worrying about the future may be attributable to anticipation of yet more career change

Table 6.5a Pathmakers and Controls reporting big worries about work

	Worry about work	
	Yes	No
Pathmakers (30)	4	26
Controls (15)	8	7
	(12)	(33)

X^2 (1, N = 45) = 8.18, $p < .001$

Table 6.5b Pathmakers and Controls reporting big worries about the future

	Worry about future	
	Yes	No
Pathmakers (30)	11	19
Controls (15)	1	14
	(12)	(33)

X^2 (1, N = 45) = 4.60, $p < .05$

in their lives—a sort of disbelieving "what's next"—that Controls don't seem to have as often, perhaps due to their calmer ascent.

Related to issues of the future, where do our subjects see themselves heading? Pathmakers were more likely than Controls to report plans for the future (and this could be thought of as an intellectualized response to their worries about the future). Compared with those who had no plans for the future, Pathmakers' future career plans more often involved new careers or education.[23] Wes Parker, who had already retired once to take his current position, when asked about retirement from his full-time *pro bono* job for $1.00 a year, said:

> I am really looking forward to finding something as challenging as this has been. I think I prefer it in the private sector. I have some hopes and there again I think that things move in mysterious ways. I had dreams and had scheduled this, that me and my older son would do something together. But I'm not sure that's right, and I'm not sure that guardian angel up there is not saying, "Look, don't do it" . . .
>
> I have about a hundred units that I'm converting to condominiums. I have bought some real estate here and there that I'm fooling around with. And then I ventured out into something that has caught my new love. I'm drilling oil wells, and I'm going to devote a lot of time to that—that's the most fun I've ever had in my life. After I raise $3 million for my church, I'm going to devote the majority of my time to drilling oil wells . . .

Wanda Perkins said:

> I would like to have the research program contribute something to the knowledge base, and wherever that takes me. That's a major investment for me. I'd love to see myself as some little grey-haired lady with a cane that people listen to for wise words of wisdom . . . a Margaret Mead type. In all humility I don't know if I've got anything to say. I have this vision of myself as something more than a distinguished professor.

In contrast, no Control males reported plans for new careers. Wendell Curtis said, when asked whether he had thought of retirement:

> I will not stay here until I'm sixty-five. I can retire at age fifty-five with a 25 percent discount off my pension. [Q. How would you spend your retirement?] I don't know. That's what I'll find out. Time goes

very fast, and it goes faster and faster . . . I expect that at some point I will retire from here whenever the next step for me comes along. [Q. How will you know when it comes?] Because it will be right, the decision will be placed before me. [Q. You'll have an option?] Sure, well I always have options to say no, too. One thing I know, I don't get bells ringing and all this. Mine comes with a sense of peace, after prayerful consideration.

Wendy Cassetta said about retirement and next steps:

No, I don't think about retirement; I probably never will. I'd leave here for a cabinet post [but then explains why she won't get one, and in an earlier comment indicates that she wouldn't want to work that hard]. Also you don't plan on being a cabinet officer. So that, you know, what are the other jobs for me? Another college presidency? The major foundations are already taken up, and those are boring jobs compared to this. There aren't a lot of things I can do after this. With luck something offbeat will come along.

About retirement Bonnie Carter said:

I'd love to—I just can't figure out a way to do it. I have no rich uncles who are about to die, I have no rich men who've offered to take me out. No, I really haven't given any thought to retirement. [Q. What do you see ahead of you?] I'm not sure, to tell you the truth. Things have just happened up to now, that's why I feel very fortunate.

Summary

In reviewing the findings presented in this chapter a number of patterns emerge. These can be divided into three areas: obtaining and leaving jobs, influences at work including the costs and benefits of work, and attitudes toward the future.

Getting and Leaving Jobs

One important variable in the study of career development is job movement, or how people obtain and leave their jobs. It is apparent that before college, Pathmakers sustained more job interruptions than Controls; they tended to leave jobs more often for family reasons. The thinness of early resources experienced by Pathmakers relative to Controls was most salient in early job movement: while Pathmakers (especially black Pathmakers) were sharing the money they made with their families and sustaining job interruptions because of them, Controls (especially males) were obtaining early jobs through family members.

After college, however, the pattern shifts. We have argued that education served as the great equalizer with this population. After college, Pathmakers were more likely to be offered jobs they hadn't applied for or to create their own jobs. Growing up amid conditions of thin resources perhaps explains Pathmakers' motivation to leave jobs for money reasons. On the other hand, the fact that Controls more often left jobs due to boredom may reflect their greater redundancy of resources. Control subjects were not motivated by money to the same degree as Pathmakers.

Influences at Work

Another important variable in studying careers involves influential forces at work. This variable includes everything from obstacles encountered, to relationships with co-workers, to support systems utilized. While we obtained a trend for Pathmakers to encounter more obstacles at work than Control subjects, they also more often turned failures connected with work into positive outcomes than did Controls. This tendency has obviously served Pathmakers well in overcoming their relatively more common obstacles and frustrations.

With respect to the support systems reported by these groups, findings followed previously reported patterns: subjects reported mentors who were the same gender and race as themselves. It is unclear whether this finding reflects identification on the part of the subjects, biases in the mentoring behavior of the mentors, or some combination of both factors. It is interesting to note that, compared to female Controls, it was the female Pathmakers who more often cited people at work as being a source of motivation and support. While this reflects the previously described pattern of these women using people at work as a substitute for lost early supports due to mobility, it also reflects constructive adaptation to loss. This finding has been discussed in greater detail in other reports (Boardman, Harrington, and Horowitz, 1987).

An interesting pattern emerges in looking at female relationships with co-workers—specifically subordinates. Female Controls had a more autocratic style with their subordinates than male Controls, while female Pathmakers sought friends at work.

Attitude toward Future Career

We obtained very consistent patterns with respect to future career orientation. Pathmakers more often worried about the future and had plans for their future careers than Controls, and these plans tended to involve a new career or continuing their education. They worried less often about their current careers.[24] Given the Pathmakers' greater reported ability to see positive experiences in failure, it is not surprising that they held different future career orientations from Controls.

One aspect of these data in need of further investigation involves patterns of mentoring. While we obtained significant patterns with respect to the race and gender of mentors, it seems logical to assume that differences in the timing of mentors might exist: we obtained differences in getting and leaving jobs before and after college between Pathmakers and Controls. Perhaps differences in mentors were important during this critical transitional period. There is also the question of how mentoring is learned. Are certain personalities more likely to mentor, or do those who get mentored mentor others?[25]

Pathmakers have been judged to report working harder than Controls, to be better able to survive adversity, and to be more likely to see new career challenges. These factors, perhaps reflecting a belief in personal control over their lives, aided their career success in spite of the thinness of early resources and relatively abundant obstacles.

We turn now to our findings concerning the current lives and families of our subjects.

7

Spouses, Children, Friends, and Health

We turn now to the personal lives of our subjects, including the families and friendships that our subjects created, as well as how they described their physical and mental well-being. Given background differences between Pathmakers and others, it seems likely that Pathmakers will construct marriages differently and with different types of people. Similarly, might not Pathmakers' children grow up in very different worlds than their parents in contrast to children of Controls? What are the consequences for their relationships with their parents? What are the consequences of the success of our subjects on friendships and personal networks? Finally, are there personal differences in lifestyles or health that separate Pathmakers from other subjects? We first examine variables concerning spouse(s), children (if any), and friends.

Spouses

Seventy of the one hundred subjects in our sample were married at the time of the interview, while eleven had never been married, and nineteen who were previously married were divorced or widowed when we interviewed them. Of all those married at least once, there was a trend for Pathmakers more than Controls to report being unmarried at the time of the interview. Fifteen of those subjects—previously married but not married at the time of the interview—were Pathmakers. If we as-

124

sume that first marriages were formed before any career developed, this could be a relational cost of success. First spouses represented original networks that they had moved away from, or outgrown (as discussed in Chapter 4, Pathmakers had more tenuous links to their homes of origin). It is in line with these expectations that Betty Powers reported that her first husband,[1] whom she married in college, was threatened by her continuing education. He became an alcoholic. She said:

> Right after [I received my doctorate] . . . a lot of things fell apart. He had begun drinking and became a very serious drinker, and still is now. Sometimes I would call and the children were home alone and I'd have to [leave graduate school—a four-hour drive], go and stay with them until I got things straight. After I finished [the doctorate] it was just not to be put back together. It couldn't, so I left then, and I [took a job] in a black school because of my agreement [that] I had to [her doctoral fellowship was designed to provide faculty for black colleges], and [I took] a job [out of state] to get away from the circumstances.

In contrast, Wendell Curtis married (while in the military) and remains married to the same woman. Further, his father-in-law became a role model, and a substitute father figure as well. Wendell's career closely paralleled his. It could be argued that the similarity of her background and his career prepared Wendell and his wife for what was coming and assured her of few surprises as his career developed. However, there were problems in other domains for which they were not prepared. Shortly after birth his second child had a serious illness:

> And at this time my father-in-law died, and then that also created problems. But I was working in the office and handling the problems at home. [Q. What problems?] Well, my wife, because of the baby and her father dying at the same time, she had all kinds of mental problems. I was working twelve hours a day at the office, and eight hours at home. Probably four hours of sleep. But in one sense one made the other work, because they were so different. I was able to get out of the problem and totally separate it from the problem there, and still keep going.

His wife recovered, and they were still married twenty-five years later. No differences in marital status were found between blacks and whites, but there was a strong gender difference: 73 percent of those not married when interviewed were women (see Table 7.1). When we coded our subjects for stability of marital status on a scale from never married to still married to the first spouse,[2] women also reported themselves less stably married than men.[3] Of the unmarried respondents who never married, nine (including Wanda Perkins and Wendy Cassetta) were women, while only two were men.[4] Wanda Perkins talks of being single as a consequence of success and her sex: "What are the costs of being successful? I think it is a problem for any single female who's over forty years old. I really do. In terms of my own personal social life it's been very costful. I still am not clear about how to deal with all of this." These findings taken together suggest that women married less often than men, and if they did marry and divorce, replaced first spouses less often than did men.[5] Comments by Bonnie Carter about her only marriage exemplify the latter trend:

I got married a year after I finished college, and I was married for, actually the marriage lasted three years. The best way I could describe it is that it was a different time—we probably just should have lived together for a while. But at the time I got married that was not ever considered to be an option. So it was very good in some ways but not that life-long partnership bit. What happened generally is that we went in different directions. I decided to leave before we started to hate each other.

In our study, stability in marriage seems to be a male characteristic, which is further supported by another finding: males reported being married more years to one person than did females, Pathmakers or not.[6] Wendell Curtis exemplifies these patterns. The gender differences on length of marriage exist even though there were no gender differences

Table 7.1 Subjects' marital status by gender

	Married	Not married[a]
Males (50)	42	8
Females (50)	28	22
	(70)	(30)

X^2 (1, N = 100) = 9.33, $p < .005$
a. Includes those never married.

for the closely related variable, age at first marriage. This suggests that males may be marrying successfully from their original home or school networks, while women's marriages from that time were more likely to fail;[7] women formed their most stable marriages after new networks formed. Many, like Betty Powers, report that husbands from this later period have helped their careers, a positive benefit for these marriages that women who did not remarry, or who never married, do not enjoy. Certainly if spouses are not supportive of their careers women in our sample of successful people may have felt they had to end such marriages—as many reported. That this was not reported to be a problem for men is perhaps linked to women's support being more expected for male career success. When Wendell Curtis was asked if his wife had been helpful in his career, he answered:

> The company doesn't require that in the sense of social support. She's a strong person in her own right, so she's helped me in the sense that she has not been negative in any way. [Q. What about when you were flying in the military?] She got an ulcer and she didn't like where I was going and what I was doing. [Q. Do you share a lot of work with her now?] Yes, and she has good insights into the people side frequently, not the business side so much.

White males also reported a more traditional division of labor in the home than other subjects.

Turning from marriage stability and length to who was chosen for a spouse, we asked the subjects to describe their spouses, and then summarized these descriptions as being either about the accomplishments of the spouse (e.g., successful businessperson) or about the personal characteristics of the spouse (e.g., good man, attractive, intelligent). Pathmakers were more likely to talk only about the personal characteristics of the spouse than Controls, who talked more about their accomplishments (see Table 7.2). Bob Price said,

> God made her and broke the mold, I guess. She's the most tolerant person I could imagine, having put up with me for eighteen years. She's very considerate and allowed me to pursue my professional career without too much interference; always very supportive of me in whatever I wanted to do professionally speaking, even when she would rather not have me do certain things. But she's done that . . . She's a

Table 7.2   Pathmakers' and Controls' descriptions of spouse

	Personal only	Mention of achievements
Pathmakers (52)	36	16
Controls (30)	14	16
	(50)	(32)

X^2 (1, N = 82) = 4.07, p < .05

smart person; too nice, people take advantage of her. It takes her a while to learn, I guess. We got married when we were kids.

Wendell Curtis, in contrast, said, "She owns a real estate agency, which she started last year. She's worked part time ever since the children went to school just because there was no way she was going to stay at home and do some sort of things . . . She's a very strong person, very independent. I support her independence." If Pathmakers discuss the spouse's personal (internal) characteristics, and not their external accomplishments, they may view their spouses as more clearly coherent, distinct persons of whom accomplishments are results, rather than focusing on the accomplishments to define the person.[8]

Not surprisingly given the patterns of our society, the spouses of our male subjects were less likely to have their own careers than the spouses of the women in our sample. All married women in the study reported spouses with careers, but only 70 percent of the black males did, and only 43 percent of the white males reported wives with careers, the difference between black and white males being a trend. Indeed 67 percent of all subjects whose spouses didn't work at the time of the interview were white males. Bob Price said, "Professionally she's always been a school teacher, and I've always encouraged her to get the big one [her Ph.D.] that might help her kind of. As a matter of fact she completed her work [on the doctorate] three years ago. She was teaching all the time and going to school at night, or whatever." Bernie Clark said:

She hasn't worked since little Bernie was born [in contrast, there was an older daughter and his wife continued working for six years]. She's been out of the system then for twelve years. I think she'd be delighted to get back in the system on a part-time basis. She talked about going back, but it's been twelve years and I think the realization has set in after talking to some of her friends that teaching is not what it was twelve years ago, especially public schools . . . going through the transition between the blacks, the Hispanics, and the Jews, and the whites. It's tough.

On the other hand, Wes Parker is an extreme example of the white male pattern:

[She's] never worked since we're married. I'm a very strong believer that a woman's place is home, and to look after the children. Very, very strong on that . . . Nancy is a perfect wife. She knows what I want her to do, and she enjoys doing what I know she wants to. I believe very strongly that it is her job to run that house. And I believe very strongly that it is her job to do the best she can and make up for my absences in raising the children . . . She has been in a mental institution . . . And probably my fault. Too hard on her. That was twenty years ago; I'm telling you something here that probably five people know. She stayed in for eight months. Came out and never been back. Perfectly normal. It was after the second birth, which is so common. She probably did not need to be hospitalized to the extent that she was. The doctor and I probably overreacted . . . You could count on your hands every time we had cross words with each other. Now we disagree and we talk things [out], but she allows me to go home at night, read the paper, talk on the telephone, have my drink, watch television, and talk to her all at the same time. And she's learned to accept that's what it takes to make me go. And the minute I quit those, I'm going to sleep. So she has accepted the fact that she's going to have to talk to me and not have my attention.

White males, married the most number of years to their spouses than any other category, were also more likely to report more traditional division of labor in their homes[9] than all women and blacks.[10] As for the black males, we note that even though Bob Price's wife had her own career, she was still carrying out the traditional roles of child raising and supportive helpmate:

She's always been very supportive . . . [when I took this job] it was going to require making myself ready. It would mean that I would have to go to school and work hard and use up our social time on weekends and at night, laboring with the books and so forth. And she quickly embraced that. She said "fine, if you want to do that, fine."

And so that is the kind of help I'm talking about. And taking care of my daughter, she actually raised my daughter, and did a pretty good job. So that's what I mean by supportive. She's done all those kinds of things that enabled me to go all out in trying to learn what this job is all about. I come to work every Saturday. A director [of the company] called me one day and asked me how she put up with all that and I said I don't know. But that's what I mean by being supportive. In other words, she has subordinated her own career to my career.[11] I couldn't ask for a more supportive person.

The disparities between male and female career trajectories described by Treiman (1985) may also account for white males' spouses' career patterns typified by the wife of Wes Parker. The literature describes the careers, when they have them, of the spouses of males as having different patterns than their husbands—more often a "dead end" trajectory (Kanter, 1977). That black males were more likely to have wives with careers is not anticipated in that literature and may reflect a white bias to data in previous studies, which therefore may err in showing general gender differences. But the careers of women in our study do not reflect these patterns. Wanda Perkins, who did not marry, was able to break out of stereotypically female teaching jobs by pursuing her Ph.D. and entering an academic career at a time when this was a decidedly male career track. Of course, she also entered academia ten years older than her male counterparts.[12]

We also asked questions about the kind of relationships subjects had with their spouses. We found no differences between Pathmakers and Controls on the main variables we examined, handling conflicts with spouse and career support by spouse, but there was a sex difference on how conflicts with one's spouse were expressed and resolved. When asked how they dealt with conflict with their spouses, female subjects more often said they shouted and yelled at them, men much less so; men were more likely to say they were likely to seek a compromise, women less so.[13] Wendell Curtis is a good example:

[Q. How do the two of you resolve conflicts?] I compromise. [She doesn't?] Infrequently. I learned very early in life that's important. She knows on certain things that I won't compromise and then there's no question. It's on the little stuff where a lot of couples I think break down and get into all sorts of hassles. I'd give in. I weigh whether it's going to cost anything. I don't hold resentments.

Betty Powers was succinct in describing how she handled disagreements with her first husband: "Yelling, screaming, eventually fighting, physical." She said her current husband is even-tempered, and while they have fights, "he won't let them get the best of him, so I end up having to adjust because he'll say, 'Well, now what you have to do is look at it a different way' . . . and I'm not always of the belief that attitude is 90 percent of a situation, but he is." It is interesting that what has changed over the years is not so much her style, but the difference in the husband's reaction—the first apparently escalating, the second not.[14] Differences like those just given between Wendell Curtis and Betty Powers, of course, may also be an indication that the males in our study were reporting what they *felt* should happen while the women subjects were more accurately presenting what they did!

Black male Controls said they used compromise more than the other categories in the sample,[15] more even than the rest of the Controls.[16] Paradoxically the black male Controls, like all black males, score high in Need for Power, suggesting again that this may be a normative response. On the other hand, remember that black males were more likely to have spouses with their own careers, and the egalitarian nature of their relationship may encourage compromise.

The black females in our study were more likely than the white female subjects to report that their spouses were not supportive of their careers.[17] This may also illuminate why we concurrently found that black female Pathmakers, whose careers faced more obstacles, tended to be least often married: remember Betty Powers's first husband!

We also found that blacks, both male and female, reported spouses to be less supportive of their careers than whites.[18] This may be attributable to the stronger difference just reported for black females, but may also reflect that black males are more likely to have spouses with their own careers, which might mean their spouses are perceived as having less time to be supportive.[19]

Children

While Pathmakers, especially women, report relational problems with spouses, they may also be more distanced from their children. For example, we found a trend for Pathmakers to be more likely than the Controls to report having used only punishment with their children (as distinct from other methods of handling conflicts such as talking or avoidance). Also, Pathmakers had constructed lifestyles for their children that were totally different from their own early experiences, which could psychologically distance the Pathmaker parent from the child in a way not true for Controls, who grew up in backgrounds similar to their child's. "Dad, can I borrow the jet [and the pilot] for the weekend?" is a request reported and granted by Wes Parker for a son. He told the story with pride, but also a little wonder over the difference between his son's life and his own at that age. Future research could be done on the children of our subjects: compared to Controls, these children are growing up in different worlds from their parents, and they seem to react in different ways. If resilience and hard work got the Pathmaker parents where they are, what will become of the more comfortable generation? For example, since he was a teenager Wes Parker has been working from six in the morning until eight at night: "I've never known anything else. I don't see how anyone lives without doing all he can do productively every day . . . I can never remember a day that I didn't go to sleep at night dreaming about what I was going to do the next day, and wake up the next morning anxious to do it. I can never remember the day."

Yet talking of his son, who recently graduated from a prestigious graduate school and turned down a job for $6,000 more from a national company to take a job at a business of which his father is a principal stockholder, Wes Parker says with no apparent irony: "Well, I was rather proud of him. He wants to go down there and prove himself. I think in one sense, being the oldest, he sees the struggles I went through, and he wants to make a name for himself, and prove that he can do it." That this contradictory logic is also a hope more than a reality is reflected in a later discussion of the same child:

> [My sons are] not even close to knowing what's going on. I think it gave me a time to reflect. I still don't know everything, and certainly I'm not worldly. But I do know how to make money. It gave me a time to say I am really giving my boys more than I realize I'm doing. It makes you think you have the capacity to start your children off so much farther. And it hit home when we were out Sunday afternoon trying to find my son a house. I'm determined he moves out of [our] house. Nancy and I have been without any children in the house for four years and then the older one moved back in. We had some readjustment to do. We went out to find him a house. And we found one that he liked, and it was $130,000 [in 1982], and had a $55,000

loan on it. And I said, OK, I'll make the down payment, which is $75,000, and you just take it from the notes. And he says, "Dad, I can't even make the payments on the notes with the salary I'm making." I said, "How does anybody in the world get started in the world?" He said, "You make the payments, and I'll pay the utilities." Those things kind of drove home to me. The last few weeks I've had some time to reflect that I hadn't took before.

It is also interesting to note that this is the first job ever held by the son.[20] Wes Parker continues:

My oldest boy looks like Nancy [Wes's wife], and acts like me. He's never lived up to his potential. But, he's never failed anything in school, but could con anybody out of anything. Would be a perfect salesman. He can maneuver, he is more of a social climber than I am. He enjoys that more than I do . . . He enjoys fine clothes, he enjoys snow skiing, enjoys water skiing, and enjoys hobnobbing with the best. He's been going with the same girl for about three years. She is from a very wealthy family. A very social-minded family. But she is a lovely, lovely girl. And he's pruned her and [knows] exactly what he wants in that he wants her to be just like Nancy . . . My other son is not as smart.

Wendell Curtis seems much more comfortable about his children when asked what they are like:

Super. My daughter is now twenty-five. She got married last September to a super guy who [is a physician]. She graduated . . . and then went on to get her master's degree in psychology. [My son] is a senior [at a school to which Wendell had been admitted but did not attend]. Doesn't know what he wants to do [he's changed his major six times]. He's going to take the law school exam and the business exam and he's interviewing with several companies on Madison Avenue. I don't think they are going to give him enough of a challenge. He probably will go back to school. If he chooses business, I hope he chooses something that has nothing remotely resembling what I do. Because he shouldn't be trying to compete with me. And hopefully I brought him up so he knows better . . . That's a trip that shouldn't be hung on any kid. I would be very happy if he chose law or something. His set of skills are entirely different from mine. I've run off at the mouth here [in our interview] but I'm much more introspective [in normal life]. My wife is an extrovert. He's taken after his mother. He can charm anybody out of the trees. He's creative and writes well, so his set of skills are kind of the opposite of mine. My daughter is smart also.

We cannot help but note differences in tone, amount of description, and the amount of career material between the son and daughter. White males in our study had the most traditional division of labor in their marriages of all our subjects.

Another example of the difference in orientations between parent and child can be seen in schooling. A number of children of Pathmaker black academics, who teach in or lead some of the nation's most prestigious predominantly white schools, were reported by our subjects to have asked to attend traditionally black schools. Did they try to regain an identity they seemed to feel their parents had distanced themselves from? One interpretation could be that they sense that class differences are replacing racial differences in terms of their salience both in their lives and in the society. Anthropological literature has for years argued (see, for example, Cohen, 1974) that as class differences develop *within* various ethnic and racial categories, that class differences will overtake ethnic and racial divisions as the most important stratification variables of that society. The desire of some Pathmaker black subjects' children to attend all-black schools could be seen as an attempt to revitalize the black-white difference in the face of such a sociological pattern—perhaps to show that their social class mobility (growing up wealthier than their parents) has not made race unimportant.

Non-academic black males reported a related sense that their children lacked roots or a sense of the struggle that they experienced. Bob Price said:

> I'm trying to build up the life of my daughter, I guess, and generations unborn. So I'm trying to put together my roots, really. My Daddy having been a bastard child, it's very difficult on this side. On my mother's side it's not quite so bad. I'm back to 1754 by going to graveyards and talking to people. So I did this as part of an overall project that I want to leave with my daughter. Of course, I'm very hopeful of writing an autobiography and I just want to leave with my daughter the kinds of experiences I had.

And when Bernie Clark found his great-grandfather's building, he "took photographs of it and everything and sent it to my kids."

Independent from parent-child relationships, study-wide we found that women reported having fewer children than the men.[21] Bonnie Carter had no children, and reported that her sister, also married but separated, had no children either.[22] This reflects Rossi's (1985) expectations that women successful in their careers would have less time to devote to raising young children.[23] Contrast them to the white males in our study, more than half of whom were married to women without careers outside the home, allowing for "traditional" divisions of labor. Childcare therefore came at no or little expense to the white males' careers. In reviewing these findings it is also important to keep in mind that we are studying these people in mid-career; women with as many children as the male subjects perhaps either are less likely to fit into our success category, or will do so later.

Friends

We also examined what our subjects said of their friends. From our data on current family we would expect Pathmakers, especially women, to have also paid some price for their success by leaving behind family and friends, and as we previously discussed, female Pathmakers more often relied upon work for social supports and friendships than did Controls. Both patterns were true for Wanda Perkins. "In a scheme of things personal friendships with folks are really very important to me. [Q. Who are your best friends?] J and C are really significant friends, and have been for a long time; they go way back ten years." She met them in her doctoral program. They all received doctorates and now teach in similar fields in the same region of the country. "They've been through ups and downs, we share a nice history."

Wendell Curtis, in contrast, has never had a circle of friends from work and is typical of the Controls' maintenance of contacts with early friends. His close friends were described this way:

> You have very few friends in life. I was counting up the other day. I'm very fortunate. I have seven. That's a lot. These are people I would do anything for. They wouldn't have to do anything but to ask. And I'd either come or do whatever it was without even asking why. And two of them are from [high school], one from [college], one from . . . [when he was in the military], and three from our days in Europe. We also have friends here [in our community] that we've gotten to know over twenty years. They're the non–country club set. They're not the tense corporate types who are always seeking the social country club.

Wendy Cassetta also reported only six close friends, none of whom are from work. Bonnie Carter said:

> My best friends have been two people who go way back—two people from the [town she went to junior and senior high school in], a core of people I met in college, and some professional colleagues I have met over the years. They were good sounding boards, and other people that I had just encountered along the way, you know, who developed into really good friends. So a small core of really close old friends, and a broader circle of acquaintances.

As previously discussed in Chapter 6, we did find a difference between Pathmakers and Controls in their use of work to form instrumental friendships. Work was used more by Pathmakers than Controls to construct friendships: a pattern, however, that was more true of the women than the men. Whatever the source of the friends, whether the long-term early-origin friendships of the Controls, or the more recent, work-related friendships of the Pathmakers, we did not find any differences between Pathmakers and Controls in who reported close friends to be important. Bonnie Carter spoke for many when she said that her friends were very special to her—"my most valuable asset."

Costs of Success

The reader has by now grown accustomed to the concept that the success of our subjects has not been without its costs. We found that women were more likely than men to report the costs of their success. Wendy Cassetta reported, "I've lost some friends as I've become more and more prominent; they just couldn't handle it, didn't know what to do about it, just couldn't handle it." Wanda Perkins said:

> Any fairly successful, assertive, secure woman has got some more problems in today's society. Finding an interesting man who's at least equally successful, equally secure, who's not threatened by what I do and who I am . . . , I don't find many of those people. And being forty-one, there aren't many men available who fit the pattern, and here a large portion of our population is gay, so that wipes out a good number. Lately I've realized there are a lot of gay men in my life who view me as another one of their girlfriends, and I've got a great relationship with these gay men, but that only goes so far. And all the

rest are married and that has its limitations. I find it's pretty dry, to be honest with you. But it depends on my mood how lonely I am . . . but I'd sure like a meaningful long-term intimate relationship someday in my life. I just don't see any possibilities. Maybe it's this city, but I've lived in other cities; maybe it's me rather than the city. Maybe it's probably me other than the city!

Wendy Cassetta, when asked about why she had always been single, said:

> Chance, chance not conscious. Chance. [Q. You didn't resist it?] I don't know. [Q. Do you think about having children?] Yes, I like children, but you know I just have a couple of friends who have had children without getting married. It's just too complicated for me to do that; it was a passing thought but not ever taken seriously. It doesn't make any sense for the kids, and it wouldn't make sense in my career.

Bonnie Carter said her chief dissatisfaction was relational: "The one dissatisfaction I'm thinking about is that my marriage didn't work out, but that's not really true. You know I'm sorry that it didn't. And perhaps a dissatisfaction in that male relationships have not been as continuous as ideally I would like for it to be. I haven't lived quite long enough to decide how I want to weigh that . . . The jury is still out on that."

Health and Emotions

We have already said in Chapter 6 that Pathmakers worked harder and talked about future career plans more than Controls. We turn now, in the remainder of this chapter and in the next, to a number of other variables that reveal more about the individual coping styles of our subjects relating to health and emotional expression. We asked our subjects if they got angry, and what made them angry. Seventy-eight percent reported feeling angry, and Pathmakers and Controls did not differ. Nor did they differ in what made them angry when they reported a specific reason (betrayal, illness, pressures of time, marriage, poverty of others, work). Like many subjects, Wanda Perkins sees a need to control her anger: "I suppress anger, I walk around anger, I avoid my own feelings. I avoid conflict as much as I can. I'm trying to find out how you behave differently. I'm better in a professional setting, better at asking questions, to get issues out on the table, to be less compulsive, more intellectual, more grown up." Yet she also admits that she does get angry, and worries about its effect on others, including her bosses:

> I have a very hard time showing anger, I have low skills. I curse a lot. That goes way back. I think I should probably, I don't say things too terrible in class, but I'll say "fuck" around the floor upstairs [her dean and department chair], and I should probably stop that. It probably goes back to gutter language, growing up the way I did, my mother calling me nasty names, and that sort of thing. [Q. What makes you angry?] A number of things make me angry now. I get angry at incompetence, injustice, sloth; I get so upset, I shock a lot of lower-class people in my neighborhood! [She lives in an urban neighborhood undergoing rapid gentrification.] I was in a grocery store the other day, and I was so angry and upset—when I see people who are poor. I was crying in a grocery store because I was just so furious that there's a woman who has no teeth [Wanda also has dental problems], who's probably thirty-five years old and has no clothes, and buying pork feed or whatever. It makes me terribly upset—I respond viscerally. I get angry when my colleagues don't carry their share of the load, when people get paid more than others for doing nothing. I get angry at a lot of things, I mean real angry. Little things or big things, I'm angry at a lot of that stuff.

Bob Price, when we asked him what he did if he became angry, said: "I seldom get really angry. I don't like myself when I get really angry. I manage by doing a number of things. If I can jog, I go running. Another thing I like to do is get together with a friend I can sit down and talk with. I believe in getting it out as opposed to internalizing . . . Internalization is a very disastrous thing to the mind and the body and I simply don't like to do that."[24]

There was a trend for white male Controls (who were less likely than anyone else to report career obstacles, but who came from more tense, unloving families of origin) to be the least likely to report anger as an emotion they must deal with in adulthood. Wendell Curtis responded to a question about what makes him angry in this way: "Twice a year I get angry whether I need it or not! I don't get angry very often. Occasionally my voice will rise. My secretary told me last week that I raised my voice twice last week with somebody. She said, '[You] don't do that with anybody; are you unwell?' When people take advantage of a situation, I guess I get [angry] . . ." It makes sense that white male Controls should feel less anger than black or women Controls: they had less to be angry about. Bonnie Carter talked about her anger:

> I try to get away from [what made her angry] and just calm down, calm down before doing whatever I'm going to do. When I get upset or angry it could be that whatever it is that I was trying to do, I couldn't, and instead of walking out or cussing somebody out, which I might do if I thought I could get away with it [laughs], I just sit down or walk away from it. And the things that make me angry would be, first thing I would think of, would be where someone is dishonest, or a betrayal in some way or other. That is what would upset me most.

Bernie Clark said two things made him angry:

> When things don't happen as I think they should happen. Or there is a goof for which I think I am responsible. There are not too many of those. [Q. How do you handle the anger?] I try to temper my feelings. I think my administrative assistant, I think I can say this with conviction, anybody you talk to around here, they'll probably say Bernie's always smiling and upbeat. I try to be upbeat. It's part of my personality!

While there were no Pathmaker/Control differences in what made people angry, we did find some evidence that Pathmakers were more self-conscious about their health than Controls.[25] For example, Bob Price said: "Yes, I'm a social drinker. I'm not a two-martini type, I stick with the wines and beer, and some of the other stuff sometimes. My wife got me on vitamin pills, so I've been doing that and I think it's working. I haven't had a cold all winter. I'm one of those persons who gets out every morning and jogs. But if I have to do it, I'll do it at night, that's when it's cold." Wanda Perkins said:

> I think I get healthier and more wholesome every year. There have been problems that are tied in to eating disorders which I guess are fairly mental, but it is manifested in a physical way and it causes me problems. My mouth is being remade for the fourth time now. My dentist cut off a $2,000 bridge yesterday. I think the rest of me is in pretty good shape. Mentally I'm about as normal as any other person. I had some free [gestalt] therapy in [doctoral school], and I uncovered some things I hadn't been aware of.

Wendell Curtis represented the other extreme.

> I don't even have a doctor. I wouldn't know where to run. I'm one of
> those: if I really feel rotten the best bet is to . . . pretend that it's not
> there and come to work and hide myself from somebody so that I
> don't give them something contagious. Fortunately I have the body
> to go with all that and it hasn't gotten me in trouble. I've really been
> sick only once: I had a slipped disk twenty years ago. And I haven't
> had any problems with that since . . . I do have high blood pressure
> [discovered in a company physical]. I take blood pressure pills and I
> don't take salt in my food. I weigh too much so I should lose weight.[26]

Bernie Clark smoked two packs of cigarettes a day, and of his exercise
habits said: "Not enough. We've got a health room here downstairs.
I've gone. I'm supposed to be in a regular program, but I don't get
involved as regularly as I should." Bonnie Carter said: "I have a very
uninteresting medical history. My health is excellent." When asked, she
admitted that she smoked. "My eating habits are good, but I drink too
much, but other than that they're good."

Differences between Pathmakers and Controls suggested health
problems could be related to the costs of Pathmakers' intra-generational mobility. Eight of the nine self-described "reformed alcoholics"
in the study were Pathmakers. Pathmakers were, like Bob Price, more
likely to report quitting smoking or drinking than Controls. He said,
"I smoked for ten years. I went to work for this other banking company,
I looked around and saw that I was the only person smoking. I said,
'Gee, there is something wrong,' so I quit. I've always been a person
with the willpower to do whatever I wanted. After ten years of two
packs of Camels a day, I just quit." Wanda Perkins said, "I don't
smoke—I used to smoke. I stopped smoking because it bothered my
mouth . . . Even now when you know what you should be doing it is
hard to change those years of bad eating habits, but I'm trying to work
on that in terms of setting a purposeful plan." Bob Price may have quit
for reasons combining other-directedness with an acute internal locus
of control,[27] or it could be simply that Pathmakers are more likely to
sense the changes in their lives, and more often accept that other
changes are possible. We will return to this theme in Chapter 9.

Men, like Bob Price, reported more regular exercise than women
(see Table 7.3); however, this could again be a result of males giving

Table 7.3   Reports of regular exercise by gender of subject

	Yes	No
Males (47)	30	17
Females (45)	17	28
	(47)	(45)

$X^2 (1, N = 92) = 6.24, p < .025$

more normative responses! The exercise finding for gender could also reflect societal patterns for subjects in this age group. Bonnie Carter, when asked whether she exercised, replied, "Sometimes. I was just in a health club like yesterday as a matter of fact. My problem is that I find it very hard to jump up in the morning and do calisthenics, so I try to get to the health club sometime in the week and swim. I can't say that I play tennis—I chase balls during the summer. I'm basically active, I think." And Wanda Perkins said, "I'm pretty good at jogging . . . for the most part. Like next month I'll be marvelous when I'm in Hawaii [for a professional conference]—I'll jog a lot, I'll exercise a lot, and I'll be really healthy in terms of nutrition and eating."

To sum up, with respect to Pathmaker/Control differences, Pathmakers were more likely to describe their spouses according to personal characteristics, and Controls more likely to describe their accomplishments. Pathmakers described different relationships with friends, and the use of friendships. Pathmakers, especially females, were more likely to have left behind family and friends, and the female Pathmakers were likely to replace these early friendships with friends from work. They were less likely to be married at the time of the interview, and their first marriages were less likely to last to the present. Pathmakers also had a tendency to use punishment in disciplining their children, to show a greater concern for their health, and to report self-reforms like quitting smoking and drinking than Controls.

With respect to personal and family issues, most differences occurred between males and females rather than between Pathmaker and Control subjects. Males were more likely to be married, and to have more stable marriages than females. Men also had more children than women, and tended to compromise more in resolving conflicts with their spouses. Males also reported getting more exercise than females. Women reported higher personal costs for their success than did men.

With respect to racial differences, whites reported more stable marriages than blacks even though black male Controls reported using compromise in handling conflicts with their spouses more than the rest of the sample. Finally, blacks were more likely to report spouses to be supportive of their careers than whites, except for black females who did not report their spouses to be helpful compared to white females.

In the following chapter we turn to a discussion of the psychological characteristics and coping styles of our subjects to further our understanding of how they constructed their paths to success.

8

The Psychology of Unusual Success

In this chapter we use the psychological variables reviewed in Chapter 2 to ascertain if Pathmakers and Controls differed in patterns of psychological structures, motivational orientation, and personal resources. Our question in this chapter is, "Are Pathmakers psychologically similar to or different from equally successful people who start out with more educated and wealthier parents?" Is there one common psychological orientation concerning success, or more? Is there one path that everyone more or less follows, or are different orientations equally likely to achieve success in different circumstances? The questions have relevance to current debates about cultural psychology,[1] or the degree to which different (sub-)cultures require the construction of different psychologies to be understood, and to critical analyses of dominant psychological models.

We will first describe the general characteristics of the sample as a whole, followed by similarities and differences we found for Pathmakers and Controls, and then turn to issues of race and gender.

Overview of the Sample

Despite the extremely different backgrounds of the subjects in our study, we discovered that their personalities were alike in several striking ways. For example, 94 percent of those interviewed were rated by us as being moderate or strong in need for achievement. This means that these individuals consistently reflected concerns for standards of excellence and good performance. Wendy Cassetta's description of her graduate school experience serves as one example: "The combination of the course work and the research assistantship was a superb training; by the time I finished my graduate work I had the equivalent in articles of a book . . . They offered me a job as an assistant professor, which was unheard of. They did not hire their own . . ."[2]

With regard to reward/cost orientation, 75 percent were judged to be reward-oriented (oriented toward potential future rewards) versus only 20 percent who were judged to be predominantly cost-oriented (oriented toward the potential costs of their choices rather than the rewards they might bring).[3] One black female Pathmaker natural scientist revealed reward orientation in her description of the initial step she took toward going to graduate school: "I had written to many people that I considered to be important in the scientific community. I did not know them. And the person was a doctor . . . He was important and he had written all these books. I wrote to him and told him all about myself and that I wanted to go to graduate school and I didn't know how. And the man wrote back, told me who to go see in [names city six hundred miles away]. I did." This is also an example of how a personality variable, in this case the reward orientation of putting oneself at risk in anticipation of future rewards, interacts with a non-replicable serendipitous event; not only did he (a white male) answer her letter, he became a sponsor of her career.

Concerning styles of coping 85 percent of our sample were coded using only the more mature (Vaillant's Level III and IV) defenses in dealing with stress and conflicts, and none used psychotic defenses. Furthermore, the defense mechanisms used most were those associated by his research (Vaillant, 1977) with constructive outcomes in life: altruism and sublimation.

Other variables showed a more even split of the sample without such overwhelming imbalances as those just discussed. For example, the sample split about evenly on need for affiliation, with 55 percent coded as being moderate or strong, and 45 percent weak or absent. As for need for power, 66 percent were coded moderate or strong and 34 percent were coded as being weak or absent. No strong preferences were found for the overall sample of successful people with respect to these variables. The need to be near people (need-affiliation) varied widely within our sample of equally successful people, and even though most demonstrated a tendency to be moderate or strong in the need to control others (need for Power), a substantial proportion did not.

A similar pattern was found for the locus of control dimension when we coded the interviews as a whole for personality orientations. The sample as a whole exhibited a preference for internal orientations: 69 percent suggested that what happened to them was a result of their own actions or factors internal to themselves.[4] Thirty-one percent were judged to see their fate as determined more by external forces beyond their control than internal factors under their control. Furthermore, 62 percent of the respondents were judged to be primarily inner-directed, that is, to use their own standards of performance to evaluate their own and others' actions, while only 30 percent were judged to be primarily other-directed, or to adopt others' standards for such evaluations.[5]

Finally 65 percent of our subjects told us that success had its costs. As we have previously described in Chapters 4, 6, and 7, they talked about incurring costs in the areas of family, intimate relationships, leisure time, and health.

Personality Differences

The main thrust of our analyses was to find what personality patterns, if any, differentiated Pathmakers from Controls, as well as to explore whatever differences existed between black and white men and women. In examining our psychological findings we will present variables in the order of their influence in distinguishing Pathmakers from Controls.[6] As we discuss each variable we will also discuss patterns of main and interaction effects for race and gender. We then go on to discuss the findings concerning styles of coping with stress or the mechanisms of defense utilized by our subjects.

Locus of Control

The key psychological difference between Pathmakers and Controls involved locus of control. Despite the sample as a whole being predominantly internal in their locus of control, Pathmakers had an even stronger belief in their ability to control what goes on in their lives than

Controls, and they were weaker in external locus of control as well.[7] When individual subjects were judged according to whether they saw the locus of control over their lives in internal factors or saw external factors predominating, Control subjects were more often predominantly external (42 percent) than were Pathmakers (23 percent) (see Table 8.1). Pathmakers, as predicted, had internal locus of control orientations which were either dominant or equal to external orientations, reflecting our expectation that a belief that fate was predominantly out of your control would make becoming a Pathmaker more difficult. Wanda Perkins exemplified the Pathmakers who emphasized internality: "Luck, effort, and ability probably played parts, but effort played, if I had to prioritize those, the greater part. And ability." But she also articulated what may be an unconscious psychological cost experienced by Pathmakers when she said: "But a lot of what debilitates me is my attribution [of my success] to ability. On the one hand I think I must know that I'm pretty bright, on the other . . . I get really frightened at times thinking I'm not bright enough. It's a force that I'm always dealing with. It's a big worry. Sort of thinking that I must be an imposter."

Wendell Curtis exemplified the external locus of control that was found more often, and more strongly, in the Controls. He said about his first big promotion: "After I had been there [Latin America] eighteen months, the head of Latin America, which was a job very senior, had a heart attack right when we had a big crisis. We had a big financial crisis and management didn't know what to do. And I was one of the few people who knew what was going on. They really didn't have any option. I had to take over and do what this other guy had been doing." When Wendell was asked about how he got his next promotion he talked about being transferred to a post just days before there was a major unanticipated upheaval in the currency of that country with which he dealt successfully. And of his getting his present position he

Table 8.1 Locus of control for Pathmakers and Controls

	Predominantly internal or equal	Predominantly external
Pathmakers (60)	46	14
Controls (40)	23	17
	(69)	(31)

$X^2 (1, N = 100) = 4.12, p < .05$

said: "It's a function of time and place, of being in the right time and place, in terms of what they were looking for in this job and who would be compatible and able to work with management, and what they saw as our needs at that point in time. And it is not strict intellect, or brain power, or whatever." Wendy Cassetta says of one key appointment: "It was good timing and being in the right place at the right time when it was breaking."

There were no differences between men and women or between races for internal locus of control, but there was a trend for whites to show more external locus of control than blacks. This is an interesting reversal of literature on the general population, which suggests the opposite. Our highly successful people do not reflect general population norms. One explanation of these findings involves the relative absence of obstacles, such as racism, for whites and Controls; for them the external environment may have been relatively more benign, hence an external locus of control would not be crippling, but might even reflect realistic appraisals of sources of support or encouragement absent in Pathmakers', especially blacks', experiences.

A number of studies have shown that this belief in personal control has a positive effect on performance, affect, and even health (Langer and Benevento, 1978; Rotter, 1966; Wortman and Brehm, 1975). Antonovsky (1983), investigating the "sense of coherence" (a belief that life events are predictable), found that those with such a belief view events in life as experiences to be coped with and challenges to be met. It seems likely to us that a strong sense of personal control played a major role in the achievement of success of Pathmakers who initially had more to overcome than Controls. This sense of personal control is clearly reflected in their orientation toward work.

Locus of Control: Attributions of Success

Another test of the subjects' locus of control was their attributions about their own success. One of the questions we asked was designed to encourage respondents to speculate about the etiology of their success: they were asked how they achieved it. While many different responses were given by the subjects, we distinguished answers which credited external forces from those in which the subject credited themselves. For example, answers such as "hard work," "being reliable/responsible," "having organizational savvy," or "being smart" were considered as crediting the self; answers such as "luck," "being in the right place at the right time," "God," "fate," "good schooling," or "being encouraged by others/mentors/parents" were considered as crediting others. We predicted that Pathmakers should make less external attributions of where they are and more internal ones. We made this prediction because Pathmakers had fewer and less redundant resources, and we thought it likely that their attributions would emphasize their own personal contributions. Similarly, Controls might have been more likely to receive external support, or to accede to a societal norm of crediting others for their own success: a myth that for Pathmakers might strain credibility.

For whatever reason, these predictions were supported by these data: Pathmakers were more likely than Controls to credit their success to variables internal to themselves, and less likely to credit variables external to themselves (see Table 8.2). Wanda Perkins said:

> There are schools that are better than other schools, more resources than other schools, more intelligent people on the faculty than other schools, but over the long haul I think you do your own thing wherever you are, and really it's up to you. If you're going to do significant writing, and if you're going to do some research, or if you're going to develop your mind in some important way, you're going to do that wherever you are.

As for Controls, Wendell Curtis said:

> For whatever reason, the Lord wants me here. I don't mean that as a flip answer. I am what I am because of the gifts He has given me. I have always used them to the best of my abilities . . . So I haven't set up a goal that's way out there and way up there that I'm striving for, and I sure as heck know that you don't have to crawl over people or

Table 8.2 Pathmakers and Controls giving predominantly internal accounts for their own success

	Yes	No
Pathmakers (60)	51	9
Controls (40)	6	34
	(57)	(43)

X^2 (1, $N = 100$) = 47.87, $p < .001$

things to get there. I think we have certain responsibilities and live to do certain things, and I'm glad to be in a position where I can influence the company toward a social good that maybe its leaders don't always agree with.

Bernie Clark attributed his success to a lucky big break, happening to be on site when an event that commanded world attention occurred. That event and his family reputation are credited by him for his call to Washington. Wendy Cassetta attributes her success to

. . . absolutely first-rate education all the way through,[8] and the world changed. I was talking to a friend who is counsel for [a governor]; first time a woman's had the job. And someone leaned over and said, "How do you account for the fact that you are counsel," and she said, "the women's movement." She was no huge feminist, but she was saying that we got breaks in our careers that we would not have gotten in another generation . . . Some of it is just prominent men that were willing to take a shot with women that were willing to be helpful. And I have a set of male friends from graduate school and [others] that I've met in other circles that have been willing to put me on boards. I sit on the most powerful boards in the country . . . And the women's movement really did have a major impact on me. I actually am one of the women that would, could have said that I would have made it without the women's movement, but I'm unwilling to say that. I'm not a Queen Bee, and I think that I represent a new generation of women. Many of the women that I know who are prominent in America are Queen Bees. They say they would have made it whether or not there was a women's movement, or they made it because of hard work, and they don't help other women, and I am absolutely the opposite. And I think I ought to use my position to help women, I think I ought to use my power to help women, and I consider that part of my agenda.

Bernie Clark said of his current job:

I'd like to be able to utilize my talents as an American and not as a black. That was my other consideration though. I didn't want to be put in a box, but your identity in going into these places [his previous jobs after the family business] had been as a black and there was nothing I could do to preclude this. I wanted to be recognized as a professional who happens to be black. You've got to understand that. Contacts had mentioned this as an enlightened company, and asked me for my vitae to send to them . . . [During negotiations the chairman] promised me that I could go as far as my talents would allow here, and he wanted me as a professional doing a job, not as a black or a white.

The Pathmaker/Control differences in their attributions were stronger than, but clearly also linked to, the more complicated psychological variable "locus of control" just reported, from which it may spring. Also, locus of control as measured here is based upon all the answers given in the interview, and assesses an individual's sense of what controls one's destiny. Clearly Pathmakers differ in what they credit for their success. It is also plausible that what one credits for past career success might be affected by the general psychological orientations to being in control.[9]

No differences in internal or external accounts of career success were obtained between blacks and whites—in fact there was a startling similarity—despite thinner resources and greater obstacles postulated for blacks, but in keeping with some more corporate familial orientations they have reported. If blacks and whites did not differ, men and women Pathmakers did differ somewhat: for those crediting external factors, males were more likely to give strong emphasis to the contribution than did females,[10] a finding which would be consistent with an argument that males receive greater support and resources than females.

A Pathmaker in the study said, "I worked very hard. I feel that I made myself but I feel I would have made a success of myself even if I hadn't gone this route . . . I would have been doing something that people would have noticed. I was determined to fulfill myself." Bob Price said:

> My sisters, my religious sisters, and my mother and my father would talk about God, they would talk about things that God has done, and those kind of things, so if you would separate that, and if you say that's a bunch of hogwash . . . [fine]. But I would also argue with you that had it not been for those people who I caught the attention of, it would have been somebody else. Because I'm simply—and I'm not saying it in braggadocio fashion—I'm simply made of the stuff that would enable me to do good no matter what. It has been like that since the cotton fields and it continues today.

Wes Parker had a strikingly internal view of luck. He said, when probed about his statement that luck had played some role:

You make the luck. Luck plays a big role. I'm not sure there's a Jesus Christ, although I'm a Methodist. I don't tell that to the bishop. There has to be a supreme being. The supreme being I worship could be the wrong one, and the one people in Asia worship could be the right one. But that supreme being put into me the capacity to do things. And as long as I use that capacity in the correct procedure, in the correct way, and to the maximum of my ability, then good things are going to happen.

Long-term Planning

A major component of need for achievement is long-term planning. We found a trend for Pathmakers to be weaker in long-term planning than Controls. We also found that males were stronger in long-term planning than females.[11] Wendell Curtis exemplifies both patterns. As we presented in Chapter 6, he chose a company that was thinly staffed so that he could rise rapidly. It was, and he did. Because of an interest in a Middle East crisis at the time, he also chose to apply to companies that would give him the opportunity to go there. His company was one of these, and he did get international experience, although he never got to the Middle East.

It makes a great deal of intuitive sense for Controls to be stronger in long-term planning than Pathmakers; how would Pathmakers engage in long-term planning? Most express astonishment when interviewed as to how far they have come. There are some interesting subtleties that need to be examined, however. How is it that Pathmakers, stronger in internal locus of control, could be weaker in long-term planning than Controls? How is it that Pathmakers were more likely than Controls to talk about new careers in their future (as reported in Chapter 6), and yet be coded as being weaker in long-term planning? An explanation is that Pathmakers' extreme belief in their own ability to control life events may preclude long-term planning! Typically Pathmakers just do it, accepting the challenge and figuring they can make it work, without long-term plans. As Wes Parker said:

> I work fourteen-hour days because I want to. If I worked seven hours a day, I would be more than half as successful as I was, probably. On the other hand, I had to believe if I only worked seven hours a day instead of fourteen hours a day, I certainly wouldn't be [even] half as successful as I was . . . Those of us who use [capacity] to the best of our ability, to the best of our knowledge, are going to fare the best.

It also makes sense that males should engage in more long-term planning than females. Considering that our subjects were between forty and fifty-five at the time of their interview in the early 1980s, females may have had fewer expectations of success, due to relatively high gender barriers in earlier years, and therefore might have planned less. In any case, none of them gave the response that Wes Parker gave to a question about goals: "I can get a new goal every day. I had two goals in college, after I decided I did not want to be a military person. I had two goals [which he met]. One is I wanted to be a millionaire by the time I was thirty-five, and I wanted to be making a million dollars a year by the time I was forty-two. They preyed on me heavily. My mistake was I didn't set any goals after that."

Wanda Perkins was tracked into teaching, then followed her mentor's advice to go to graduate school, and by "luck" wound up in the multi-disciplinary doctoral program that became number one in her discipline after she entered it, so she followed the strength of the program in selecting her discipline. She said:

> I've never really had a vision what options were. So there must have always been a lack of information, either because I lacked the skills or knowing where to go, or it just wasn't naturally available to me in any way. I think it is only now that I'm beginning to see that there are lots of choices, that I might do any number of things. No time in my life until recently was I ever aware that there were other choices. I just moved into whatever next step was open to me. And there was always a next step open. So it's hard to say it was purposive . . .

It may be that long-term planning comes late to Pathmakers like Wanda Perkins, so that at the time of the interviews they do talk about new careers for the future, and do so more than Controls (see Chapter 6), but they report less previous planning.

Furthermore, Rossi (1985) has explained that women frequently sustain career disruptions or start careers at a later time than their male counterparts due to bearing and raising children. This might require a more flexible orientation focused upon short-term goals. Consider Bonnie Carter's response compared to Wes Parker's goal speech above: "I've never had the kind of plan as of five years from now I want to be a fill-in-the-blank. But I have dealt with a kind of experience that I wanted to get over a period of time, or an opportunity to make a contribution over a period of time. And I do like being in a position where you can make things happen. Now that's the best part of it all!" Wendy Cassetta thought she would have a career in journalism, and doesn't even like academics. Of her future she says: "There's no strategy for me. There's nothing I can do in terms of a strategy. I've never had [long-term] goals. There's some places I'd like to see, and some things I'd like to do."

Reward Orientation

Despite the theoretical importance of this variable, no differences were obtained between Pathmakers and Controls, or between blacks and whites. However, females were found to be weaker in reward orientation[12] than males.[13] Wanda Perkins talked about her first job opportunity after her doctorate:

> I went to A for an interview way early on. And I got scared. A was far away from everything, I mean like culture shock, and I just, you know, it was really weird . . . It was so far away from everything that I knew. I was then East coast–oriented, and I was in love with this guy, and it was going to be away from him. You know, stupid things. [It was a very good professional opportunity.] So I stalled around, and finally said no even though there were no prospects for anything else.

In contrast, Wendell Curtis, after taking over a job in his second year held by someone with twelve years' seniority, got a raise, but not up to the incumbent's level.

> So they were giving me overly generous raises every six months, but then they were going to find out I was still unhappy. I complained. Complained is not the right word. Every opportunity I let them know that I knew what job I was filling in, what a bargain they were getting. And when they would give me a raise and look for a big response and how super it was, they got a [sad face]—I'm not being facetious, I drove them crazy. I would not have the guts to do that if I didn't feel that I didn't have a lot of financial pressures behind me. Also I have confidence in myself, so the downside of this was negligible to me. I really didn't have any question.

The fact that men differed from women leads us to believe that weaker reward orientation may be largely a woman's issue. That is, women may have had less exposure to salient external rewards than men (the existence of sexism would support this), or be less likely to ask, or know how to ask effectively for more. Our analysis revealed a trend that individuals who were high in internal locus of control were less likely to be reward-oriented than those who were low in internal locus of control. From this one might argue that for some successful women, a strong internal locus of control, coupled with the absence of external rewards, seemed to reinforce self-sufficiency. Alternately one could argue that some women relied on their strong internal locus of control as a personal resource to achieve success, while others relied on reward orientation, even though it was not typical of women. Wendy Cassetta, for example, was strong in reward orientation and quite weak in internal locus of control. Remember, all of our subjects were successful, but they appear to have taken different paths to get there.

Need for Power

No differences were found between Pathmakers and Controls in their need for power. However, there were differences between races and between genders. Black subjects were coded as being stronger in their need for power than whites.[14] Males were stronger in need for power than females.[15] Black males were stronger than the other three categories.[16] It may be that the black males accounted for much of the overall race and sex differences, although black women were not without a need for power, as Betty Powers illustrates in describing her application for a job at the college she wanted to attend: "I just went to the President's office. I thought that was the place to be. I was always wanting to be with people who could make decisions, you know things such as that." When asked about her interest in politics, she said, "I don't know . . . when I was in high school I always ran for office, [also in] church, and I was always the president. In college I ran as president, and I was the first woman to run."

Such individuals notwithstanding, that men were stronger in the need for power than women is not surprising, since American men have been traditionally judged by themselves or others on the amount of power or authority they have. In such circumstances the black male is particularly vulnerable since societal prejudices would impede advancement to positions of power, perhaps resulting in their strongest need for power in our study. Women, including black women, often followed a different route since they were weaker in need for power, although they occupied similarly powerful positions in their careers as the men. The weaker need for power of black women is especially interesting since black women had the strongest affiliation needs in the sample. We turn to those findings now.

Need for Affiliation

Since we are presenting our results in descending order of contribution to an understanding of Pathmaker/Control differences, we have no overall Pathmaker/Control differences to report with respect to being primarily motivated by the need to be near or affiliated with people. However, the importance we have reported elsewhere of friendships and relational issues at work for the women Pathmakers in our study, especially for black female Pathmakers (see Chapter 6), is supported by our data: black females as a whole tended to be stronger in need for affiliation[17] than the other categories. White males were also strong, while black males were the weakest in their need for affiliation (which makes sense given that they were also the strongest in need for power, a traditional opposite of need-affiliation). However, black female Controls were the strongest in need for affiliation of all the other categories.[18] White male Controls were next strongest and black male Controls the weakest of all categories. The gender difference between black Controls was startling since both groups presumably shared a family tradition of successfully overcoming societal racism, but it illustrates even more clearly how different were the personalities of the black male and female subjects.

Wanda Perkins, who was coded strong in need for affiliation, talked about her "rejection syndrome": "I have this rejection syndrome, it goes way back to those early years' experiences, and so when somebody says that 'we don't want you' that really weighs pretty heavy, and I generate all of these 'I must be stupid' responses." Wendy Cassetta was quite weak in need-affiliation, but also quite strong in need for achievement, to which we now turn.

Achievement Motivation

Our main need-achievement variable involved striving to meet standards of excellence and welcoming competition with competent others. Like the findings for affiliation, white males and black females were

stronger in need for achievement than the other subjects.[19] Why were
the two most divergent categories similar, and why were the findings
consistent across Pathmakers and Controls? Since these findings parallel the findings we just reported for need for affiliation, perhaps the
key to their similarity lies in their divergence.[20] The fact that white
males, who had a leg up, and black females, who had the most odds
against them, looked alike on need for achievement and need for affiliation does not mean that they were strong for the same reasons, but
it does emphasize that they were different from the black males and
white females in their motivation. As we shall see, they also shared a
number of defense patterns.

Maturity of Defenses and Styles of Coping

Before collecting data we were uncertain as to how differences in styles
of adaptation or ego defenses would be played out in our study. On the
one hand, it could be argued that since defenses are formed early in life
Pathmakers could be expected to have more "immature" defenses. This
assumed that the sociological disadvantages accompanying Pathmaker
status were accompanied by psychologically negative factors. We now
know this to be the case. We reported in Chapter 4 that Pathmakers
were more likely to have lost a parent during childhood, and to have
grown up in disintegrated homes. Wanda Perkins is an example of both
these patterns, and she exhibits the "immature" defenses that such patterns would predict.[21] On the other hand, immature defenses are also
thought to be severely crippling and unproductive as coping strategies.
It could be that Pathmakers, with all the other strikes against them,
would need more productive strategies than Controls to be successful.
For Controls, unproductive defenses (for whatever reasons they might
have occurred) should be less crippling due to their other advantages.
If this were true, Pathmakers should have more productive, or mature,
defenses than the Controls.

   Although our data do not allow a definitive answer as to which of
these assumptions is more fruitful, they do provide some evidence for
each position, and both may be true for different people. As we have
said, eighty-five subjects in the sample had only the more mature (Level
III and IV) defenses as Vaillant defines them (see Chapter 2). As Vaillant
found for his sample, successful functioning appears correlated with
these defenses. On the other hand, of the fifteen equally successful
subjects who do exhibit "immature" defenses (no one had only "im-

mature" defenses) in their lives, eleven were Pathmakers, and only four were Controls. These numbers are too small to demonstrate a difference, yet how do these fifteen people with immature defenses, who Vaillant implies do not become successful, in fact succeed?

The data just presented in the last paragraph using coders' judgments of the relative strength of Vaillant's four categories are too aggregated to allow us to fully understand the role of defenses in the functioning of these individuals. We transformed our scores on each of the individual defense codings into one score for maturity of defenses for each subject.[22] We found no differences in this score between Pathmaker/Controls or between men and women, suggesting that differences in maturity of defenses are not correlated with these categories. We did find a trend for whites to have more mature defenses than blacks. The analysis provides some support for the position we took concerning the findings for "immature" defenses and Pathmakers: the highest mean maturity score was in the white male Control cell, the lowest maturity score was in the black female Pathmaker cell, suggesting limited evidence that immaturity of defenses was again more a Pathmaker issue than a Control issue. We find little support for the second argument that Pathmakers would need more mature defenses to overcome greater obstacles. Perhaps the overall maturity of one's ego defenses is not a sign that individual coping strategies are unavailable. Perhaps when viewed as coping strategies we should think of a repertoire from which choices can be made. Overall, the findings are consistent with a position that there are different paths to success among our subjects, including a possibility of success being achieved by people who differ markedly on their mechanisms of defense.

Since Vaillant's work continues to reintroduce defenses to a professional literature which had moved away from such perspectives, we want to allow the interested reader additional opportunities to review the role of defense mechanisms by presenting the findings for each of the defense mechanisms studied. The defenses will be presented in the order of, and accompanied by, the number of the entire sample coded as using the defense.[23] Other readers may skip to the summary on p. 164.

Intellectualization (n = 75)

Intellectualization occurs when an idea is conscious but the accompanying affect (feeling) is not. No differences were found between Pathmakers and Controls, nor between males and females. However, there was an interaction such that, for males, Controls more often used intellectualization than Pathmakers, but for females, Pathmakers more often used intellectualization than Controls.[24] We also found that when intellectualization did occur, among the white males it was the Controls who were stronger on intellectualization, whereas for white females it was the Pathmakers who were stronger, suggesting that the general finding was influenced by the white subjects alone.[25] These findings taken together suggest that intellectual distancing from feelings was most predominant for whites, especially white male Controls and white female Pathmakers.

An observation is in order concerning our results on intellectualization, a "neurotic" defense on Vaillant's scale. We feel that the ranking of intellectualization as the dominant defense for both Pathmaker and Controls above all other defenses is certainly an artifact of our methodology. A life history interview of the kind we constructed virtually predisposes the subject to give intellectualized accounts of one's life. Our interviews were the sole source of the material to be coded. Similarly, note that fantasy may be as rare as it is in our coding (see below, $n = 4$) because our techniques implicitly discouraged fantasy—for example, we asked no "what if" or "magic man" questions.

Altruism (n = 69)

Given the operationalization problems with intellectualization, we feel that altruism should be regarded as truly the most used defense in our sample, and it is tied, with sublimation (discussed next), in the number of Pathmakers coded for it: forty-one. Altruism, a "mature"[26] defense in Vaillant's scheme, is defined as vicarious but gratifying service to others. It was also the one defense that differentiated Pathmakers from Controls. While altruism is reported present as often for Pathmakers and Controls, when it is present Pathmakers use it more strongly than the Controls.[27] This suggests that while altruism is widespread in the sample, Pathmakers are stronger altruists, which may relate to their greater internality of control beliefs. Internals may be more likely to think that they have the power to help others as well. For example, Wanda Perkins said: "I really think it's important. I always feel that you have to pay back something and I feel like I'm—a lot of what I do— links to that. It doesn't motivate me to act, but I'm aware that there's some kind of paying back that's important for me to do." One Pathmaker academic described a long-term intense involvement in community affairs and the development of a community health clinic which came to dominate her life:

> We had community meetings, whether they were big ones or small ones it didn't matter. The thing that mattered to me was to really listen to what people said they felt they needed . . . It was really like educating your community on issues like health care . . . if you got sick you had hospitals, period. Poor people had nowhere else to go . . . and we kept saying there must be another way. Why must people suffer because they cannot get health care? . . . We came up with the idea of having a free neighborhood clinic, and a year later we opened with a group of volunteers.

Despite these examples, over the whole sample men were more often coded altruistic than women.[28] Bob Price said:

> I wouldn't mind being somebody who could cure cancer. I wouldn't mind being somebody who could do some very much needed service in this world, and make it a little bit better. And sometimes you think about things like that. I don't think I could ever be satisfied with my life in the sense that I'm prepared to lay back on my laurels or my past or forget about that. I don't think I could ever be contented enough with whatever I'm doing to really do that. I think what you have is people who are intimidated somewhat by certain conditions . . . so they build up this wall, this defense mechanism, to protect themselves from society. I could never really be satisfied, and I'm not talking about being satisfied from the point of wealth. But as long as there are people I see suffering, as long as I see a role that I can play in helping to make the world a little better, I think I would probably strive for that.

An interaction with race was found such that for males, whites were more likely to be altruistic than blacks, while for females the reverse was true; white males had the most altruism and white females the least.[29] These findings suggest that women, especially white women, were less likely to report concern for the welfare of others than men. Given the stereotype of women as socioemotional support givers, this finding might be interpreted to suggest that women who make it are less likely to help others to make it. This could be due to any number of reasons, such as having less time or energy due to more consuming family obligations (such as caring for children). It seems unlikely that it could be due to having fewer resources to help others since our subjects were equally successful and therefore, at least theoretically, equally powerful. It could also be that having to work harder to get where they are makes them less likely to manipulate situations or people to give others a leg up. There is a suggestion, however, that black females were more like the males. When altruism was present, black females and white males were the strongest in their reports of altruism than all other categories.[30] Since it is the black females who have faced the most obstacles, it is interesting to note that they demonstrated equally strong altruism as the white males. This will not be the last defense with this pattern of similarity between white males and black females; indeed our next most prevalent defense shows a similar pattern.

Sublimation (n = 68)

Sublimation is also a "mature" defense. It involves indirectly expressing emotions or needs through a creative constructive outlet (such as Wanda Perkins becoming a teacher in response to defending against dependency). Wendell Curtis sublimated when he responded to his wife's breakdown and son's illness by continuing to work twelve hours a day. No Pathmaker/Control differences or gender differences were found. However, whites were found to sublimate more than were blacks,[31] and to use it more strongly.[32] There was again an interaction showing that white males and black females were alike—this time strong in sublimation.[33]

Dissociation (n = 60)

Dissociation is defined as a temporary but drastic change in character in order to avoid emotional distress; for example, a temporary denial of reality. Since dissociation is not under conscious control it is not a very productive defense, and Vaillant calls it "neurotic" (Level III). Therefore its high frequency in these successful people is mildly surprising. Once again there was a finding linking black females and white males: both were stronger on dissociation when it occurred.[34]

Anticipation (n = 50)

The "mature" defense anticipation involves the realistic anticipation of, and preparing for, future inner discomfort. For example, individuals would be using anticipation when they make extra time in their schedule to prepare for a difficult meeting with their boss when they anticipate that their boss will disagree with their proposal.

We obtained a trend for females to use anticipation more than males. This trend is interesting when coupled with the fact that women reported long-term planning less than men. Perhaps, given the relative disadvantages of being female (for example, sexism and child care responsibilities), women's future planning was more likely to be limited to anticipating short-term future difficulties. For males there was also a trend for Pathmakers to use anticipation more than Controls; however, for females, Controls used it more than Pathmakers. It is perhaps not surprising that it was the male Controls who exhibited the least anticipation, as they were the category (at least the white males) with the least obstacles; they didn't have as many potential situations in which to anticipate future inner discomfort! This doesn't mean they didn't plan—in fact males were the strongest in the use of long-term planning—rather, that they did not plan around future discomfort.

Repression (n = 39)

Repression, a "neurotic" defense, is defined as being aware of an emotion or feeling, but not being aware of the idea or reason behind it (for example, feeling sad but not knowing why). Pathmaker/Control differences were found, but only when controlling for gender, and with a reversal: there was a trend for male Pathmakers to be stronger on repression when it occurred than male Controls, while female Controls were stronger repressors than female Pathmakers. This trend is linked to a finding that it is the white male Pathmakers who were the most likely to repress of all the male groups, and the white female Pathmakers who were the least likely repressors of the female groups.[35] Finally, there was an interaction: white males and black females again have a similar pattern: when it occurs, they have stronger codings of repression than other subjects.[36]

Reaction Formation (n = 39)

Reaction formation is defined as behaving in a fashion diametrically opposed to an unacceptable instinctual impulse. If one were defending against aggressive impulses, one might be excessively pleasant to a person one really hated. Reaction formation is not, theoretically or practically, a productive defense; Vaillant classifies it as a "neurotic" defense.

No main effect differences were found for the presence or strength of reaction formation for Pathmakers by race or gender. However, there was a finding that when the defense occurred, white males and black females again were similar, this time coded stronger in reaction formation.[37]

Humor (n = 35)

The use of humor as a "mature" defense involves the expression of painful ideas and feelings without individual discomfort or unpleasant effects on others. Typically this is accomplished by joking, a gentle kind of having fun at the expense of oneself or others. The joking is genuinely funny, but at the same time respectful enough not to arouse feelings of discomfort. We had high hopes for humor as a defense: it was a great favorite of the interviewers since a subject with humor as a dominant theme was likely to be more fun. However, just as there was no pattern for interviewers' favorites to have been more likely Pathmakers or Controls, so was there no difference in the use of humor between Pathmakers and Controls, nor was there any difference for gender. However, a trend was found between whites and blacks: white subjects were more likely to use humor as a defense than black subjects. Further, when humor occurred, whites were more likely than black subjects to exhibit it strongly.[38] Perhaps whites felt freer to use self-deprecating humor: remember that because of our paired interviewer strategy, a white interviewer was present for many black respondent interviews.

Suppression (n = 33)

Suppression, a "mature" defense according to Vaillant's scheme, can be defined as the conscious or semiconscious decision to postpone paying attention to a conscious impulse of conflict. So, for example, if one were worried or confused about an impending meeting, one would temporarily block it from one's mind in order to continue working on the task at hand without disruptive anxiety about the meeting. Wendell Curtis was coded for suppression for his responses to illness; he reported getting through the crisis of his wife's illness, her father's death, and his son's illness by not thinking about them the twelve hours a day he was at work. Suppression is considered a "mature" defense by Vaillant since it acts to temporarily suspend anxiety in order for productive work to continue. It can also enable the user to take time to reflect on solutions: thinking it over, or "I'll sleep on it" can be suppressive responses and can be constructive in certain settings. For example, one female manager told us that if certain things happened at a meeting she was running, she knew she would react emotionally and lose control. Her solution was to adjourn meetings when such things happened, and reconvene them later when she was able to cope. This is an interesting positive use of suppression but it does not tell us what she used as a defense against those things before she became powerful enough to singlehandedly adjourn meetings.

Again, no general findings for background, race, or gender were obtained. There was a trend that white males (like Wendell Curtis) and black females were once again linked, and this time they were the strongest on suppression.

Other Defenses

Our next six defenses were little used by our sample of successful people. Except for displacement, the other five are "immature" or Level II defenses on Vaillant's scale. Thus his general point that the most successful people exhibit the most mature defenses is supported by our data. However, while they are the most rare of the defenses exhibited by subjects in this study, "immature" defenses do exist even among these highly successful individuals. Future research might question how success can be achieved using these defenses.

Since these six psychological defenses—Displacement[39] ($n = 15$), Passive-Aggressive behavior[40] ($n = 12$), Projection[41] ($n = 10$), Acting Out[42] ($n = 5$), Fantasy[43] ($n = 4$), and Hypochondriasis[44] ($n = 3$)—were coded relatively infrequently in our sample, the decreasing number of subjects in each category would lead to relative instability in our statistical analysis, and we will not discuss them further.

Psychotic Defenses

The three psychotic defenses on Vaillant's scale did not occur in our sample. They are delusional projection, which is defined as frank delusions about external reality, usually of a persecutory type; denial, a complete denial of external reality; and distortion, the gross reshaping of external realities to suit inner needs. Since psychotics generally live in worlds not shared with the rest of us, it is not surprising that such defenses were completely incompatible with the levels of success achieved by our sample.

Summary

We felt that the most theoretically important differences between the Pathmakers and Controls were the stronger internal locus of control of the Pathmakers coupled with their greater internality of attributions for their own success. The only other difference for Pathmakers was their stronger altruism. We did obtain several interactions in which Pathmaker/Control differences were important. Specifically we found intellectualization to be more characteristic of male Controls (especially white male Controls) and female Pathmakers (especially white female Pathmakers). Male Pathmakers and female Controls on the other hand were similar in their stronger use of dissociation, anticipation, and repression.

We found differences for race and sex as well. Specifically blacks were coded as having stronger need for power (especially black males), stronger passive aggression and projection, and weaker sublimation and humor. Males were found to have stronger long-term planning, reward orientation, need for power, and altruism[45] than females. We also found that black females and white males were curiously alike in a number of variables: both having stronger need-affiliation, need-achievement, altruism, sublimation, dissociation, repression, reaction formation, and suppression.

In commenting on our psychological findings, we remember a point made the first time our findings were presented several years ago in New Zealand. A philosopher there noted that anyone who could have an "internal locus of control" when they grew up black in the rural South as the son of a sharecropper was simply "crazy," and that what we were studying was in fact people who were simply too crazy to know that they should quit. Bob Price anticipated his comment:

> Shortly after I became president of the first bank somebody asked me what I figured my success to and I finally got out that I guess I'd have

to give some credit to my stupidity. My inability, my refusing to say no to challenges, my refusing to refuse to accept challenges . . . But then you sit down and try to figure out a process to cope with the situation, to solve the problem, and then you find that it was not so hard after all. So I told this person that part of my success was my simply refusing to say no. That's crazy! But I guess that otherwise I would not have done. And after saying that I would, being to some extent ridiculed by friends and buddies and so forth, saying that, "Who do you think you are? You can't do that, we tried that!" And so forth. Being crazy enough to accept a challenge and then making them out a lie. I got a big kick out of that!

We think that a combination of need for power and internal locus of control is a more theoretically useful conceptualization than craziness. But in the sense that all of our Pathmakers were in fact flying in the face of convention and the forces of social reproduction, and therefore statistically deviant, we are studying the positive aspects of being deviant, or "crazy." Since we have only studied successful people, however, we have no way of knowing how precisely the same personality traits we have described can lead to other than positive outcomes. Our data suggest that traits like internal locus of control produced successful outcomes for the Pathmakers of our study.

9

Conclusions and Implications

The research we have undertaken was untraditional in a number of respects. For anthropology, we have taken a rare stance by "studying up"; that is, studying segments of a population at the higher strata. To interview one of our subjects who personally controlled over $50 billion was a rare anthropological experience. We would like to encourage more anthropologists to study elites, particularly in contemporary societies. It is advice more often given than followed in that discipline.

For sociology, our research was unusual in that we focused upon the cells for which sociological theory does not work: in focusing on Pathmakers we have concentrated our attention on those cells of a distribution normally dismissed as "error" or noise in sociological investigations. We would argue that no adequate sociology can dismiss issues of resilience, resistance, and defiance of normative expectations. Indeed, it is possible to argue that in examining such phenomena we are studying the aspects of being human which directly bear on what social scientists have come to call agency (see, for example, Harris, 1989; Whiting and Edwards, 1988)—that persons are active participants in deciding among behavioral choices within any culture. People who construct careers which are unanticipated on the basis of sociological variables not only help us to understand the limitations of the sociological variables, but illuminate individual agency in decisions that transcend social constraints.

166

For psychologists, the focus on the statistically unusual, seen as "deviant," is commonplace, but psychologists often equate deviance with pathology, and in this study we decidedly do not. Pathmakers are statistically rare: they do not follow norms, but they operate at high levels of success. Further, we argue that we need to focus on the advantages atypical psychological orientations can afford, not just for the individual in one's actualization, but also for the society over the long haul. Were our subjects "too crazy" to know they couldn't succeed? As to pathology, while most of our subjects evidence healthy ego integration by standard definitions, some of them also appear to possess some degree of psychopathology. These latter Pathmaker subjects succeeded against both sociological odds and the psychological "impediments," which can, in certain settings, apparently be turned to advantage. In anthropology the notion that what is "crazy" is culturally determined has been long accepted (see Benedict, 1935). Here we are arguing that differing psychological orientations can only be understood against a situational ground, to which they may or may not be adaptive.[1]

Summary of Findings

Pathmaker/Control Differences

In considering families of origin, we found that Pathmakers were somewhat more likely than Controls to have had a parent die in childhood (the finding was stronger for the women, especially black women). Perhaps, in part, as a consequence of the remaining parent having to assume dual roles, Pathmakers proportionally grew up twice as often in egalitarian homes (regarding division of labor for males and females in the home). However, Pathmakers were also more likely to have grown up in disintegrated homes (due to abusive parents or an unstable family structure), and more likely to feel hate upon returning to their home of origin as adults. As a result, they reported leaving home to get away from bad environments more often, and they were less likely to maintain contact with their families of origin. Their families of origin were described as being somewhat more religious, as having larger numbers of children, and as being located in neighborhoods of lower SES than Controls' families of origin. In contrast to female Controls, female Pathmakers reported that their siblings were as occupationally successful as they were, but male Pathmakers reported the opposite relative to male Controls. With respect to schools, not surprisingly in the face of the thinner family resources, Pathmakers reported teachers to be important to them more often than did Controls.

Pathmakers were less likely to attend private school at elementary, secondary, or collegiate levels. They reported somewhat more obstacles to school success, and described themselves as loners in high school more often than Controls did. This is also reflected in their dating patterns: they more often reported not dating until meeting their spouse.

In considering their careers, Pathmakers were far more likely to give internal than external accounts of how they became successful. At least for the males, Pathmakers less often reported getting jobs before college through family connections than did Controls. Furthermore, they reported leaving jobs before college for family and school reasons somewhat more often. Pathmakers were also somewhat more likely to share the money they earned with their families (this is especially true for black Pathmakers as compared to white Pathmakers). After college, however, Pathmakers were more likely to create jobs or be offered jobs for which they had not applied. From this point on they were also more likely to leave jobs for more money, and less likely to leave because they were bored. When asked what they found satisfying at work, female Pathmakers were more likely to mention contact with people than female Controls. Furthermore, it was the female Controls and male Pathmakers who were more likely to use an autocratic style with their subordinates. Not only did Pathmakers report obstacles to school success as previously mentioned, they also had a tendency to encounter obstacles at work, and reported more obstacles per person than Controls reported. Pathmakers were more likely to make a positive outcome out of a failure, to have career plans for the future, and to plan for new careers or additional education.

In looking at differences that existed within their created families, we found that Pathmakers were somewhat less likely to be married at the time of the interview, but, if married, they were more likely to describe their spouse's personal characteristics, rather than their achievements. Furthermore, Pathmakers were somewhat more likely to handle conflicts with their children through punishment.

Considering friendship and mental and physical health patterns, female Pathmakers were somewhat more likely to report friends from work as being important than female Controls. Pathmakers were somewhat more likely to describe themselves as reformed smokers or drinkers (which might be thought of as the consequences of their origins on the one hand, and attempts to undo them on the other). Pathmakers (especially the men) worried more about the future and less about their jobs than Controls. Finally, Pathmakers were also somewhat less likely to participate in politics if it was not part of their job.

With respect to psychological patterns, Pathmakers were coded as being more strongly internal in their locus of control and success attributions, and less strongly external than Controls. Control subjects were stronger than Pathmakers in long-term planning, while Pathmakers were stronger in altruism. We did obtain several interactions in which Pathmaker/Control differences were more complicated: we found intellectualization to be more characteristic of male Controls (especially white male Controls) and female Pathmakers (especially white female Pathmakers). Male Pathmakers and female Controls on the other hand were similar in their stronger use of dissociation, anticipation, and repression.

Gender Differences

Outside the area of created family we obtained relatively fewer gender differences in our study than Pathmaker/Control differences. For example, we found no differences in the families from which men and women came, except that the men maintained somewhat less contact than women with their families of origin at the time of the interview, and to some extent reported fewer siblings with more education than themselves. One of the two gender differences found for schooling involved school influences: men were more often influenced in their schooling by men; women were more often influenced by women. In addition, for Pathmakers, females performed better than males in school. Finally, only two gender differences were found in the area of employment: men were more likely to leave their jobs after college for better opportunities, and while men reported male mentors somewhat more often than women reported male mentors, women reported women mentors somewhat more often than men reported them (although women still reported having more male mentors overall than women mentors).

However, in the area of created family we described a number of gender differences. Most significantly, women reported more costs of success than did men, with interpersonal (relational) costs being the most frequently mentioned. So for these women, career success often came at the expense of their personal lives. In contrast, men were more likely to be married at the time of the interview than women, and men were married to one person for more years than the female subjects.[2] Women also had fewer offspring, and yelled more and compromised less with their spouses than men.

Two other gender differences were obtained in the areas of success attributions and health. When external success attributions were made, male Pathmakers had stronger external attributions than female Pathmakers. This is interesting in light of the differences obtained between women and men in their personal lives. Women clearly incurred greater costs than men in their personal lives as they became successful. It makes sense that women, especially female Pathmakers, would make more internal success attributions. Men also reported getting regular exercise more often than did women.

Concerning differences in psychological patterns, males were stronger in long-term planning, reward orientation, and need for power than females. In addition, men were coded more often for altruism[3] than women, but women were coded more often for anticipation than men.

Race Differences

Turning to differences between blacks and whites within the family of origin, blacks were more likely to have had extended families in their homes when they were growing up; to some extent to have mothers (who were more likely to be working) with higher school attainment; to have reported more loving, less tense homes; and to have reported feeling more pleasure on returning home as adults. Black families of origin were also described as being religious more often than were white families of origin.

With respect to racial differences in schooling, blacks were influenced in their schooling by other blacks more than by whites, while whites were more influenced by whites than by blacks. Black males achieved higher levels of educational attainment than did the rest of the subjects, despite the fact that blacks encountered more obstacles to school success than did whites, and were more likely to make aggressive responses to such obstacles when they occurred.

The only difference we obtained in the realm of work between blacks and whites involved influences on careers: blacks were more likely to report black mentors, and whites only reported white mentors. Black males reported being less influenced by their bosses than the rest of the subjects. However, with respect to their created family we obtained a few differences. Blacks were married for fewer numbers of years to one person than were whites. Perhaps their shorter-term marriages were due to the fact that blacks were less likely than whites to have spouses who were described as supportive of their careers. This was especially true for the black women in our sample as compared to the white women. In addition white males more often reported marriages with a traditional division of labor than the rest of the subjects.

With respect to psychological differences, whites were more external in their locus of control than blacks. We also found blacks had a stronger need for power (especially black males), and that they had stronger scores on passive aggression and projection, and weaker scores on sublimation and humor. We also found that black females and white males were curiously alike in a number of variables: both were stronger on need for affiliation, need for achievement, altruism, sublimation, dissociation, repression, reaction formation, and suppression.

Conclusions

Our final analysis concerns the balance of costs, or disadvantages, and resources, or sources of support. How do Pathmakers counterbalance early disadvantages in order to construct paths to success, at least in terms of their careers? What resources do they use? How do individuals overcome racism and sexism, and how do Pathmakers overcome these obstacles in combination with others they face? We found several suggestive patterns in our data that help us begin to answer these questions.

Resources

Our subjects utilized two types of resources: psychological and social. We describe the importance of these below, with emphasis on how different subjects utilized different combinations of resources, hence constructing different paths to success.

Psychological Resources   Although we found evidence of the additional disadvantages Pathmakers, blacks, and females faced in their families, we also found evidence of reliance upon psychological resources that helped to overcome them. Pathmakers exhibited several psychological characteristics that have also been seen to play a central role in studies of resilient children—children growing up in families that put them psychologically or developmentally "at risk" but who do not develop the predicted pathology. The most important of these is having an internal locus of control. Indeed, a number of researchers studying the psychology of the resilient child found that these children had an internal locus of control, often coupled with a positive sense of self, or high self-esteem[4] (Werner and Smith, 1982, 1992; Farrington, 1993; Felsman, 1989; Garmezy, 1981).[5] These were particularly good predictors of a positive outcome in the face of family psychopathology, something with which some of our Pathmakers were familiar.[6] Anthony (1974) suggests that when psychopathology is present the danger for the child is involvement in the parental pathology. An internal locus of control, avoidance of helplessness, and belief in one's efficacy are good insulation. In another example of internal locus of control, Cohler (1987) points out that more resilient children showed a strong capacity for comforting themselves during times of emotional stress rather than depending on others for solace. This would be particularly adaptive for children living with various forms of social disorganization. Finally, an internal locus of control appears to reduce risk for severe psychiatric disorder (Lefcourt, 1976) as well as chronic depression (Abramson, Seligman, and Teasdale, 1978).

What psychologically distinguished Pathmakers from Controls, and in a sense was responsible for their different paths to success, was their belief that they were personally in control of their own life outcomes. We believe their strong internal locus of control played an important role in Pathmakers' subsequent achievement, while externality was a feature of the Controls. These differences are also strongly reflected in Pathmakers' attributions of credit for their success to factors internal to themselves, while Controls credited factors external to themselves.[7] Weiner's (1985) model suggests that in assessing success or failure at specific tasks individual responses are in part a result of their disposition to invoke internal or external influences. A short-term explanation of internal attributions is whether one succeeded or not at the task being evaluated, but all of our subjects were equally successful in the task being evaluated. Therefore we tend to explain their attributions as a result of their locus-of-control dispositions.

Pathmakers' greater internality is contextualized by the fact that virtually all of our subjects were also strong in need for achievement, and that most were reward-oriented and used only mature defenses, characteristics our Pathmakers shared with our Controls. Strong internal locus of control and achievement motivation are a formidable mix, producing standards of excellence and confidence that one holds the power to achieve them. For Pathmakers this was also coupled with greater altruism: they were more determined to "pay back" and to help others—perhaps a belief in their own ability to recreate their paths in others. Controls saw themselves as more dependent upon external factors to achieve. Their lower altruism may be a reflection of this lower efficacy: a paradox since they, of all people, ought to recognize how others can be important to people achieving success.

Black subjects in our study describe greater obstacles to school success and encounters with racism in the larger society. However, black males appear to have utilized their stronger need for power to achieve success. In addition to internal locus of control and positive self-esteem, Garmezy (1981) found that a sense of personal power was an important factor in the resiliency of disadvantaged black children. In light of this literature, it is not surprising that blacks in our study were coded as being significantly stronger in need for power than whites, males stronger than females, and black males the strongest of all our subjects. Since the greatest significance for these differences was obtained for the main effect of race as well as the interaction between race and gender, it would appear that this characteristic is important for a combination of these categories, but particularly for race. This need for power is reflected in two other findings: relative to whites, blacks were coded as using aggressive responses to obstacles in school. Furthermore, black males claimed that their bosses were less of an influence on them than any other cohort.

On the other hand, women, who like black women reported greater personal and relational costs of success, exhibited different patterns of resilience. They apparently utilized a combination of high internal locus of control with weaker reward orientation, which may have contributed to self-sufficiency in another way. If you have an internal locus of control, external rewards may be less salient. One subject's comment is illuminating: "I never knew we were poor until I grew up—then it didn't matter." She learned to respond to emotional warmth, which she had in abundance,[8] rather than to material goods, which she did not.

Furthermore, perhaps women's greater use of anticipation (to offset future difficulties) coupled with *weaker* altruism may also have aided their achievement. Although the gender difference we observed for altruism may have reflected differential access to resources with which one could help others, it may also be that women preferred to conserve their energy and channel it to their own career development. Indeed, the greater focus on their own careers of the Pathmaker women in our study may have been required for them to offset the additional obstacles associated with being female, and for some, being black as well.

Social Supports   A second category of resources we observed involves the social or interpersonal supports that our subjects utilized. We have argued that Pathmakers come from home environments with less redundant resources than Controls, the implications being that, as they grew up, Pathmakers might be more likely to call upon resources external to those provided by their immediate family. This pattern is supported by literature on resiliency in children. As Felsman (1989) argues: ". . . the most direct impact on how these children regard themselves results from the nature of their social supports, their relationships with peers, and members of their community. Their lack of traditional family magnifies the importance of these relations" (p. 75). A number of other researchers have also emphasized the role of people in the community as sources of social support for resilient children (Werner and Smith, 1982, 1992; Anthony, 1987; Garmezy, 1983; Rutter, 1979). Research has shown that resilient children and adolescents make use of an extended network of support: teachers, ministers, peers, friends' parents, extended family members, etc. Indeed, Rutter (1979) found that when children had at least one warm, supportive relationship in their lives, the percentage showing conduct disorder dropped from 75 percent to 25 percent, in spite of extreme stress.[9] Felsman and Vaillant (1987), in their longitudinal study of high-risk inner city youth, found that resilient individuals were not solitary or isolated as children, and successfully maintained object relations through adulthood.

We have evidence that Pathmakers also utilized social support resources: relative to Controls, Pathmakers cited teachers as being much more important to them than did Controls. This spontaneous admission in answer to the question of who influenced them in school is very important. It is, for example, also reflected in research on resiliency.

Werner (1993) found that all of the Kauai Longitudinal Study's resilient high-risk children had at least one teacher who was a source of support. Rutter et al. (1979) report similar findings for inner city London secondary schools. In light of the fact that Pathmakers claimed somewhat more obstacles to school success than Controls, as well as poorer relations with high school peers[10] (they were self-described "loners"), teachers probably represented the most important resource for Pathmakers to cope with school demands. Remember that our research showed the importance of education as an equalizer. Schools themselves were utilized as resources, and successfully coping with school was important in becoming a Pathmaker. Growing up, Pathmakers also claimed their families to be somewhat more religious than Controls, with black females coming from the most religious families[11] (a pattern which continued in adulthood).

As Pathmakers became adults, the females continued to utilize a network of social and emotional support discussed earlier: relative to female Controls, female Pathmakers cited people as primary motivators at work (perhaps as resources in overcoming their somewhat greater work obstacles as well as their greater relational costs). They also cited friends from work as an important part of their friendship network. Female Pathmakers were more likely to rely on work and career as a source of interpersonal support and a place to invest emotional energy. They make work into an environment which fits their needs. Their friendship networks come from work, and this means that even their play is linked to work.

This constellation of variables would appear to have profound implications for what these Pathmakers expect of work and what work may reasonably demand of them. It seems especially likely that they will wind up devoting more time to their work than Controls do, which may not be incidental to their career success. Some may find their devotion to work neurotic, but it is one example of a cost of success—the disruption of early support systems and discontinuity with the past—becoming an asset as it leads these people to direct more and more energy toward their work and the people with whom they work.

These findings concerning Pathmakers' social resources are very interesting in light of research linking internal locus of control and social support. Not only has social support been shown to reduce vulnerability to psychological problems (Cobb, 1976; Cohen and McKay, 1984; Gottlieb, 1978; Holahan and Moos, 1981), but it appears that people with an internal locus of control benefit most from social support when under stress (Lefcourt, Martin, and Saleh, 1984)—presumably because it encourages autonomy and initiative which Pathmakers believe can have an effect. They may also use social support givers instrumentally, so that social support systems provide networks that can help, not just support.

We believe an important component in being able to construct social resources and to make environments was the Pathmakers' belief that they could determine their own future: their internal locus of control. They report this especially clearly when they were asked to account for their success. In a very real sense they were saying that their single most important resource was themselves.

It may be that their internality is a consequence of their success: "I beat the odds without outside help, therefore I must have done it myself," but we think it more likely to be a trait of long duration that was important to them from the very beginning, since, as we have seen, the trait is often reported in the resiliency literature. This is some reassurance that people's capacity as adults to "rewrite the story of one's own life" (see Cohler, 1987: 401) is not the source of our finding. Further, in a number of studies which focus on adults under stressful circumstances (Rodin and Langer, 1977; Bettelheim, 1943, 1960), the presence of a strong internal locus of control continued to be a major factor in coping with adversity. So, although we believe in maturational changes over the life span with respect to coping styles and emotionality, our Pathmakers in adulthood seem to share those psychological characteristics deemed important by other studies for overcoming adversity. This supports a presumption that our Pathmakers possessed these characteristics in childhood and continued to rely on them in adulthood. However, as we mentioned, we have no way of testing the reasonableness of this assumption in our present design, nor was our study aimed at understanding the etiology of these characteristics, although this seems a good area for future research.

Although we have discussed the importance of need for power for blacks with respect to the multiple paths argument and social resources, we want to highlight the apparent importance of a more closely knit, warmer family of origin as a form of social support for all blacks. Relative to whites, blacks had more extended family members in their home, had more loving, less tense homes, expressed more pleasure upon returning home, had a more religious upbringing, and had a greater number of siblings.[12] Furthermore, in terms of role models, blacks' mothers had greater educational attainment than whites' and more often worked (although this difference could have been more of a cost than an advantage). Taking into account the literature on the black family reviewed in Chapter 1, we found general support for positive effects of the black family among the black subjects in our study.

Another potential form of social support in the family involves parenting styles. Researchers have found that a combination of family warmth (leading to basic trust) and good supervision with balanced discipline (the presence of structure and rules) may protect a child from a high-risk background (Rutter, 1979; Werner, 1993). In fact Wilson (1974) found that strict parental supervision was more effective in preventing delinquency under conditions of chronic poverty than a happy family atmosphere. Black and female Pathmakers received stricter parenting which, if the literature is correct, may have been to their advantage. If the white males had relatively greater advantages in their particular gender and race than women and blacks, strict parenting might not have been as important.[13] Finally, the family was an important social resource for women as well, and women maintained contact with their family of origin more often than men did.

Tolerance for Ambiguity

Some researchers (Rutter et al., 1975) cite adaptability or malleability as a primary characteristic that protects against childhood psychiatric disorder. We observed a remarkable pattern of tolerance for the ambiguity that change brings in the lives of our Pathmakers. Given the incredible social mobility they have achieved, it seems obvious that adaptability and tolerance for ambiguity and change are a necessary psychological characteristic for people from disadvantaged backgrounds to become Pathmakers.[14]

Is this a result of all of the change in their lives, given the extraordinary intragenerational mobility the Pathmakers have experienced? If so, it also seems to make them more able to adapt to change in the future. Or is it that they were psychologically always able to handle change? Perhaps because of their high internality they thought change posed less of a threat? Consider the range of the changes they either have experienced or have chosen beyond their own extraordinary social mobility: Pathmakers were more likely to have had a parent die in their own childhood, and were less likely to maintain contact with their families of origin. They "replaced" their parents with teachers, and they overcame more obstacles to school success. Pathmakers were more likely to create jobs, to leave jobs for better money, to have overcome more obstacles at work (indeed, to make positive outcomes out of such failures), and to have plans for new careers and more education.[15] Pathmakers were more likely to report themselves as reformed drinkers and smokers. Further evidence that they were open to change in their interpersonal relations is that they were more likely to report relying upon work for developing friendships than Controls were. Altogether these experiences of change and orientation to change may result from the Pathmaker process itself. Perhaps it also stems from their high internality and is instrumental in making them more adaptable, which might itself help with career challenges. As one Pathmaker said about opportunities that were made available to him: "I always said yes." It is interesting to note that despite the evidence that Pathmakers have a greater tolerance for change, they are reported in Chapter 8 to have less reward orientation than Controls. Reward orientation is generally thought to be correlated with risk-taking, which many assume means change. It is interesting to learn that tolerance for change is in fact a separate variable, at least for these subjects. Aside from a willingness to leave jobs for more money there are few reward themes in the findings reported for Pathmakers. Therefore, apparently it is possible to have a high tolerance or experience of change, but not be motivated to change by considerations of reward. This high tolerance for ambiguity and internal locus of control may also explain why Pathmakers were weaker in long-term planning.

The patterns of the use of external social resources, high internality, and tolerance for the ambiguity that change brings that were typical of Pathmakers in our study bear some psychological costs for Pathmakers (in addition to the interpersonal costs we have reported), which are evident in some of our data. Sustaining internality in the face of early experiences of external obstacles may be a useful defense against internalizing others' negative expectations, and it apparently works for these subjects. But there may be a cost, epitomized by Wanda Perkins's worrying that she was really an imposter who did not belong where she was. It seems to us that she freely verbalized what may be an unconscious anxiety for many Pathmakers, and that this may best account for the otherwise anomalous finding that these strongly internal people with tolerance for change were more likely to worry about the future than Controls. Perhaps there was a nagging doubt that others' negative expectations might be correct after all, or that the external forces may yet succeed.[16]

Implications

We believe that our exploratory research has indicated that there may be multiple paths to career success, not one path, and that these multiple paths for the populations we studied are not predicted well by more mainstream literature. In many ways Pathmakers were similar to Controls, but in several significant ways they were different. In many ways blacks were not different from whites, but other variables produced significant differences. In many ways men and women were similar, but in several crucial areas they proved to be different. Further, the three variables—status, race, and gender—sometimes interacted, revealing some combination of status, gender, or race differences for only some subjects.

Given that the research reported here was exploratory in nature, it is premature to think of specific policy implications of our research until further confirmatory analyses are done with larger data banks. However, a number of key issues emerge from our study which should inform future researchers in ways that seem likely to have implications for education and employment policy issues. These issues can be summarized as follows:

1. We agree with Scarr (1988) that research that allows for comparisons among subjects of different genders, races, SES, and educational backgrounds should be encouraged and strengthened. Important differences in the nature of the paths followed to achieve career success may be masked by studies that aggregate across these characteristics. For example, we note that there appear to be fundamental differences between many men and women in their orientation to and expectations of work, what they can get out of work, their fellow workers, and their perceptions of their own success. Further, Pathmakers accounted for their success differently than Controls. In addition, we found evidence that race and sex have fundamental and lasting effects on mentoring and perhaps access to educational opportunity.

Not only were there similarities and differences in the social resources used by individuals to construct paths to success, there were similarities and differences as well in the psychological resources they brought to bear which would have been masked if we had not considered these subject variables in combination as well as separately. Some findings could only be understood by examining several background variables at once: for example, white males and black females were strongest in such defenses as altruism, sublimation, dissociation, and need for affiliation, but black male Controls were weakest in need for affiliation. Within the white male group, Controls were stronger in intellectualization, but within the white female group, it was Pathmakers who were stronger. These brief examples are indicative of the complexity and the diversity of issues that our study uncovered. We anticipate that future research on career success will be much more finely grounded and yield much more fertile results when such distinctions are observed.

2. There are several implications for educational research and policy. First, research on the role of education in preparation for career success must also be attentive to the variables of SES and educational status, race, and gender. While it should be noted that our subjects' ages (40–55 years old between 1981 and 1984) tilted our sample toward those who suffered more exclusionary forms of racial and gender prejudice than would current school populations, reviews of the survival of de facto segregated schooling (see Barnett and Harrington, 1985) strengthens the relevance of our findings. Remember that our subjects all made it to the top no matter what the obstacles: our main research objective was the narrow question of how successful careers are built by men and women, both black and white, from economically and educationally disadvantaged households, and how their paths to career success may differ from those growing up in more advantaged circumstances. While we found the paths were not completely distinct, important differences in the paths taken among these groups did exist. Equally important, in some cases we found that Pathmaker/Control differences can be masked unless race and gender are taken into account.

Second, given the high proportion of students in school districts with lower expenditures per pupil than average (especially the poorer urban and rural districts) who share the sociological categories we have used to describe Pathmakers, a curious imbalance is obvious: those with the least redundant resources outside of schools are often in the school districts with the thinnest resources. In the 1980s, the Supreme Courts of Montana, Kentucky, and Texas struck down their states' school financing systems because of disparities in what is spent in rich and poor districts. Similar rulings are possible in other states.[17] Even if such judicial efforts were to equalize per-pupil expenditures across districts where legislative ones have not (see Shalala, Williams, and Fischel, 1973), given the importance of teachers for such subjects, there is probably a need for greater per-pupil expenditure in districts in which potential Pathmakers go to school compared to wealthier districts with greater redundancy of resources. However, it could be argued that other education differences between Pathmakers and Controls, such as the quality of teachers, are not necessarily predicted by per-pupil expenditures.

We found evidence that teachers may be filling more important roles for the Pathmakers than for the Controls. This relates to the lesser redundancy of the resources of the Pathmakers compared to the Controls, but places greater burdens on the teachers of potential Pathmakers. Teachers are role models. They must challenge and support. We reported in Chapter 8 that variables not necessarily conducive to good classroom control—such as internal locus of control and the risk-taking associated with reward orientation—may be critical to later life success. We may be meddling at some peril to Pathmakers' long-term development if in order to achieve short-term management goals we retard obviously adaptive traits. The paradox here is that one of the most consistent views our Pathmaker subjects have of their parenting—when they think it was successful—is a combination of love and rules. A black male Pathmaker said, "Mama was the carrot and Daddy was the stick." Betty Powers says, "It was strict. It was loving. Mama always cared about what we were doing. School and the church were very important. We didn't get a lot of beatings, but when we got one we really got one, and all those times it had to be [problems with] the school or the church." It would seem likely that it is not discipline that is a problem, but a perceived inequity in how it is applied or feeling that rules are carried out in an uncaring way or by uncaring people. Remember that the white female Controls reported less family support even though they had the strictest, most traditional homes. Teachers, like parents, can combine caring with a structured environment in which the work of learning can go forward.

Finally, we found evidence that race and gender stratification can be seen to have fundamental and lasting effects on access to educational opportunity and to mentoring. Schorr (1988) has found that mentors can provide sustained access to competent, caring role models who can help improve problem-solving and communication skills, and promote self-esteem. The presence of minority teachers may be important not only to provide role models, but as a powerful promotion of mentoring to promote school performance. This is especially the case since blacks and whites seem to have different responses when they encounter obstacles to their schooling, and blacks reported greater obstacles to school success. Blacks' more frequent use of aggressive responses could be linked to frustration over the unequal distribution not only of rewards, but within the formal and informal structures of the school and the absence of black teachers. They may also have different cultural attitudes toward violence. Mentors could mediate this conflict and provide a greater range of responses when obstacles do occur. A good example is Betty Powers's discussion of her second husband's influence:

> He helped me take off the hard angry surface and also you know that fellow helped . . . He showed me how accomplishing a little at a time could get you there eventually. Keep down all the anger; it wasn't until I met him that I became less angry. I used to be angry with the system, I couldn't understand the lackadaisical attitude of legislators. I couldn't understand. I was angry all the time and he helped me see how unhealthy that was . . .

For many of our subjects, teachers carried out such functions.

3. Implications of our findings for schools, colleges, and even companies that consciously recruit, try to retain, and otherwise encourage women, blacks, and other traditionally under-represented populations would suggest that such programs should not assume that what makes these people successful is always the same as what makes anyone successful. The fact that we found differences not only between Pathmakers and Controls, but differentially for blacks and women as well should not be overlooked and cannot be underestimated, given common (and we would argue self-defeating) confusions among status, ethnicity, and gender.

4. Not only do we encourage research that looks at status, ethnicity, and gender in combination as well as separately, we argue that more research needs to consider the influence of the individual's socio-cultural situation on personal and professional development. For example, as to the main distinction between Pathmakers and Controls—their

attribution of success to factors internal to themselves and a correlated internality in the psychological variable of locus of control—we believe more research is crucial to understanding the development and etiology of internality or a sense of personal control. Given the environments in which these subjects were born, the belief that one could still exert control over one's life outcomes must be quite important. For the more advantaged groups, however, an external locus of control in and of itself would not be limiting. Such a person could succeed simply by following paths of least resistance! It is therefore important to consider the additional complication of the interaction of personal styles and resources with the socio-cultural situation in which people are embedded. In certain situations such personality variables might be crucial, but they might not matter in others.

We should also emphasize the socio-historical context of the psychological variables we have addressed. Our subjects were alive for all or part of World War II, and many grew up remembering the Great Depression and the New Deal.[18] They therefore grew up at a time of national commitment and, not unimportant, success at overcoming odds. Thus the internal locus of control that our successful subjects exhibit was itself, to some degree, supported by the historical context of the country in which they were raised. Some of the younger subjects were growing up during the Korean conflict, which was far more ambiguous both in its process and its outcome. The generation that grew up during Vietnam would receive far different kinds of reinforcement. This losing war against an intractable opponent might reinforce externality, a locus of control that would be more crippling for people growing up in the same circumstances as our Pathmakers did. Thus it is a point to ponder whether the kinds of extreme intergenerational mobility we have characterized as belonging to Pathmakers will be as likely for this generation. The countervailing force of the late 1960s is presumably that equal opportunity programs provided opportunities for advancement and greater hope. However, these programs were targeted not toward Pathmakers but toward blacks, other minorities, and women and are as likely to be used by Controls from those categories as by Pathmakers. It is therefore a plausible hypothesis that the phenomena we study will, for that generation at least, become more rare. As a new generation watches the disintegration of the Soviet Union, and the deposing of Communist regimes in Eastern Europe and the former Soviet Union, however, the socio-historical forces may once again shift. We have argued elsewhere (Adler and Harrington, 1970; Harrington, 1979b) that more attention should be paid to situational and historical influences on personality. Ogbu (1974) has specifically argued that his data show the importance of historical factors to the understanding of differences among blacks and other minorities in the United States.

At its most general level, our research suggests that a diversity of psychological traits may lead to similar outcomes, i.e., success. This is a view consistent with the concept of culture, as described by Anthony Wallace (1961), as an organization of diversity. Our subjects are producing similarly successful behaviors but, apparently, for a variety of reasons.

Finally, listening to the stories of these one hundred people we have found reason to agree with an observation of Booker T. Washington: "Success is to be measured, not so much by the position that one has reached in life as by the obstacles overcome while trying to succeed." In this sense, our Pathmakers and Controls are equal on the first variable insofar as they now occupy similar positions in life. But they differ in what they have overcome to get there. Women and blacks each have faced obstacles peculiar to their gender or race. The process of confronting these obstacles is, we believe, ultimately responsible for the somewhat different paths taken to success by our various subjects. Specifically, Pathmakers have had to construct social supports which others did not, which explains our finding that teachers were more important to Pathmakers than Controls, were more dependent upon an internal locus of control in order to succeed, and show a greater acceptance of change than other subjects. In several significant ways the paths taken to success by our Pathmaker subjects are different from Controls, despite the many other characteristics, most notably educational attainment, that they share with other successful people. Since educational attainment is the main route Pathmakers use to level the playing field with Controls as adults, the importance of teachers to children sharing backgrounds with our Pathmakers is doubly critical. For if the teachers are not there, or do not make themselves available, or do not allow themselves to become resources for the child, educational attainment becomes even more problematic for these children. The divergent paths of our subjects are worthy of future study by those broadly interested in how persons and collectivities shape each other, as well as those who would better understand the narrower relationships among education, social stratification, and social mobility in American society.

Appendixes

Notes

References

Index

Appendix A

Interview Procedures

In this appendix we describe the methods of our research—the interviews and their analysis—that generated the data reported in this book.

Interviewers and Procedures

Interviewers were approximately the same age as (at least the youngest of) those to be interviewed, a characteristic we believed to be important for obtaining the serious cooperation of the respondents. In addition to the principal investigators, we hired as interviewers mid-career persons from the fields of psychology and anthropology, as well as several advanced psychology and anthropology doctoral students who fit the age requirement. The interviewers were both male and female, and black and white.

All of the interviews were conducted by two-person teams (with the exception of one cross-country interview due to serious, sudden illness of one of our team members). We first utilized this two-interviewer strategy in our pilot work developing the interview described in this section. We used a team of two interviewers in each interview because two (Gumpert and Harrington) were involved in planning the study and developing the instrument. During this process, we observed that in a four-hour interview it was useful to have two interviewers: one to keep track of making sure everything was covered, the other to concentrate on feedback and encouragement to the subject. We thought that a two-person interview team would help to make the lengthy interview less onerous for the respondent by doubling the possibility of having good rapport with an interviewer. The bulk of the interviewing was done by the authors of this book, either together or with another team member.

In addition to issues of age and status, we also felt it would be useful to make certain that at least one member of the interviewing team was of the same gender and race as the respondent, and two-person teams obviously made that more likely to be achieved. Existing survey research literature is quite ambiguous on these issues. There seems to be a consensus that blacks will give different responses to black interviewers than white interviewers, but the differences are not easy to predict (see Hyman, Cobb, Feldman, Hart, and Stember, 1954; Williams, 1964; and Cannell and Kahn, 1968). There is less consensus that gender affects the outcome, but the absence of consensus that it does not is itself problematic. We had sufficient staff resources to allow us to match gender and ethnicity between interviewers and respondents. In many cases both interviewers shared one variable with the subject. In our view the two-interviewer strategy for life-history research is promising. In future research, we would strengthen it by tightening choices of interviewers—the two interviewers might be unambiguously and systematically matched on the one hand, and mismatched on the other. Our criterion was that one had to be the same race and gender as the respondent. This meant that in interviewing a black female, one interviewer could have been a black male if he were matched with a female, white or black. We would now recommend a design which required a black female as one interviewer, with the second being opposite on both characteristics. The possibility that the presence of a white interviewer would matter for blacks, for example the trend for black males to use less self-deprecating humor, suggests the need for this strategy to improve comparability of all the interviews.

The decision to use two people and the partial matching technique employed relate to fundamental questions about social research. On the one side is the position that you must be female to study a female, or black to study a black. We believe this perspective to be overdrawn and in fact to put an end to most of anthropology if not all of behavioral science. It is the nature of anthropology that the anthropologist be a stranger. This allows questions to be asked that insiders could not venture to ask. On the other hand, neither as anthropologists nor psychologists do we feel that you must be a sociological outsider to study a population (see Merton, 1973 on insiders and outsiders). For readers' reference Harrington was born in New York City, and has been a specialist in psychological anthropology in the urban United States throughout his career. Boardman was born in Philadelphia, and has specialized in the social psychology of conflict management and gender issues in career success. Both are white.

When the rhetoric is removed, the point of this methodological debate is simply that people will say different things to an insider than they will to an outsider, and that this must be taken into account in an adequate research design. We tried to do so by having, at least in some ways, both insider and outsider present, and our strategy enabled us to probe both perspectives during the interview. Certain subjects clearly played to the interviewer with whom they shared the most characteristics with statements such as, "*you* know what I mean". Other subjects played to the other, or non-linked, member. For example, some females virtually ignored the female interviewer and played to the male. A few blacks played to the white member of the team. Certain males played to the female exclusively, no matter what her race. By having both insider and outsider on the team we took away the necessity for subjects to follow only one strategy, and allowed different styles to play out so long as the interview generated the data needed. By sidestepping the need to decide whether or not to match ethnicity and gender, and by choosing to both match and not to match, the technique enabled a productive interview to proceed by allowing the subject to set the style to be followed. The preferred style then was the one that established the best rapport and resulted in the most information shared by each particular subject.

As part of their training, interviewers were interviewed using the instrument by other staff. These (along with the later pre-test interviews) were also used by staff as training opportunities for coding. Since the interviewers were also doing the coding, this meant that each coder was aware of what it was like to be interviewed, and, in many cases, to assess the coding their own interview had generated. The training of coders included extensive review of the theoretical antecedents of the psychological variables to be coded, as well as joint coding to determine the meaning of the main definers of the categories to be coded (described in the Analysis section, below).

When the prospective respondent was first contacted, the purpose of the research was fully explained, and the general nature and length of the interview was described. The interview is indeed a long one—it takes three to five hours—and we believe it is preferable to conduct it with willing and informed subjects. The study is, of course, biased in unknown ways by the fact that these 100 people were all willing to talk with us. The people who turned us down after a personal discussion had shown they were likely to fit our criteria, and were not observed to differ in any external way from those who participated, i.e., were not reportedly more or less successful, younger or older, etc. The reasons given for not participating varied, with lack of time and other commitments heading the list. Occasionally other—perhaps more central—reasons emerged: we will always remember the subject, whose name is a household word to most, who agreed to participate in the study, and then called the day before the interview to say that he had decided it was going to be one of those "who did you knife to get where you are" interviews and (despite our assurances that this was not the case) that his interests would be better served by withdrawing. Only this one respondent, however, explicitly used the possible content of the interview as an excuse for not participating. Respondents were assured of the confidentiality of the data, and the means we chose to protect their anonymity were explained.

The interview was conducted in a private place chosen by the respondent, where he or she felt comfortable discussing autobiographical material: often in the respondent's home, office, or an equally comfortable and private place provided by the interviewing team. We placed the priority on the comfort and preference of the respondent. The cost was that we could not obtain comparable data on the respondent's home or office based on interviewer observations. Our intuitive notions of what such differences might be reflect gender differences, not Pathmaker/Control or race differences. That is, women's offices, and the treatment accorded us in them, seemed to take the interviewer's comfort into account more often than men's offices with respect to their hospitality. Except when necessary we expected to avoid the respondent's office as a site for the interview during regular business hours. Our concern was that there would be interruptions. When the rule was broken due to subject's preference (really insistence), interruptions were not a problem (we had underestimated the power at the top to control access), and the rule was dropped. In only two instances were significant interruptions allowed by subjects: both were emergencies.

According to the persons who have participated in our research, the interview we devised was interesting and stimulating to the respondent. It began with a re-statement on the part of the interviewing team of the purposes of the research, and an explanation of the structure of the interview. The respondent was told that the structure served primarily as a guide for the interviewers who would not ordinarily interrupt the respondent's narrative flow, except to obtain clarification or additional information about points of particular interest. In retrospect, more attention must be given to ensuring that all the material is covered in each interview, hopefully without compromising spontaneity. Many tables are characterized by missing data for small numbers of subjects. This was a result of our decision to go with the subject's "flow" to encourage spontaneity and reduce redundancy. Some teams developed more liberal interpretations as to whether or not something had already been covered, and by choosing not to return to the topic this optimism sometimes resulted in an inability of our coders to later retrieve comparable information in such cases. While we think it fruitful not to anticipate with whom the subject will establish rapport, we do think that there should be a clear decision ahead of time as to who is responsible for monitoring whether questions have been spontaneously answered. If the subject turns out to prefer one interviewer—to insist on eye contact, exhibit signs of discomfort toward the other interviewer— a shift of the responsibility can take place.

Analysis

The interviews were all tape-recorded, and notes were taken by the interviewers. The tapes were transcribed verbatim, and these materials together were content analyzed for the variables discussed in this volume. While audiotape was used, in future research we would consider using videotape. This would be useful for interviewer training, but would also allow for more accurate coding of psychological variables by allowing coders to see nonverbal gestures. A cost, as yet unknown, of such a procedure would be its inhibitory effect on subject spontaneity.

Psychological coding judgments were made by social and clinical psychologists, or psychological anthropologists with relevant assessment experience. For the psychological material (personality variables and defenses), coding was done by listening to the audiotape at the same time the written transcripts of the interview were read. This allowed the coders to hear the inflections which often gave meaning to the written work. The transcripts were also marked for correction at this stage, but since the priority was on the coding, transcripts were re-verified by a later reading solely for that purpose. A seven-point coding scale (ranging from "absent" to "strong") was used for each of the variables described in Chapter 2. The four major points on the scale were defined as follows: if evidence of the psychological theme was pervasive in the subject's life, characterizing many thoughts, responses, and approaches, it was coded as being strong. If the theme was present, characterizing frequent responses and approaches but not pervasive, it was coded moderate. Weak ratings were given in instances in which the psychological theme was present in only a few responses and approaches; otherwise an absent coding was given. Three intermediate points on the scale (strong-moderate, moderate-weak, and weak-absent) separated these major points. Each protocol was coded twice and Intercoder reliability for ratings used in this book were .79 or better; coding divergences were all resolved between the original two coders.

Since psychological attributes are subject to development and change throughout life, the burden of the interview and its interpretation was even greater for these variables. An alternative would have been to use normed instruments to directly assess them. While we are persuaded that using normed tests gains us little for our research design on such an extraordinary population, and would raise additional practical obstacles, they could have facilitated comparisons with other research. More confirmatory designs than ours could use such instruments— accepting the cost that some subjects may not "sit still" for them. It was our judgment that subjects at this level of success would not sit still for standardized instruments. Further, since the population is exceptional, we felt little would be gained by a normed instrument. However, enough subjects might have submitted to allow partial use of such instruments, even though those who agreed would probably not be typical of the cohort as a whole. The standardized test results for only a part of our sample would have enabled us to assess the construct validity of our own psychological coding for these variables by comparing our interview coding judgments and the instruments. This would have enabled us to assess, for example, how strong our category "strong internal locus of control" was in terms of nationwide samples. In the end we felt the costs outweighed the benefits and we decided not to use standardized tests.

Life history material (number and types of jobs, number of children, school history, etc.) was coded separately from the psychological material. Each transcript and the notes of the interviewers were coded by staff not involved in the psychological coding for that subject, who were also blind to the Pathmaker status of the subject. These coders used only written material to record life history material, and did not listen to the tapes, as this coding task was more clerical.

The code book used followed the variable order of the interview, and was created by a preliminary scanning of twenty-four interviews, selected from the longest conducted, to exemplify the material which would be expected. The codes included "laundry lists" of responses, as well as judgments requiring the coder to summarize, for example, whether accounts of success were predominantly internal or external, or interpretive codings in which a number of responses could be considered, for example, tolerance for hard work. The codings were then finalized and put into a format which could be entered into a computer program for analysis.

Whenever appropriate, analyses included log-linear analysis, chi square and Fisher tests of association, analysis of variance, and corelational analyses. For the psychological data additional analyses included factor analysis for the defenses, and multiple discriminant analysis to order the material presented in Chapter 8.

Selectivity of college data was gathered from college guidebooks from the time our median-aged subjects would have been in college. The undergraduate college attended was coded from 0 to 5 with 5 being the most selective.

The process of selection of subjects for detailed presentation in this book is described in the text. After the quantitative results were clear and the early draft of these findings had been prepared, these transcripts were read repeatedly by the authors, who marked the text with symbols showing to which findings the text related. The text selections were then made by inserting all the relevant materials in the text for each individual separately, then reducing and editing these materials down for clarity, to eliminate redundancy, and to improve the flow of the presentation. When subjects failed to exemplify the finding, this was noted in the text or in the notes, and sometimes quotes are provided as well. By and large, however, the quotes provided exemplify the findings.

A final point of data analysis: the reader is reminded that the research reported here is more exploratory than confirmatory. The in-depth study of people's lives severely limits the number of people who can be examined. Since the purpose of this study was not to test hypotheses, but rather to probe the usefulness of existing theory to generate hypotheses for future study, most of our findings are not presented in terms of hypothesis testing but rather descriptively. It was necessary, however, to lay out some ground rules for when we recognize a difference between Pathmakers and Controls strong enough to report. In a hypothesis-testing study we would describe this as a decision about where to set alpha. Given the exploratory nature of our research and the size of our sample, in such a study it would make sense to set alpha at the high end of traditional levels, specifically at $p<.05$. Convention allows the reporting of distributions whose probability of occurring by chance was somewhat greater than .05 but less than .10 as "trends." We have used these guidelines to help us determine when a difference is significant. That is, we will only describe as different distributions which in more confirmatory research would have achieved these levels of significance.

Of course, given that there are more variables than subjects in our study, a certain number of comparisons would reach significance levels by chance alone. We do not see this as being as much of a problem in exploratory research as it would be in a confirmatory design. What we have done, until more confirmatory designs can be carried out, is to limit ourselves to reporting findings showing differences that can be contextualized or triangulated with other findings from our own study, or with other findings in the existing literature for these variables on comparable subjects, and to suspect idiosyncratic findings which cannot be so supported.

Appendix B

INTERVIEW SCHEDULE

The questions served as guidelines for the interviewer rather than questions to be asked in a fixed order. We intended to achieve an open interview format with sufficient probing to obtain the necessary information.

I. Biographical material: Place and date of birth; parents' occupation; marital status; ages of children; wife's or husband's occupation; estimate of original and present socioeconomic status.

II. Employment, including general issues about the relationship between the respondent and his/her work.

1. History of employment: What was your first job? Next job, etc.? (The remainder of the questions in this section were repeated for each job/position.) Exactly how did you obtain the job/position? What network or institutional supports were available? What obstacles emerged, and how were they overcome? How satisfying was it: Did you dislike anything about the job, and did you make any attempt to change that? How?
2. How did your job decisions come about? Who and what influenced career decisions? Was your family of origin influential or supportive? How?
3. Attitudes regarding responsibility in jobs/positions: Were there differences from one job to another in degree of responsibility involved? How did you respond?
4. Preferred work atmosphere and relations with co-workers: How do you get along with subordinates, colleagues, and bosses?
5. In case of problems, disagreements, or conflicts in jobs, how do you deal with them? Was there any difference among handling of conflicts with boss, co-workers, and subordinates?

6. What has been most satisfying about your work? What factors have made your work particularly difficult?

7. Have there been events or persons that have been particularly influential in your career?

8. Were you consciously aware of learning to behave in ways that might facilitate upward mobility (dress, speech, etc.)?

9. Have there been failures in work or career that you consider particularly difficult?

10. How do you feel about retirement? Have any plans been made?

11. Where do you feel you are heading? What are your long-term career goals?

III. Schooling History

1. Parents' and siblings' education: Were there any striking differences between their education and your education? How do you account for differences?

2. Types and locations of schools: Is minority/socioeconomic status a factor in each?

3. How good were you at school subjects? In what subjects did you excel? Like? Do poorly? Dislike?

4. Did you like school in general? What were your feelings about the teachers? Were any obstacles to mobility encountered, such as prejudice or discrimination? How were these overcome?

5. How did your teachers feel about you?

6. How did your family feel about school and school performance/achievement?

7. Was anyone particularly important in encouraging your efforts in school?

8. How did you get along with peers at school? How did you and your peers feel about one another?

9. Did you have any extracurricular activities? Hobbies? How was leisure and vacation time spent?

10. Were any changes in schooling history experienced in college? Graduate/professional school?

11. Did you date in high school? College? What were your dating patterns?

IV. Family and Community of Origin

1. Who were the most significant figures/influences in your childhood (inside or outside nuclear family)? In what way were they significant?

2. How do you characterize the way you were raised?
3. Was your family traditional with respect to sex-role socialization? How?
4. How do you characterize the "atmosphere" at home during childhood, and your own response to it?
5. How about the neighborhood you primarily grew up in? What was it like? Was it integrated? Ethnically heterogeneous?
6. What role did religion play in your family? What are your feelings about religion now? (What role, if any, does it play in present life?)
7. Did the composition of your family change as you grew up? How so?
8. When did you leave home, and under what circumstances?
9. Do you see your family now? How frequently?
10. Do you ever return to the place where you grew up? What feelings are generated about seeing those places/people?

V. Current Family

1. Describe your first marriage. What happened with other ones, if any?
2. How do members of your current family share work and responsibilities?
3. Can you describe your husband/wife? Tell me a bit about him/her.
4. To what extent and how has your spouse been helpful in your career?
5. What are your children like?
6. How do you handle/resolve disagreements with your spouse and children?
7. When your child misbehaves, what happens?
8. How do you spend leisure time now? How are vacations spent? With whom? How often?

VI. Health

1. How would you describe your health? Have there been any significant changes? How did you deal with them?
2. What about your eating, smoking, drinking, medication-taking patterns? Do you sleep well? Do you have an exercise routine, such as jogging?
3. Do you become upset/angry/depressed? How do you deal with it? What usually precipitates it? What are your big worries?

4. When you have health problems (physical), how are they dealt with? Do you use a physician?
5. When you have problems, do you try to work them out alone, or turn to family? Friends? Professional help?

VII. Psychological/General

1. How do you account for where you are now in life? What part did sheer luck play?
2. Who and what were the significant persons and factors contributing to your success? Who and what hindered it?
3. Who have been your best friends? Do you keep in touch with old friends? What places do friends have in your current life?
4. What do people criticize or find irritating about you? What do people tend to admire?
5. How do you feel about your life overall? What satisfactions and dissatisfactions do you feel with yourself and your life?
6. How do you feel in regard to your accomplishments in your career and personal life?
7. What role has political activity played in your life?
8. Do you have any questions for the interviewers?
9. Do you wish to receive information about the results of our study when they are available?
10. Now that you have been involved in our study, can you recommend anyone else who might be willing to participate?

Notes

Preface

1. The quotes and information are taken from an interview Elders gave to Claudia Dreifus, reported in the *New York Times Magazine*, January 30, 1994.
2. Quoted in Dreifus (1994).
3. *Policy Review*, Fall 1991.
4. The quote and other biographical material in this paragraph are taken from *Current Biography Yearbook*, April 1992, p. 567.
5. The quotes from Elders are from Dreifus (1994).

1. Introduction

1. We used this term in early publications about our study. See Boardman, Harrington, and Horowitz (1987).
2. Stella Chess uses the defiance metaphor in reporting findings of the New York Longitudinal Study, as in her title "Defying the Voice of Doom" (1989).
3. See Garmezy (1983) for an example.
4. See Werner and Smith (1982) for an example.
5. See Anthony (1974).
6. See Felsman and Vaillant (1987).
7. See also Werner and Smith (1992), and Anthony (1974).
8. See, for example, Long and Vaillant (1989).
9. Felsman (1989) is an exception in using resilience metaphors to focus on social factors facing street gamins in Colombia.
10. "Transcenders" or "Surpassers" (of negative predictions) have been suggested to us as labels, and they do carry the implication of obstacles. Another suggestion is the awkward term "overcomers," which would explicitly link them to the ideology of the civil rights movement. We find "odds beaters" awkward as well.
11. Gail Sheehy has already used "pathfinders" for those who survive obstacles in adulthood like divorce and illness.

12. The senior author has investigated the world of work through the study of occupational histories of men who were hospitalized for social and mental problems to see the degree to which downward occupational mobility is a path to, or consequent of, personal disintegration (Harrington and Wilkins, 1966). He has also studied the mental hospitals themselves with their rhetoric of cure and rehabilitation for poorly functioning populations and the reality of their treatment (Harrington, 1970); studied, with others, schools which are supposed to be providing a more equalized opportunity to children from across the spectrum (Harrington, 1973, 1975, 1976; Adler and Harrington, 1970; Gumpert and Harrington, 1972); examined bilingual programs which are specifically designed to improve a child's ability through schooling to compete for resources in the larger English-dominated society (Harrington, 1978); reviewed the processes of migration by which individuals and populations seek geographically to improve their ability to compete for resources (Harrington, 1975, 1979b); and examined political processes by which people might collectively seek to create a more balanced distribution of resources for themselves and for society (Harrington, Adler, and Smith, 1969; Adler and Harrington, 1970; Harrington and Adler, 1971; Harrington, 1973, 1980).

13. Among the most noted is Jencks et al.'s (1972) research. For a useful review of input-output studies of education, see Bridge, Judd, and Moock (1979).

14. See Chapter 3.

15. This pattern was found in pilot interviews for our study, but it was not a pattern for many of our subjects.

16. However, this argument is directly contradicted by the Hispanic migration literature (see Alvarez, 1987) and also work by Leguerre (1987) on Haitian migration to New York City.

17. See Harrington (1979b), Chapter 2.

18. See Sternberg (1988) on triarchical theories of intelligence.

19. See Coleman et al. (1966); Coleman, Hoffer, and Kilgore (1982); Natriello and McDill (1986); Alexander and Pallas (1985); Corwin (1974); and Waller (1965).

20. Harrington (1981) has argued that this tendency to put money into programmatic action and not into research (either to plan or to evaluate) is a peculiarly American trait.

21. Merton (1968) once observed that to whom it was given more would be given, while from whom it was taken more would be taken. He pointed to the multiple positions of successful people, success breeding success, and essentially observed the rich getting richer and the poor poorer.

22. Ryan and Sackrey (1984) is limited to autobiographical essays of white, largely male, academics who come from working class backgrounds. Zweigenhaft and Domhoff (1991) is limited to thirty-eight interviews with black men

and women from low income families; most are successful, some are not. The study was intended to assess the effectiveness of "A Better Choice," a program designed to select such low income blacks into prestigious prep schools.

2. *Personal Resources*

1. Garmezy attributes this quotation to Robert Louis Stevenson.

2. For a useful review of the literature on interpersonal approaches to psychoanalysis, see Lionells, Fiscalini, Mann, and Stern (1995).

3. See Grey (1993) for a thorough and useful elaboration of differences between interpersonal and endogenous perspectives of self.

4. Particularly notable is work by Anthony (1972); Anthony and Koupernik (1974); Becker (1973, 1976); Garmezy (1975a, 1975b); Gould (1972); Levinson et al. (1978); Lifton (1976); and Vaillant (1975, 1976, 1977).

5. See Gumpert, Thibaut, and Shuford (1961); and Canavan-Gumpert (1977).

6. The work on achievement motivation has been criticized by Canavan-Gumpert, Garner, and Gumpert (1978), and Entwisle (1972) on a variety of conceptual and methodological grounds. We are nevertheless persuaded that there is much of interest in this large and highly diverse body of research.

7. We should note that research on the questionnaire measure of locus of control devised by Rotter and his colleagues indicates that respondents' ideas about the degree to which people in general have control over what happens to them are best viewed as distinct from their ideas about the extent to which they themselves have control, and that most of the research findings relate particularly to personal locus of control rather than to more general control ideology. Due to this research tradition, as well as to the fact that we believe personal locus of control to be more germane to our research, we define locus of control for this study as personal.

8. See, for example, Werner and Smith (1982, 1992); Farrington (1993); Felsman (1989); and Garmezy (1981).

9. There is also a link with attribution theory to which we shall return in Chapter 9.

10. Riesman et al. (1950) suggested a trichotomy: tradition-directed persons, other-directed persons, and inner-directed persons. The meaning of Riesman's original distinctions has been partially lost. From the perspective of these investigators, tradition-directed persons were seen as highly fearful and dependent on tradition for a basic sense of comfort and security. Other-directed persons were seen as tending strongly to conform to the values and adopt the standards of those around them, while inner-directed people were seen as responsive to (or rather conforming to) rules and principles rather than persons.

11. See especially Murphy (1962, 1976). For a useful and concise review relating classic theories of defense to more modern ego and self perspectives see Cohler (1987).

12. The conceptual overlap between ego-defense mechanisms and certain so-called "cognitive styles" such as Byrne's (1964) distinction between "repressors" and "sensitizers" is considerable; it is as easy to see the similarity between "sensitization" as a coping style and "anticipation" as an ego defense as it is to note that the term "repression" has the same general meaning in both theoretical contexts. Similar parallels can be shown with other notions about coping styles.

13. For example, of the self-report measures of ego defenses currently in existence, most are usually limited to a very few defenses; the ones most frequently studied have been denial, rationalization, and projection (see a review by Plutchik, Kellerman, and Conte, 1979).

14. See Haan (1982).

15. In 1967, Vaillant became associated with the "Grant Study," a major longitudinal study of Harvard College undergraduates begun in 1937 by Henry Murray, Arlie Bock, and others. Participants in the study were selected because they were deemed particularly promising, sound, stable young men. The more than 260 Harvard men so chosen over a period of five years were tested and interviewed extensively during their college years, and were then followed up periodically during the thirty years between their graduation and the mid-1970s. Vaillant randomly selected a sub-sample of about half of the men who had graduated from the last three classes studied (1942–1944) and conducted an extensive interview of these ninety-four men to assess the quality of their adjustment as adults (including career, family and other interpersonal relations; physical and psychological health; their career and general life satisfaction; their ego-defense preferences; and the quality of adjustment of their children). We note that while these men came from socioeconomically heterogeneous backgrounds, none of them were black or Hispanic, and probably few, if any, of these Harvard men would meet our background criteria for Pathmakers.

16. Among the thirty men whose life outcomes (as indicated by Vaillant's adult adjustment scale) were judged to be the worst, the psychotic defenses (delusional projection, denial, and psychotic distortion) and the immature defenses (projection, schizoid fantasy, hypochondriasis, passive-aggressive behavior, and acting-out) were relatively frequent—over 20 percent of the codable defenses in their interview protocols were in these categories. Only slightly more than 20 percent of the codable defenses in the interview protocols of men in this "worst outcome" group were in the "mature" category (which includes humor, anticipation, altruism, suppression, and sublimation). In dramatic contrast, the codable defenses in the group of thirty men whose life outcomes were judged "best" included only 2 or 3 percent defenses in the

"immature" category and nearly 45 percent in the "mature" category. Defenses that would be categorized as "neurotic" (dissociation, reaction formation, repression, intellectualization, and displacement) appeared about equally frequently in both groups.

17. Vaillant's recent work has extended his work on defense mechanisms to at-risk populations making use of a research cohort of inner city youth now in their late forties (Vaillant, 1993; Long and Vaillant, 1989). The focus of his research, like the research on resiliency, is on who makes it and who doesn't.

18. At least some of the Pathmakers may well resemble the surprisingly invulnerable children of schizophrenic parents and other extreme forms of adversity studied by Anthony (1972); Anthony and Koupernik (1974); Garmezy, and others (Garmezy, 1975a, 1975b; Garmezy and Devine, 1977). We will return to this in Chapter 9.

19. See, for example, Vaillant (1993), Chapter 4. The point is also discussed in Cohler (1987). However a fruitful area for future research the malleability of defenses may be, our study was not designed to address this point since our method is not longitudinal. We do discuss in Chapter 9 how this issue may affect the interpretation of our data.

20. See Stacey (1967), Klein and Riviere (1964), and Klein (1948).

21. It could also be argued that marginality might free the individual from his past and help ease the mobility. As John Cumming once suggested in a conversation, there have been few studies of the positive consequences of being neurotic. In Chapter 8 we will consider how ours may fill the gap.

3. The Study Design

1. When we say poor by local definition, we indicate that even in a community with a low SES by national standards, for example, rural Appalachia, our subjects would have been poor compared to the norm in that community.

2. This is a somewhat more stringent standard than requiring only that one parent not be a high school graduate. For the reasons just given, and also given possible gender links to educational attainment in which children might differentially identify with an educated parent based on gender, we felt that neither parent was a more severe but conceptually purer test.

3. A small number of academic physicians, or lawyers active in government, academia, or business were included in these other relevant categories.

4. The presence of some subjects lacking just one criterion might have allowed us to assess whether parental education or occupation is contributing most to the findings differentiating Pathmakers from Controls. After completing our research, however, we felt that there were insufficient numbers available. In future research we might clarify definitions so that it would be possible to isolate effects of poverty and parental education by examining each

variable separately and not by combining them into one index for either Path-makers or comparisons.

5. Rutter (1979, 1983) reported about 10 percent of his study of invulnerable offspring of psychotics exhibited genuine "creativity," for example. Those who are able to achieve the level of mobility studied here and construct successful careers would be a fraction of that.

6. See Dollard (1935) on this point, and Langness and Frank (1981) for a good review of life history research.

7. No more than two subjects could come from any one source for each of the occupational domains selected.

8. Although one subject, Bernie Clark (see the end of this chapter for a description of him), was a veteran of the Korean war, and reported that GI bill benefits helped him complete college.

9. A later stage of our research, still to be conducted, is designed to accomplish two aims that the present study was unable to accomplish: (1) to provide, via larger, more representative samples and additional Controls, evidence relating to the tentative assertions generated in this stage; and (2) to extend our findings to other ethnic groups of interest.

10. There is a national society whose headquarters are in New York City's Rockefeller Center that is devoted to the cultivation and perpetuation of the story of Horatio Alger! Felsman and Vaillant (1987) link the study of "invulnerability" to Horatio Alger themes that one is solely responsible for one's own progress.

11. With alpha set so that $p < .05$ is the cutoff; $p < .05$, but $> .10$ will constitute a "trend."

12. Adequate disguising of exemplary narratives in published work, however, can only be achieved if great care is exercised, as we have tried to do with the quotes included here. The tension for us in disguising any material is to retain enough to make it useable for the reader. If we call a physicist a lawyer to disguise her identity, we also do violence to the career line one would expect, or the nature of the rewards experienced. We rejected "composite" presentations since they would do violence to the presentation of each person as a life which must be understood in its own terms. So we changed as little as possible, but still protected the identity of the subject in ways that would be generally acceptable to social scientists reporting this type of research.

4. Family Resources

1. See Whiting and Edwards (1988), Chapter 2.

2. Wanda Perkins reports idealizing her father after he left: "I had always fantasized that my father must be a good person and he must be out there

looking for us somewhere. [Her mother] had destroyed most pictures of him, but I found a few, and I thought he was this marvelous good-looking Italian, tall man." She wrote him by cadging the address off a package he sent to her mother [for her] and lived with him for almost a year when she fled from home. Of her first meeting with him she reports disillusionment: "So I did meet him and I was really a little turned off by him. He wasn't tall, he was short. He was chunky, and he had sweaty hands, and he wanted to kiss me all the time, and hug me, and I mean no one has ever hugged me around the house. And this was just terribly offensive. And he was crying, and for a man to cry, I mean . . . I just thought it was terrible."

3. Her fondest remembrance of a work environment in academia was working with graduate students in large collaborative research projects in which both faculty and students participated.

4. The second was when his college sweetheart was killed right after they graduated from college.

5. $X^2(1, n = 25) = 5.24, p < .025$.

6. $X^2(1, n = 29) = 4.88, p < .05$.

7. $X^2(1, N = 98) = 5.3, p < .025$; and $X^2(1, n = 59) = 6.29, p < .025$ respectively.

8. However, Bonnie Carter's mother was a housewife until two years ago, "after the kids were up and out," when she "rejoined the work force."

9. $X^2(1, N = 83) = 8.84, p < .005$.

10. The degree of family disintegration of Wanda Perkins is unusual in our sample.

11. We will discuss later in this chapter what educational and occupational success siblings had compared to our subjects.

12. $F(1, 99) = 7.53, p < .01$. These differences probably reflect class differences in the larger society.

13. $X^2(1, n = 58) = 6.33, p < .025$.

14. $X^2(1, n = 49) = 4.42, p < .05$.

15. The quote exemplifies themes of power and reward orientation which characterize Wendy throughout her life—see Chapter 8.

16. $X^2(1, n = 48) = 5.41, p < .025$.

17. There were no SES differences between white and black Pathmakers, thanks to our sampling frame. Nor did blacks in the overall sample come from poorer neighborhoods than the white subjects. While it is indeed very difficult to obtain comparability on financial and status differences between these two categories, in view of these facts we do not see a somewhat greater resource redundancy for white as opposed to black Pathmakers to be an explanation for this finding. Further, there were no differences in use of earnings from early jobs among the blacks and whites in the comparison groups.

18. Bernie Clark's mother, for example, was a teacher in the South when he was growing up, but left teaching after the divorce for a waitress job in the North because it paid more money.

19. $X^2(1, n = 37) = 4.85, p < .05$. Support was defined as having high expectations, encouraging and actively helping the subjects. Wendy Cassetta was an exception: when she was asked if her parents "pushed education," she said, "Yes, yes they did. My mother, I think most people thought, would [as a teacher], but it's really my father, though, that had more of a mark on me because of the fact that as a leader in [our ethnic] community and a very traditional male, he felt very strongly about women's education. [He] not only made a difference with my sister and myself, but for a whole generation of women in [our community] because my father was just adamant about his friends' . . . sending their daughters to college."

Also an exception was Wanda Perkins whose mother "never wanted either of us [her sister] to go to school. She thought we ought to be putting our money into the household and so get jobs. Going to school was frivolous and that's what communists do. There was always this whole set of names she called the enemy and we were the enemy. I mean school was always important to me, I had always done well, I liked going . . . Maybe it was an escape for me."

20. $X^2(1, N = 90) = 7.30, p < .01$.

21. $F(1, 97) = 4.07, p < .05$.

22. $X^2(1, N = 98) = 5.18, p < .025$.

23. $X^2(1, N = 98) = 6.97, p < .01$.

24. $X^2(1, n = 47) = 6.34, p < .025$. Bonnie Carter is somewhat different from the typical black female Control: She said now she seldom went to church, but then added: "I'm at the place where I want to get back to church, but I'm not sure which church I want to get back to."

25. Wanda Perkins said, "I don't participate in organized religion. I think I got pretty turned off. I've been recently active in a Unitarian church . . . I kind of flit in and out. I still think I'm a fairly religious person in terms of a core of beliefs that I have, though."

26. $F(1, 92) = 4.52, p < .05$.

27. Four of Bob Price's siblings died in childhood "for a lack of proper medical attention," another concomitant of rural poverty.

28. Since these are self-reported data, we must consider an explanation that female Pathmakers and male Controls are more likely to see their siblings as equals while female Controls and male Pathmakers are more likely to elevate themselves over their siblings.

29. Male Pathmakers and female Controls are similar in their stronger use of dissociation, anticipation, and repression.

30. The finding is even stronger when white males are excluded [$X^2(1, n = 65) = 9.43, p < .005$.], because, interestingly, the white male Controls

report less current contact than the other Controls [$X^2(1, n = 33) = 8.00$, $p < .01$]. The white male Controls could be interpreted as reacting against too close an identification—i.e., an attempt to distinguish themselves as individuals from their own successful fathers.

31. $F(1, 86) = 5.62, p < .02$.

32. $X^2(1, N = 84,) = 5.44, p < .025$. Wanda Perkins won't return home: "No, I don't see my mother, nor the two boys. There are some problems, some unfinished business I have with that. She's still alive."

33. $X^2(1, N = 90) = 35.77, p < .001$.

5. Education and Schooling

1. Research on literacy carried out in the Institute for Urban and Minority Education by Denny Taylor would argue that these family variables do not predict less support of school in specific black families in the Northeast, however. She reports very low SES families, often having only one parent, which provide enormous support for schooling and childhood literacy. We must once again be chary of predictions based on aggregate data in understanding the specific populations under study (Taylor and Dorsey-Gaines, 1988).

2. Eighteen of the subjects reported one parent as a negative influence on their schooling: four were Controls, fourteen were Pathmakers. In most cases these were offset by a parent who was a positive influence.

3. College guides from the time of their college attendance were used to assess this variable. The scales obtained showed Pathmaker/Control differences ($p < .05$).

4. They did interact in a trend for black Pathmakers to attend less selective schools than the other categories combined, however.

5. As we will see in Chapter 8, the first part of this quote also exemplifies the fact that Pathmakers were more likely to report a need to "pay back" people, communities, and institutions with which they feel affinity, and such institutions who accept Pathmakers might therefore expect the loyalty shown by Pathmakers such as Wes Parker. It was in college that Wes set the goals for his life that he describes in Chapter 8.

6. There is reinforcement for our argument in a trend for the most re-source-redundant group, white male Controls, to be less likely to mention teachers than white female Controls.

7. $X^2(1, n = 57) = 6.01, p < .025$.

8. This can be related to Loury's cultural capital argument in Chapter 1, but remember that all our subjects are successful.

9. Apparently it was useful, in light of her comments in Chapter 6 about being an "insider" at the time of the interview who was clearly a member of the "establishment."

10. But a cultural capital point of view might find the fact that Pathmakers attended less selective colleges and less often attended private colleges to somewhat impede its development, relative to Controls. Yet Pathmakers became successful nonetheless.

11. $X^2(1, N = 112) = 10.41, p < .005$. More than one obstacle could be reported by each subject.

12. "High yellow" refers to someone socially classed as black who has a light complexion and is upper to upper middle class.

13. It is unclear whether or not Wanda Perkins was aware of the sexism in her teachers channeling females into teaching, but what is clear is that she was docile in following the path they set. Working harder as a response to obstacles may be, for white female Pathmakers, a combination of needing the teacher more and seeing the system as fair and just, possibly because their teachers were also likely to be white females.

14. Fisher's exact test, $n = 23, p < .01$.

15. $X^2(1, N = 100) = 6.65, p < .01$.

16. As we said before, and discuss in more detail in Chapter 8, black males scored higher in Need for Power than the others studied. Perhaps the family support of education combined with this need to suggest educational attainment as a route to power, even though their concern with power resulted in a greater "distance" from school teachers than the female subjects who were not as concerned with power.

6. Work and Careers

1. He provides a good example of the depth of resources typifying the Controls, which he describes as black middle-class tradition.

2. These quotes (for Bonnie Carter and Bernie Clark) suggest their families had a more corporate orientation, but not the necessity reported by black Pathmakers.

3. $X^2(1, n = 32) = 4.8, p < .05$.

4. Being more likely to create jobs may also reflect Pathmakers' greater sense of internal control (see Chapter 8).

5. Spiralism is now interacting with his need for power.

6. Control males were stronger on long-term planning than Pathmakers (see Chapter 8).

7. Fisher's exact test, $n = 14, p < .025$. Other reasons for leaving jobs showed no Pathmaker differences: better opportunity (56 percent), to enter graduate school (12 percent), fired (5 percent), family reasons (4 percent), or because of the people (2 percent).

8. As he ages, Bob Price is starting to become less cost-oriented (when he

made his move to the first bank he asked for a thirty-day guarantee of salary in case he didn't work out!) and more overtly achievement-oriented—psychological themes to which we shall return in Chapter 8.

9. $X^2(1, n = 50) = 6.59, p < .025$.

10. That the finding is not as strong for the male Pathmakers is perhaps linked to the greater likelihood of their being in stable marriages (see Chapter 7).

11. Remember, as discussed in Chapter 5, this was also true for obstacles reported to school success.

12. $X^2(1, n = 44) = 9.03, p < .01$.

13. $X^2(1, N = 73) = 12.36, p < .001$.

14. We have reported in Chapter 5 that such processes were also said to be important to educational success by these same subjects. It is interesting to note that 39 percent of Pathmakers and 33 percent of Controls volunteered that it was a teacher or former teacher who influenced their career decisions.

15. For example, Betty Powers said: "I did have people I admired but they were not, their encouragement was not on a sustained basis, like you ought to do this, or you ought to do this, or when are you going to do this . . . I've always been encouraged by someone in the environment all the time, at every level, but I don't have a mentor. I've always had a strong inner spirit." Later in the interview, however, she refers to a teacher as a mentor, and credits her current husband with being a major influence on her current career. Still later she talks about various people (national politicians she thought successful) who have helped her believe she could have an effect: "You know you really can't get up off that chair and go do anything until you believe it's going to have some meaning and purpose." So despite her disavowal, consistent with her personality, she was coded as reporting mentors and others influential to her career.

16. These data are interesting when compared with (1987) Census Bureau studies (*The New York Times*, September 20, 1987: p. 28) that show that businesses owned by women and white men are most likely to be without minority employees. The study, financed by the Minority Business Development Agency and the Small Business Administration, did not cover large corporations, but found that only 2.5 percent of black-owned businesses had no minority employees, while 48.3 percent of companies owned by women had no minority employees, virtually the same as the 52.1 percent of the white male–owned companies who reported no minority workers. We cannot tell the minority status of these women. Women were, however, least likely to own businesses with no female employees (10.4 percent), while 20.8 percent of white male–owned businesses had no women, virtually the same as the 21.5 percent of the black-owned businesses without women.

17. $X^2(1, N = 97) = 9.21, p < .005$.

18. In Chapter 8 we describe black males as being stronger in Need for Power than any of the other categories.

19. She also knows its limits: "And sometimes it is to recognize that you've gone as far as you can and that you have to catch it another time."

20. $X^2(1, n = 40) = 6.14, p < .05$.

21. $X^2(1, n = 56) = 6.09, p < .05$.

22. $X^2(1, n = 21) = 6.39, p < .025$.

23. $X^2(1, N = 35) = 4.73, p < .05$.

24. These attitudes are very consistent with the psychological differences (for example, locus of control) we discuss in Chapter 8.

25. See Harrington and Flaxman, in press, for a presentation of research on related issues.

7. *Spouses, Children, Friends, and Health*

1. Betty Powers remarried, but Pathmakers typically did not.

2. "Married, now not" and "now married but not to first spouse" were intermediate steps.

3. $F(1, 99) = 11.68, p < .001$.

4. One told us he was gay and chose to lead a lifestyle which was characterized by a succession of intense but short-term relationships.

5. Sixty-eight percent of those previously married but not at the time of the interview were women and 32 percent were men; but the difference was perhaps attributable to the finding for Pathmaker women.

6. $F(1, 90) = 18.83, p < .001$.

7. Given the ages of our subjects, it may be that women were more pressured to get married when relationships became serious. Bonnie Carter suggested that in her comment about her marriage.

8. This difference in how Pathmakers describe their spouses may be related to our finding reported in Chapter 8 that Pathmakers were more likely to credit themselves for their own accomplishments.

9. Wendell Curtis is an exception to these patterns: his wife works and he also enjoys housework and cooking: "I do at least my fifty percent share—I do sixty percent of my share of household tasks. I like to cook. When I'm home on weekends, I probably cook as much or more than she does. Housework to me is a catharsis. I run the vacuum, do all that kind of stuff. She hates it. So we have a cleaning lady who comes twice a week. But if she can't come because she's on vacation, I do more of it."

10. $X^2(1, N = 68) = 4.83, p < .05$.

11. Apparently the support he reported for her career earlier in this chapter was not intended to redo this priority. Also, later in this chapter we report that

the black female subjects told us that their spouses were not supportive of their careers. We wonder what Bob Price's wife would tell us.

12. She also left home later.

13. $X^2(1, N = 37) = 6.92, p < .01$.

14. Of course, the first also gave her more to be angry about.

15. $X^2(1, N = 67) = 6.20, p < .025$.

16. Fisher's exact test, $n = 25, p < .025$.

17. $F(1, 80) = 7.78, p < .01$.

18. $F(1, 80) = 4.90, p < .05$.

19. This was certainly not true for Bob Price's wife, who he felt was helpful despite her career.

20. Note also that at age sixteen the son asked his father for a new car for his birthday, and received it.

21. $F(1, 90) = 10.87, p < .001$.

22. Her married brother has no children either, and her parents are "dying for grandchildren."

23. Or women would delay their careers until after child-raising, a pattern not found as much in this sample since the women overall were younger than the men.

24. See our discussion about psychological defenses in the next chapter for findings relating to his assertion.

25. We think this is related to the finding reported in Chapter 8 that Pathmakers are stronger in internal locus of control.

26. It is worth noting that his father died of a sudden stroke when he was three years older than Wendell Curtis at the time of the interview, so avoidance of this risk cannot be treated lightly.

27. It is perhaps the more internal locus of control of the Pathmakers that accounts for the Control/Pathmaker differences (see Chapter 8).

8. *The Psychology of Unusual Success*

1. See Shweder (1991).

2. Nor did she take the job.

3. Five percent were judged to be equally oriented to both rewards and costs.

4. Seven of these were judged as being equal in their orientations to internal/external factors.

5. Eight were judged to be equal in inner/other direction.

6. We did a post hoc analysis of the relative contribution of the different variables to an understanding of what might differentiate Pathmakers from Controls. Utilizing a multiple discriminant function analysis we derived the relative strength of the variables reviewed here in differentiating them, and we

will discuss the variables in that order. Since the data do not conform to the assumptions of that test, we do not use the results of that analysis for any other purpose except the heuristic one just described.

7. We had three separate measures relating to internal/external locus of control: two separate judgments for internality and externality themes in the life history, and then a summary judgment on which of the two themes was stronger for each individual. The first two measures varied from strong to absent on a seven-point scale; the second was a trichotomy: internal, external, or equal. The first two measures allowed us to assess the strength of each dimension separately. The third assessed which was dominant in the life of each individual.

8. In fact, she went to a technical high school and a private college not known for academic distinction, and has a doctorate from a good program in a private university.

9. We are unable to further explore the relationship between locus of control and attributions in this study because the variables as measured here are confounded: the attribution question was one variable which could have been considered in the overall locus-of-control coding.

10. $X^2(1, n = 51) = 4.87, p < .05$.

11. $F(1, 99) = 4.36, p < .05$.

12. No significant differences were found for the strength of cost orientation.

13. $F(1, 99) = 5.23, p < .025$.

14. $F(1, 99) = 6.85, p < .01$.

15. $F(1, 99) = 5.07, p < .05$.

16. $F(1, 99) = 6.85, p < .01$.

17. $F(1, 99) = 6.16, p < .025$.

18. $F(1, 99) = 4.73, p < .05$.

19. $F(1, 99) = 5.20, p < .025$.

20. Riesman, Glazer, and Denney (1950) argued that continua were not necessarily linear, but could be curved. The two extremes of a continuum, therefore, can start to look alike in surprising ways.

21. On the other hand many Pathmakers did not report such crippling family circumstances.

22. We performed a factor analysis for all defenses. The first factor, by definition the one controlling the most variance, was clearly interpretable as a continuum of maturity of defenses, with passive-aggressive as the immature pole (.82) and sublimation as the mature pole (–.42). Factor scores were then obtained for subjects by multiplying their scores on each variable by the factor loadings and summing. Vaillant has used a different procedure in his analyses.

23. In the case of a tie the defense with the most Pathmakers coded will go first, in line with our main research focus on the antecedents and consequences of their success. Analyses reported are based upon three-way analyses of variance for each defense discussed.

24. $F(1, 99) = 6.41, p < .025$. We also obtained a trend that Control females were the weakest on intellectualization of all the categories.

25. $F(1, 74) = 6.19, p < .025$.

26. Level IV.

27. $F(1, 68) = 5.05, p < .05$.

28. $F(1, 99) = 4.92, p < .05$.

29. $F(1, 99) = 9.11, p < .005$.

30. $F(1, 68) = 5.05, p < .05$.

31. $F(1, 99) = 5.05, p < .05$.

32. $F(1, 67) = 3.99, p < .05$.

33. $F(1, 67) = 9.08, p < .005$.

34. $F(1, 59) = 5.89, p < .025$. There was a trend that, for males, Pathmakers were stronger on dissociation than the Controls, but for females, Controls were stronger than Pathmakers.

35. $F(1, 99) = 4.24, p < .05$. A trend showed the same pattern for strength of repression when it occurred.

36. $F(1, 38) = 6.18, p < .025$.

37. $F(1, 38) = 5.58, p < .025$.

38. $F(1, 34) = 4.62, p < .05$.

39. Displacement is defined as the redirection of feelings toward a relatively less cared-for object than that arousing the feelings. An example would be a manager who, upset with his wife, is short with his secretary. Since the individual is unaware of the displacement, the defense is unproductive for two reasons: it can lead to trouble with individuals where none existed, and second, it does nothing to deal with the real source of the difficulty. There were no differences regarding the use of displacement.

40. Passive-aggressive behavior is not only an immature defense but a destructive one as well. It involves aggression toward others which is expressed indirectly and ineffectually through passivity, and ultimately toward the self. The underpaid fast food clerk who deliberately slows the level of service, the aggrieved auto worker who delays the line, are engaging in behaviors which exemplify passive-aggressive syndromes. No differences were found.

41. Projection is defined as attributing one's own unacknowledged feelings to others. An immature defense, it can result in serious miscommunication. For example, the individual who projects her own unacknowledged aggressive impulses onto her boss and then acts as if it were her boss who was the aggressive party is in for trouble. Even though projection was coded in only

10 percent of our sample, there was a difference between black and whites suggesting that when it occurred blacks were more likely to use projection than whites ($F(1, 99) = 5.52, p < .05$).

42. No differences were obtained for acting out, defined as the direct expression of an unconscious wish or impulse in order to avoid being conscious of the affect that accompanies it. Engaging in self-destructive drinking, or driving dangerously as expressions of an unconscious need for independence or a way of expressing anger are two examples. Dugan (1989) has argued that for adolescents "acting out," a quite immature defense, has positive functions of trying out things, a kind of practice of alternative roles, which can be growth-producing behaviors linked to resiliency. Our findings would suggest that this pattern, if it exists, would not continue after adolescence, or does not characterize Pathmakers.

43. We have already alerted the reader that fantasy is likely to be underrepresented in our sample due to methodological issues. There was a trend for blacks to be coded for fantasy more than whites.

44. Hypochondriasis is the transformation of reproach toward others into self-reproach and then into complaints of pain or illness that have no basis in physiological fact. All three subjects coded for hypochondriasis were female.

45. This is especially the case for white males.

9. Conclusions and Implications

1. Scarr and McCartney (1983) have stressed that people may make their own environments, or seek out more appropriate environments so as to maximize their ability to function effectively.

2. This may be due in part to age differences, since the men in the sample were slightly older than the women.

3. This is especially true for white males.

4. Although we did not specifically study the self-esteem of our subjects, a number of researchers have discussed the close relationship between an internal locus of control and the development of a higher self-esteem (Murphy, 1976; Deutsch et al., 1992). In fact some researchers have cited successful school attainment as being related to higher self-esteem, as well as being a predictor of positive outcomes (Rutter et al., 1975). In light of this, it is interesting that female Pathmakers reported significantly better school performance than did female Controls.

5. Wallerstein and Blakeslee (1989) also found internal locus of control to be important to children's positive adaptations to the divorce of their parents.

6. Remember, Pathmakers more often came from disintegrated homes (Chapter 4).

7. See Dweck, Hong, and Chiu (1993) and Dweck, Chiu, and Hong (1995a, 1995b).

8. Werner (1993) stresses the importance for resilient girls of having reliable support from a female caregiver, whether mother, grandmother, or older sister.

9. This relationship was especially effective if it was with a parent; remember that although Pathmakers came from significantly more disintegrated homes, many described warm relations with at least one parent. Pathmakers were able to utilize resources other than parents if necessary.

10. This is in contrast with Garmezy's (1974) finding that strong peer relations are important to competence in disadvantaged youths, and Biller's (1974) work which sees peer relations as a source of support for fatherless boys. Peer relations therefore may be important for competence, but may not be adaptive for long-term success by Pathmakers. One reason for this is that the peers of Pathmakers may distract or inhibit them from becoming different, having success orientations, or perhaps even just leaving the community to go to college.

11. See Clark (1983) for more on religion and resilience in black children.

12. More siblings could be seen as a resource on the one hand (greater social support potential), and a drain on the other hand (having to share parental attention, money, etc., with more siblings).

13. These findings are somewhat different than the sex difference reported by Werner (1993), who showed that structure was more important for boys than for girls in Kauai.

14. This flexibility is also reflected in Pathmakers' use of resources outside their immediate families, which we discuss in more detail later.

15. On the other hand, they were also more likely to worry about their futures, although it may be that they were anticipating future changes more than Controls. See the discussion of psychological costs for another view.

16. Indeed there is some evidence in our research that this can happen. Five years after the interview a black male Pathmaker lost his job amid a major financial reversal. A white female Pathmaker was fired after a financial scandal in her firm. Two Pathmakers suffered premature deaths related to stress. Anecdotal though these examples are (our follow-up data are incomplete), we are unaware of any Controls suffering similar fates.

17. *New York Times*, March 11, 1990, A1.

18. See Elder (1986) and Elder, Liker, and Cross (1984) for a discussion of the effect of the Depression on children and parents.

References

Abramson, L. Y., Seligman, M. E. P., and Teasdale, J. D. 1978. Learned help-lessness in humans: Critique and reformulation. *Journal of Abnormal Psychology* 87(1): 49–74.

Adams, B. N. 1968. *Kinship in an urban setting.* Chicago: Markham.

Adler, A. 1930. *Problems of neurosis.* New York: Cosmopolitan Books.

Adler, N., and Harrington, C. 1970. *The learning of political behavior.* Glenview, Ill.: Scott-Foresman.

Alexander, K., and Pallas, A. 1985. School sector and cognitive performance: When is a little a little? *Sociology of Education* 58(2): 115–128.

Alvarez, R. R., Jr. 1987. *Familia: Migration and adaptation in Baja and Alta California, 1800–1975.* Los Angeles: University of California Press.

Anthony, E. J. 1972. Primary prevention with school children. In H. H. Barten and L. Bellak, eds., *Progress in community mental health*, vol. 2 (pp. 131–158). New York: Grune and Stratton.

——— 1974. The syndrome of the psychologically invulnerable child. In E. J. Anthony and C. Koupernik, eds., *The child in his family: Children at psychiatric risk.* International Yearbook, vol. 3. New York: John Wiley.

——— 1987. Children at risk for psychosis growing up. In E. J. Anthony and B. J. Cohler, eds., *The invulnerable child.* New York: The Guilford Press.

———, ed. 1975. *Explorations in child psychiatry.* New York: Plenum Press.

Anthony, E. J., and Cohler, B. J., eds. 1987. *The invulnerable child.* New York: The Guilford Press.

Anthony, E. J., and Koupernik, C., eds. 1974. *The child in his family: Children at psychiatric risk*, vol. 3. New York: John Wiley.

Antonovsky, A. 1983. The sense of coherence: Development of a research instrument. *Newsletter and Research Reports* 1 (March): 11–22.

Atkinson, J. W. 1966. An approach to the study of subjective aspects of achievement motivation. In J. Nuttin, ed., Proceedings of the 18th International Congress in Psychology, Symposium 13, Moscow, 21–32.

————, ed. 1958. *Motives in fantasy, action, and society: A method of assessment and study.* Princeton: Van Nostrand.

Atkinson, J. W., and Feather, N. T., eds. 1966. *A theory of achievement motivation.* New York: John Wiley.

Atkinson, J. W., and Raynor, J. O. 1978. *Personality, motivation and achievement.* Washington, D.C.: Hemisphere.

Averill, J. R. 1973. Personal control over aversive stimuli and its relationship to stress. *Psychological Bulletin* 80: 286–303.

Bandura, A. 1977. *Social learning theory.* Englewood Cliffs, N.J.: Prentice-Hall.

———— 1990. Reflections on non-ability determinants of competence. In R. Sternberg and J. Kolligian, Jr., eds., *Competence considered.* New Haven: Yale University Press.

Barnes, J. A. 1972. *Social networks.* Addison-Wesley Module in Anthropology 26, 1–29.

Barnett, M. R., and Harrington, C. C. 1985. *Race, sex, and national origin: Public attitudes of desegregation.* Readings on Equal Education, vol. 8. New York: AMS Press.

Becker, E. 1973. *The denial of death.* New York: Free Press.

———— 1976. *Escape from evil.* New York: Macmillan.

Bell, R. 1965. Lower class Negro mothers' aspirations for their children. *Social Forces* 43: 130–138.

Berryman, S. E. 1988. *Who serves: The persistent myth of the underclass army.* London: Westview Press.

Bettelheim, B. 1943. Individual and mass behavior in extreme situations. *Journal of Abnormal and Social Psychology* 38(4): 417–452.

———— 1960. *Informed heart: Autonomy in a mass age.* New York: Free Press.

Biller, H. 1974. *Paternal deprivation: Family, school, sexuality and society.* Lexington, Mass.: Lexington Books.

Billingsley, A. 1968. *Black families in white America.* Englewood Cliffs, N.J.: Prentice-Hall.

Blau, P. M., and Duncan, O. D. 1967. *The American occupational structure.* New York: Wiley.

Block, G. 1971. *Lives through time.* Berkeley: Bancroft.

Boardman, S. K., and Harrington, C. C. 1984. Strategies for career success. In L. L. Moore (Chair), *Paths for women to the corporate fast track.* Symposium conducted at the conference on Women and Organizations (August), Simmons College, Boston.

———— 1991. Successful men: A psychological investigation of the antecedents of career success. Paper presented at the meetings of the Eastern Psychological Association (April), New York.

Boardman, S. K., Harrington, C. C., and Horowitz, S. V. 1987. Successful women: A psychological investigation of family, class, and education origins. In B. A. Gutek and L. Larwood, eds., *Women's career development.* Newbury Park, Calif.: Sage Publications.

Boardman, S. K., and Horowitz, S. V., eds. 1994. Constructive conflict management: An answer to critical social problems? *Journal of Social Issues* 50 (Spring): 1.

Bott, E. 1971. *Family and social network.* 2nd ed. New York: Free Press.

Bottomore, T. B. 1964. *Elites and society.* Middlesex, England: Penguin Books.

Bourdieu, P., and Passeron, J. C. 1977. *Reproduction in education, society and culture.* London: Sage.

Bowles, S., and Gintis, H. 1976. *Schooling in capitalist America: Educational reform and the contradictions of economic life.* New York: Basic Books.

Brewington, D., and Comerford, J. 1974. A look at the Kin family network of black and white families. Master's thesis, Washington, D.C.: Howard University, School of Social Work.

Bridge, R. G., Judd, C., and Moock, P. 1979. *The determinants of educational outcomes.* Cambridge, Mass.: Ballinger.

Byrne, D. 1964. The repression sensitization scale: Rationale, reliability, and validity. In B. A. Maher, ed., *Progress in experimental personality research.* New York: Academic Press.

Canavan-Gumpert, D. 1977. Generating reward and cost orientation through praise and criticism. *Journal of Personality and Social Psychology* 35(7): 501– 513.

Canavan-Gumpert, D., Garner, K. A., and Gumpert, P. 1978. *The success-fearing personality.* Lexington, Mass.: Lexington Books, D.C. Heath and Co.

Canavan-Gumpert, D., and Gumpert, P. 1979. Student heterogeneity: Teaching more of the people more of the time. Proceedings of the Fifth International Conference on Improving University Teaching, London.

Canavan-Gumpert, D., Gumpert, P., and Garner, K. A. 1978. When success-fearers succeed: The effects of cooperation and competition. Paper presented at the 86th Annual Convention of the American Psychological Association, Toronto, Canada.

Cannell, C. F., and Kahn, R. L. 1968. Interviewing. In G. Lindsey and E. Aronson, eds., *The handbook of social psychology* (2nd ed., pp. 526–595). Reading, Mass.: Addison-Wesley.

Chess, S. 1989. Defying the voice of doom. In T. F. Dugan and R. Coles, eds., *The child in our times.* New York: Brunner/Mazel.

Chess, S., and Thomas, A. 1984. *Origins and evolution of behavior disorders: From infancy to early adult life.* New York: Brunner/Mazel.

Clark, R. M. 1983. *Family life and school achievement: Why poor black children succeed or fail.* Chicago: University of Chicago Press.

Cobb, S. 1976. Social support as a moderator of life stress. *Psychosomatic Medicine* 38(5): 300–314.

Cohen, A. 1974. Introduction: The lesson of ethnicity. In A. Cohen, ed., *Urban ethnicity*, A.S.A. Monograph No. 12, London: Tavistock Publications.

Cohen, S., and McKay, G. 1984. Interpersonal relationships as buffers of the impact of psychological stress on health. In A. Baum, J. E. Singer, and S. E. Taylor, eds., *Handbook of psychology and health* (pp. 253–267). Hillsdale, N.J.: Erlbaum.

Cohler, B. J. 1987. Adversity, resilience, and the study of lives. In E. J. Anthony and B. J. Cohler, eds., *The invulnerable child* (pp. 363–424). New York: The Guilford Press.

Coleman, J. 1988. Social capital in the creation of human capital. *American Journal of Sociology* 94. Supplement.

Coleman, J., Campbell, E., Hobson, C., McPartland, J., Mood, A., Weinfeld, F., and York, R. 1966. *Equality of educational opportunity*. Washington, D.C.: U.S. Government Printing Office.

Coleman, J., Hoffer, T., and Kilgore, S. 1982. *High school achievement: Public, Catholic and other private schools compared*. New York: Basic Books.

Collins, R. 1971. Functional and conflict theories of educational stratification. *American Sociological Review* 36(6): 1002–1019.

Corwin, R. 1974. *Education in crisis: A sociological analysis of schools and universities in transition*. New York: John Wiley.

Cremin, L. 1970. *American education: The colonial experience, 1607–1783*. New York: Harper and Row.

——— 1976. *Public education*. New York: Basic Books.

Deutsch, M., Mitchell, V., Zhang, Q., Khattri, N., Tepavac, L., Weitzman, E., and Lynch, R. 1992. The effects of training in cooperative learning and conflict resolution in an alternative high school. Final report. New York: Teachers College, Columbia University, International Center for Cooperation and Conflict Resolution.

Dollard, J. 1935. *Criteria for the life history, with analysis of six notable documents*. New Haven: Yale University Press.

Dreifus, C. 1994. Joycelyn Elders. *New York Times Magazine*, January 30.

Dugan, T. F. 1989. Action and acting out: Variables in the development of resilience in adolescence. In T. F. Dugan and R. Coles, eds., *The child in our times*. New York: Brunner/Mazel.

Duncan, O. D., Featherman, D. L., and Duncan, B. 1972. *Socioeconomic background and achievement*. New York: Seminar Press.

Dweck, C., Hong, Y., and Chiu, C. 1993. Implicit theories: Individual differences in the likelihood and meaning of dispositional inference. *Personality and Social Psychology Bulletin* 19(5): 644–656.

Dweck, C., Chiu, C. and Hong, Y. 1995a. Implicit theories and their role in judgements and reactions: A world from two perspectives. *Psychological Inquiry* 6(4): 267–285.

———— 1995b. Implicit theories: Elaboration and extension of the model. *Psychological Inquiry* 6(4): 322–333.

Dweck, C., and Legget, E. L. 1988. A social cognitive approach to motivation and personality. *Psychological Review* 95(2): 256–273.

Elder, G. H. 1986. Military times and turning points in men's lives. *Developmental Psychology* 22: 233–245.

Elder, G. H., Liker, K., and Gross, C. E. 1984. Parent child behavior in the Great Depression. In T. B. Bates and O. G. Brim, eds., *Life span development and behavior*, vol. 6. New York: Academic Press.

Ellis, Robert A., and Lane, W. C. 1963. Structural supports for upward mobility. *American Sociological Review* 28(5): 743–756.

———— 1967. Social mobility and social isolation: A test of Sorokin's dissociative hypothesis. *American Sociological Review* 32(2): 237–253.

Entwisle, D. R. 1972. To dispel fantasies about fantasy-based measures of achievement motivation. *Psychological Bulletin* 77(6): 377–391.

Epstein, A. L. 1969. The network and urban social organization. In J. C. Mitchell, ed., *Social networks in urban situations: Analyses of personal relationships in Central African towns.* Manchester: Manchester University Press.

Erikson, E. 1950. *Childhood and society.* New York: Norton.

———— 1959. Identity and the life cycle. *Psychological Issues* 1(1): 18–100.

———— 1965. The concept of identity in race relations: Notes and queries. *Daedalus* 95: 200–215.

Farrington, D. P. 1993. *Protective factors in the development of juvenile delinquency and adult crime.* Cambridge: Institute of Criminology, Cambridge University.

Felsman, J. K. 1989. Risk and resiliency in childhood: The lives of street children. In T. F. Dugan and R. Coles, eds., *The child in our times* (pp. 56–80). New York: Brunner/Mazel.

Felsman, J. K., and Vaillant, G. E. 1987. Resilient children as adults: A forty year study. In E. J. Anthony and B. J. Cohler, eds., *The invulnerable child* (pp. 289–314). New York: The Guilford Press.

Flaxman, E., Ascher, C., and Harrington, C. 1988. *Youth mentoring: Programs and practices.* New York: Institute for Urban and Minority Education, Teachers College, Columbia University.

Fortes, M. 1949. *The web of kinship among the Tallensi.* London: Oxford University Press.

Freud, A. 1937. *Ego and the mechanisms of defense.* London: Hogarth Press, Ltd.

Furstenberg, F. F., Brooks-Gunn, J., and Morgan, S. P. 1987. *Adolescent mothers in later life.* New York: Cambridge University Press.

Gandara, P. 1979. Early environmental correlates of high academic attainment in Mexican Americans from low socio-economic backgrounds. Ph.D. diss., University of California, Los Angeles.

Garmezy, N. 1975a. The experimental study of children vulnerable to psychopathology. In A. Davids, ed., *Child personality and psychopathology: Current topics*, vol. 2. New York: John Wiley and Sons.

—— 1975b. Intervention with children at risk for behavior pathology. *The Clinical Psychologist* 28(2): 12–14.

—— 1981. Children under stress: Perspectives on antecedents and correlates of vulnerability and resistance to psychopathology. In A. I. Rabin, J. Aronoff, A. M. Barclay, and R. A. Zucker, eds., *Further explorations in personality* (pp. 196–270). New York: John Wiley and Sons.

—— 1983. Stressors of childhood. In N. Garmezy and M. Rutter, eds., *Stress, coping and development in children* (pp. 43–84). New York: McGraw-Hill.

Garmezy, N., and Devine, V. D. 1977. Longitudinal vs. cross-sectional research designs in the study of children at risk. In J. Strauss, ed., *Longitudinal studies in psychopathology*. New York: Plenum Press.

Gary, L. E., ed. 1981. *Black men*. Beverly Hills, Calif.: Sage Publications.

Goertzel, M. V., and Goertzel, T. 1978. *Three hundred eminent personalities*. San Francisco: Jossey-Bass.

Gottlieb, B. H. 1976. Lay influences on the utilization and provision of health services: A review. *Canadian Psychological Review* 17: 126–136.

Gould, R. 1972. The phases of adult life: A study in developmental psychology. *American Journal of Psychiatry* 129(5): 521–531.

Grey, A. 1993. A spectrum of psychoanalytic theories of self. In J. Fiscalini and A. Grey, eds., *Narcissism and the interpersonal self*. New York: Columbia University Press.

Gumpert, P., and Canavan-Gumpert, D. 1980. Situational and personality factors in the creation of intrinsic motivation. Proceedings of the Fifth International Conference on Improving University Teaching, Lausanne, Switzerland.

Gumpert, P., Canavan-Gumpert, D., and Garner, K. A. 1978a. Fear of success and family dynamics. Paper presented at the 86th Annual Convention of the American Psychological Association, Toronto, Canada.

—— 1978b. Social structure, interpersonal relations and teaching effectiveness. Paper presented at the 86th Annual Convention of the American Psychological Association, Toronto, Canada.

Gumpert, P., and Garner, K. A. 1976. Competence and incompetence beliefs: A reconceptualization of intrinsic motivation and psychological stress. Mimeograph, New York: Teachers College, Columbia University.

Gumpert, P., and Gumpert, C. 1968. The teacher as Pygmalion: Comments on the psychology of expectation. *The Urban Review* 3: 21–25.

Gumpert, P., and Harrington, C. C. 1972. Intellect and cultural deprivation. *Teachers College Record* 74(2): 261–273.

Gumpert, P., Thibaut, J. W., and Shuford, E. 1961. Effect of personality and status experience upon the valuation of unobtained statuses. *Journal of Abnormal and Social Psychology* 63(1): 47–52.

Haan, N. 1963. Proposed model of ego functioning: Coping and defense mechanisms in relationship to IQ change. *Psychological Monographs* 77(8) (whole no. 571): 1–23.

——— 1964. The relationship of ego functioning and intelligence to social status and social mobility. *Journal of Abnormal and Social Psychology* 69(6): 594–605.

——— 1972. Personality development from adolescence to adulthood in the Oakland growth and guidance studies. *Seminars in Psychiatry* 4: 399–414.

——— 1977. *Coping and defending: Processes of self-environment organization.* New York: Academic Press.

——— 1982. The assessment of coping, defense and stress. In L. Goldberg and S. Breznitz, eds., *Handbook of stress.* New York: Free Press/Macmillan.

——— 1989. Coping with moral conflict as resiliency. In T. F. Dugan and R. Coles, eds., *The child in our times.* New York: Brunner/Mazel.

Haggerty, R., Garmezy, N., Rutter, M., and Sherrold, L., eds. 1994. *Stress, risk and resilience in children and adolescents.* New York: Cambridge University Press.

Hallinan, M. 1985. Sociology of education: The state of the art. In J. Ballantine, ed., *Schools and society: A reader in education and sociology.* Palo Alto: Mayfield.

Hargreaves, D. H. 1967. *Social relations in a secondary school.* London: Routledge.

Harrington, C. C. 1970. *Errors in sex-role behavior.* New York: Teachers College Press.

——— 1973. Pupils, peers, and politics. In J. Burnett and S. Kimball, eds., *Learning and culture* (pp. 131–162). Seattle: University of Washington Press.

——— 1975. A psychological anthropologist's view of ethnicity and schooling. *IRCD Bulletin* 10(4).

——— 1976. Psychological anthropology and educational practice. *Teachers College Record* 78(1): 69–76.

——— 1978. Psychological anthropology and education: A delineation of a field of inquiry. In *Anthropology and education.* Washington: National Academy of Education.

——— 1979a. The pedagogical relevance of culture. In E. Gordon, ed., *Human diversity.* Washington, D.C.: National Institute of Education.

——— 1979b. *Psychological anthropology and education.* New York: AMS Press.

———— 1980. Textbooks and political socialization. *Teaching Political Science* 7(4)(July): 481–500.

———— 1981. *Bilingual education: A view from 1980.* New York: Teachers College, Columbia University. ERIC/CUE Urban Diversity Series no. 68.

Harrington, C. C., and Adler, N. 1971. Political socialization implications of grade school textbooks in New York State. Albany: New York State Commission on the Quality, Cost and Financing of Elementary and Secondary Education in New York State.

Harrington, C. C., Adler, N., and Smith, D. 1969. *Political socialization: An annotated bibliography.* New York: Horace Mann Lincoln Institute, Teachers College, Columbia University.

Harrington, C. C., and Boardman, S. K. 1990. *Educational antecedents of unlikely career success* (Occasional Paper Series, no. 10, July). New York: Teachers College, Columbia University, National Center on Education and Employment.

Harrington, C. C., and Flaxman, E. In press. *Youth mentoring.* New York: Teachers College Press.

Harrington, C. C., and Wilkins, M. L. 1966. Treating the social symptoms of mental illness. *Hospital and Community Psychiatry* 17(5): 136–139.

Harris, G. G. 1989. Concepts of individual, self, and person in description and analyses. *American Anthropologist* 91(3): 599–612.

Hartmann, H. 1958. *Ego psychology and the problem of adaptation.* New York: International Universities Press.

Hays, W., and Mindel, C. 1973. Extended kinship relations in black and white families. *Journal of Marriage and the Family* 35(1): 51–57.

Hill, R. 1972. *The strengths of black families.* New York: National Urban League.

Hillman, S., Wood, P., and Sawilowsky, S. 1992. Externalization as a self-protective mechanism in a stigmatized group. *Psychological Reports* 70: 641–642.

Holahan, C. J., and Moos, R. H. 1981. Social support and psychological distress: A longitudinal analysis. *Journal of Abnormal Psychology* 90(4): 365–370.

Hollingshead, A., and Redlich, F. 1958. *Social class and mental illness: A community study.* New York: John Wiley.

Horney, K. 1950. *Neurosis and Human Growth: The struggle towards self-realization.* New York: Norton.

Hyman, H., Cobb, W. J., Feldman, J. J., Hart, C. W., and Stember, C. H. 1954. *Interviewing in social research.* Chicago: University of Chicago Press.

Jencks, C., Smith, M., Acland, H., Bane, M., Kohen, D., Gintis, H., Heyns, B., and Michelson, S. 1972. *Inequality: A reassessment of the effect of family and schooling in America.* New York: Basic Books.

Jordaan, J. P., and Heyde, M. B. 1978. *Vocational maturity during the high school years.* New York: Teachers College Press.

Jung, C. G. 1963. *Memories, dreams, reflections.* New York: Pantheon Books.

——— 1964. *Man and his symbols.* Garden City: Doubleday.

——— 1969. The archetypes and the collective unconscious. *Collected works* 9(1). 2nd ed. Bollingen Series. Princeton: Princeton University Press.

——— 1971. The stages of life. In J. Campbell, ed., *The portable Jung.* New York: Viking.

Kahl, J. A. 1953. Educational and occupational aspirations of "Common Man" boys. *Harvard Educational Review* 23: 186–203.

——— 1957. *The American class structure.* New York: Rinehart.

Kandel, D. 1967. Race, maternal authority and adolescent aspiration. *American Journal of Sociology* 76(6): 999–1020.

Kanouse, D., Gumpert, P., and Canavan-Gumpert, D. In press. The semantics of praise. In J. Harvey, R. Kidd, and W. Ickes, eds., *New directions in attribution research,* vol. 3. Hillsdale, N.J.: L. Erlbaum Associates.

Kanter, R. M. 1977. *Men and women of the corporation.* New York: Basic Books.

Kilpatrick, D. G., Dubin, W. R., and Marcotte, D. B. 1974. Personality, stress of the medical education process, and changes in affective mood state. *Psychological Reports* 34: 1215–1223.

Klein, M. 1948. *Contributions to psychoanalysis.* London: Hogarth Press.

Klein, M., and Riviere, J. 1964. *Love, hate, and reparation.* New York: Norton.

Kroeber, T. 1963. The coping functions of ego mechanisms. In R. White, ed., *The study of lives* (pp. 178–198). New York: Atherton Press.

Lacey, C. 1970. *Hightown grammar: The school as a social system.* Manchester: Manchester University Press.

Langer, E. J., and Benevento, A. 1978. Self-induced dependence. *Journal of Personality and Social Psychology* 36(8): 886–893.

Langer, E. J., and Rodin, J. 1976. The effects of choice and enhanced personal responsibility for the aged: A field experiment in an institutional setting. *Journal of Personality and Social Psychology* 34(2): 191–198.

Langness, L., and Frank, G. 1981. *Lives: An anthropological approach to biography.* Novato, Calif.: Chandler and Sharp Publishers.

Lefcourt, H. M. 1972. Recent developments in the study of locus of control. In B. A. Maher, ed., *Progress in experimental personality research,* vol. 6. New York: Academic Press.

——— 1976; 1982. *Locus of control: Current trends in theory and research.* 1st and 2nd eds. Hillsdale, N.J.: Erlbaum.

——— 1980. Locus of control and coping with life's events. In E. Staub, ed., *Personality: Basic aspects and current research.* Englewood Cliffs, N.J.: Prentice-Hall.

Lefcourt, H. M., Martin, R. A., and Saleh, W. E. 1984. Locus of control and social support: Interactive moderators of stress. *Journal of Personality and Social Psychology* 47(2): 378–389.

Leguerre, M. S. 1987. American odyssey: Haitians in New York. In L. Lamphere, ed., *From working daughters to working mothers*. Ithaca, N.Y.: Cornell University Press.

Lengner, T. S., and Michael, S. T. 1963. *Life stress and mental health*. Glencoe: Free Press.

——— 1968. Emotions and adaptation: Conceptual and empirical relations. In W. T. Arnold, ed., *Nebraska symposium on motivation*. Lincoln: University of Nebraska Press.

Levinson, D. J., Darrow, C. N., Klein, E. B., Levinson, M. H., and McKee, B. 1978. *The seasons of a man's life*. New York: Ballantine Books.

Lifton, R. J. 1976. *The life of the self: Toward a new psychology*. New York: Simon and Schuster.

Lionells, M., Fiscalini, J., Mann, C., and Stern, D., eds. 1995. *A handbook of interpersonal psychoanalysis*. Hillsdale, N.J.: Analytic Press.

Lipset, S. M., and Bendix, R. 1959. *Social mobility in industrial society*. Berkeley: University of California Press.

Litwak, E. 1960. Geographic mobility and extended family cohesion. *American Sociological Review* 25: 385–394.

Long, J. V. F., and Vaillant, G. E. 1989. Escape from the underclass. In T. F. Dugan and R. Coles, eds., *The child in our times* (pp. 200–213). New York: Brunner/Mazel.

Loury, G. 1995. *One by one from the inside out: Essays and reviews on race and responsibility in America*. New York: Free Press.

Luthar, S., and Zigler, E. 1991. Vulnerability and competence: A review of research on resilience in childhood. *American Journal of Orthopsychiatry* 61(1): 6–22.

Macleod, J. 1987. *Ain't no making it: Aspirations and attainment in a low income neighborhood*. Boulder: Westview Press.

Marx, K., and Engels, F. 1973 edition. *The communist manifesto*. New York: Pathfinder Press.

Maslow, A. 1954. *Motivation and personality*. New York: Harper and Row.

——— 1968. *Toward a psychology of being*. 2nd ed. Princeton: Van Nostrand Reinhold.

——— 1971. *The farther reaches of human nature*. New York: Viking.

Masten, A. S., Best, K. M., and Garmezy, N. 1991. Resilience and development: Contributions from the study of children who overcame adversity. *Development and Psychopathology* 2, 425–444.

McAdoo, H. P., and McAdoo, J. L. 1985. *Black children: Social, educational and parental environments*. Beverly Hills: Sage Publications.

McClelland, D. C. 1955. Some social consequences of achievement motivation.

In R. M. Jones, ed., *Nebraska symposium on motivation, 1955*. Lincoln: University of Nebraska Press.

———— 1961. *The achieving society*. Princeton: Van Nostrand Reinhold.

McClelland, D. C., Atkinson, J. W., Clark, R. A., and Lowell, E. L. 1958. A scoring manual for the achievement motive. In J. W. Atkinson, ed., *Motives in fantasy, action and society* (pp. 179–204). Princeton: Van Nostrand.

Merton, R. 1968. *Social theory and social structure*. New York: The Free Press.

———— 1973. *The sociology of science: Theoretical and empirical investigations*. Chicago: University of Chicago Press.

Mitchell, J. C. 1969. The concept and use of social networks. In J. C. Mitchell, ed., *Social networks in urban situations: Analyses of personal relationships in Central African towns*. Manchester: Manchester University Press.

Moos, R., and Billings, A. 1982. Conceptualizing and measuring coping resources and processes. In L. Goldberger and S. Breznitz, eds., *Handbook of stress: Theoretical and clinical aspects*. New York: Free Press/Macmillan.

Munroe, R. L., Munroe, R. H., and Daniels, R. E. 1969. Effect of status and values on estimation of coin size in two East African societies. *Journal of Social Psychology* 77: 25–34.

Murphy, L. 1962. *The widening world of childhood: Paths toward mastery*. New York: Basic Books.

———— 1976. *Vulnerability, coping, and growth: From infancy to adolescence*. New Haven: Yale University Press.

Myers, J. K., and Roberts, B. H. 1959. *Family and class dynamics in mental illness*. New York: Wiley.

Natriello, G., and McDill, E. 1986. Performance standards, student effort on homework, and academic achievement. *Sociology of Education* 59(1): 18–31.

Nieva, V. F., and Gutek, B. A. 1981. *Women and work: A psychological perspective*. New York: Praeger.

Ogbu, J. 1974. *The next generation: An ethnography of education in an urban neighborhood*. New York: Academic Press.

———— 1981. Origins of human competence: A cultural-ecological perspective. *Child Development* 52(2): 413–429.

Pareto, W. 1916 (1963). *The mind and society: A treatise on general sociology*. New York: Dover.

Pearlin, L., and Schooler, C. 1978. The structure of coping. *Journal of Health and Social Behavior* 19(1): 2–21.

Phares, E. J. 1976. *Locus of control in personality*. Morristown, N.J.: General Learning Press.

Plutchik, R., Kellerman, H., and Conte, H. 1979. A structural theory of ego defenses and emotions. In C. E. Izard, ed., *Emotions in personality and psychopathology* (pp. 229–255). New York: Plenum.

Rabkin, J. G., and Streuning, E. L. 1976. Life events, stress, and illness. *Science* 194: 1013–1020.

Rainwater, L. 1965. The crucible of identity: The lower-class Negro family. *Daedalus* 95: 258–264.

Raynor, J. O. 1978. Motivation and career striving. In J. W. Atkinson and J. O. Raynor, eds., *Personality, motivation, and achievement* (pp. 199–219). Washington, D.C.: Hemisphere.

Raynor, J. O., Atkinson, J. W., and Brown, M. 1974. Subjective aspects of achievement motivation immediately before an examination. In J. W. Atkinson and J. O. Raynor, eds., *Personality, motivation and achievement* (pp. 155–171). Washington, D.C.: Hemisphere.

Rhodes, W. A., and Brown, W. K., eds. 1991. *Why some children succeed despite the odds.* New York: Praeger.

Riesman, D., Glazer, N., and Denney, R. 1950. *The lonely crowd: A study of the changing American character.* New Haven: Yale University Press.

Rodgers-Rose, L., ed. 1980. *The black woman.* Beverly Hills: Sage Publications.

Rodin, J., and Langer, E. J. 1977. Long-term effects of a control-relevant intervention with the institutionalized aged. *Journal of Personality and Social Psychology* 35(12): 897–902.

Rosen, B. 1959. Race, ethnicity and the achievement syndrome. *American Sociological Review* 24: 47–60.

Rosenfeld, R. A. 1978. Women's intergenerational occupational mobility. *American Sociological Review* 43: 36–46.

Rossi, A. S., ed. 1985. *Gender and the life course.* New York: Aldine.

Rotter, J. B. 1966. Generalized expectancies for internal versus external control of reinforcement. *Psychological Monographs* 80(1): 260–296 (Whole no. 609).

Rutter, M. 1979. Protective factors in children's responses to stress and disadvantage. In M. W. Kent and J. E. Rolf, eds., *Primary prevention of psychopathology,* vol. 3. *Social competence in children* (pp. 49–74). Hanover: University Press of New England.

———— 1983. Stress, coping and development: Some issues and some questions. In N. Garmezy and M. Rutter, eds., *Stress, coping and development in children.* New York: McGraw-Hill.

Rutter, M., Cox, A., Tupling, C., Berger, M., and Yule, W. 1975. Attainment and adjustment in two geographical areas. I: The prevalence of psychiatric disorder. *British Journal of Psychiatry* 126: 493–509.

Rutter, M., Maughan, B., Mortimore, P., and Ousten, J. 1979. *Fifteen thousand hours: Secondary schools and their effects on children.* Cambridge, Mass.: Harvard University Press.

Ryan, J., and Sackrey, C. 1984. *Strangers in paradise: Academics from the working class.* Boston: South End Press.

Scarr, S. 1988. Race and gender as psychological variables: Social and ethical issues. *American Psychologist*, 56–59.

Scarr, S., and McCartney, K. 1983. How people make their own environments: A theory of genotype. *Child Development* 54(2): 424–435.

Schorr, L., and Schorr, D. 1988. *Within our reach: Breaking the cycle of disadvantage.* New York: Anchor Press/Doubleday.

Scribner, S., and Stevens, J. 1989. Experimental studies of the relationship of school math and work math (Tech. Rep. no. 4, April). New York: National Center on Education and Employment, Teachers College, Columbia University.

Sewell, W., and Hauser, R. 1980. The Wisconsin longitudinal study of social and psychological factors in aspiration and achievements. *Research in Sociology of Education and Socialization* 1: 59–99.

Shaffer, W. F. 1968. Tests of hypotheses relating psychopathology to extreme upward mobility. Ph.D. diss., Teachers College, Columbia University, New York.

Shalala, D. E., Williams, M. F., and Fischel, A. 1973. *The property tax and the voters: An analysis of state constitutional referenda to revise school finance systems in California, Colorado, Michigan, and Oregon in 1972 and 1973.* New York: The Institute of Philosophy and Politics of Education, Teachers College, Columbia University.

Sherif, M., and Cantril, H. 1947. *The psychology of ego-involvements, social attitudes and identifications.* New York: Wiley.

Shostrom, E. L. 1965. An inventory for the measurement of self-actualization. *Educational and Psychological Measurement* 24(2): 207–218.

——— 1966. Manual for the Personal Orientation Inventory. Princeton: Educational and Industrial Testing Service.

Shweder, R. 1991. *Thinking through cultures.* Cambridge, Mass.: Harvard University Press.

Simmel, G. 1955. *Conflict: The web of group affiliations.* New York: Free Press.

Smith, L. 1954. *The Journey.* Cleveland: World Publishing.

Sorokin, P. 1927. *Social mobility.* New York: Harper.

Srole, L., Lengner, T. S., Michael, S. T., Opler, M. K., and Rennie, T. A. C. 1962. *Mental health in the metropolis: The Midtown Manhattan study.* New York: McGraw-Hill.

Stacey, B. 1967. Some psychological consequences of inter-generational mobility. *Human Relations* 20: 3–12.

Stack, C. B. 1974. *All our kin: Strategies for survival in a black community.* New York: Harper and Row.

Sternberg, R. 1988. *The triarchic mind: A new theory of human intelligence.* New York: Viking.

Sun, B. 1975. The development of reward-cost orientation: An investigation of direct and indirect reward-cost training. Unpublished ms., Columbia University, New York.

Taylor, D., and Dorsey-Gaines, C. 1988. *Growing up literate: Learning from inner city families.* Portsmouth, N.H.: Heinemann.

Thibaut, J. W., and Kelley, H. H. 1959. *The social psychology of groups.* New York: John Wiley.

Treiman, D. J. 1985. The work histories of women and men: What we know and what we need to find out. In A. S. Rossi, ed., *Gender and the life course* (pp. 213–231). New York: Aldine.

Vaillant, G. E. 1971. Theoretical hierarchy of adaptive ego mechanisms. *Archives of General Psychiatry* 24: 107–118.

——— 1975. Sociopathy as a human process: A viewpoint. *Archives of General Psychiatry* 32(2)(February): 178–183.

——— 1976. Natural history of male psychological health, V: The relation of choice to ego mechanisms of defense to adult adjustment. *Archives of General Psychiatry* 33(5): 535–545.

——— 1977. *Adaptation to life.* Boston: Little, Brown.

——— 1993. *The wisdom of the ego: Sources of resiliency in adult life.* Cambridge, Mass.: Harvard University Press.

Vincent, J. 1971. *African elite: The big men of a small town.* New York: Columbia University Press.

Wallace, A. F. C. 1961. *Culture and personality.* New York: Random House.

——— 1978. *Rockdale: The growth of an American village in the early industrial revolution.* New York: Knopf.

Waller, W. 1965. *The sociology of teaching.* New York: John Wiley.

Webb, C., Waugh, F., and Herbert, J. 1993. Relationship between locus of control and performance on the National Board of Medical Examiners. Part I: Among black medical students. *Psychological Reports* 72: 1171–1177.

Weiner, B. 1985. An attributional theory of achievement motivation and emotion. *Psychological Review* 92: 548–573.

Weinstock, A. 1967. Longitudinal study of social class and defense preferences. *Journal of Consulting Psychology* 31: 539–541.

Werner, E. E. 1993. Risk, resilience, and recovery: Perspectives from the Kauai Longitudinal Study. *Development and Psychopathology* 5: 503–515.

Werner, E. E., and Smith, R. S. 1982. *Vulnerable but invincible: A longitudinal study of resilient children and youth.* New York: McGraw-Hill.

——— 1992. *Overcoming the odds: High risk children from birth to adulthood.* Ithaca: Cornell University Press.

Whiting, B. B., and Edwards, C. P. 1988. *Children of different worlds: The formation of social behavior.* Cambridge, Mass.: Harvard University Press.

Williams, J. A. 1964. Interviewer-respondent interaction: A study of bias in the information interview. *Sociometry* 27: 338–352.

Wilson, H. 1974. Parenting in poverty. *British Journal of Social Work* 4: 241–254.

Wilson, W. J. 1987. *The truly disadvantaged: The inner city, the underclass, and public policy.* Chicago: University of Chicago Press.

Winter, G. 1973. *The power motive.* New York: Free Press.

Wohl, R. R. 1966. The rags to riches story: An episode of secular idealism. In R. Bendix and S. M. Lipset, eds., *Class status and power.* 2nd ed. New York: Free Press.

Wortman, C. B., and Brehm, J. W. 1975. Responses to uncontrollable outcomes: An integration of reactance theory and the learned helplessness model. In L. Berkowitz, ed., *Advances in experimental social psychology*, vol. 8 (pp. 277–336). New York: Academic Press.

Zweigenhaft, R. L., and Domhoff, G. W. 1991. *Blacks in the white establishment? A study of race and class in America.* New Haven: Yale University Press.

Index

Note: Page numbers in italics indicate direct quotations.

231